JACQUES-LOUIS DAVID'S
MARAT

This book focuses on Jacques-Louis David's *Marat,* one of the key works of art created during the period of the French Revolution and one of the most important works of Western painting. Beginning with an introduction that outlines the general history of the painting, this volume provides six new essays, each specially written (with one exception) for this title, which examine the work using a variety of methodologies, including feminist, psychoanalytic, and material analysis approaches. Each of these essays provides for a broader and deeper understanding of the painting, the circumstances in which it was created and commissioned, and its critical and art historical reception over two centuries.

William Vaughan is professor of the history of art at Birkbeck College, University of London. A scholar of nineteenth-century European art, he is the author of *German Romantic Painting* and co-editor of *Art in Bourgeois Society,* among many other publications.

Helen Weston is professor in the Department of History of Art at University College London. She has contributed to *Oxford Art Journal, Art History,* and *RES* and is currently working on a book about Pierre-Paul Prud'hon.

This series serves as a forum for the reassessment of important paintings in the Western tradition that span a period from the Renaissance to the twentieth century. Each volume focuses on a single work and includes an introduction outlining its general history, as well as a selection of essays that examine the work from a variety of methodological perspectives. Demonstrating how and why these paintings have such enduring value, the volumes also offer new insights into their meaning for contemporaries and their subsequent reception.

VOLUMES IN THE SERIES

Masaccio's "Trinity," edited by Rona Goffen, Rutgers University

Raphael's "School of Athens," edited by Marcia Hall, Temple University

Titian's "Venus of Urbino," edited by Rona Goffen, Rutgers University

Caravaggio's "Saint Paul," edited by Gail Feigenbaum, New Orleans Museum of Art

Rembrandt's "Bathsheba with David's Letter," edited by Ann Jensen Adams, University of California, Santa Barbara

David's "Marat," edited by William Vaughan, Birkbeck College, University of London, and Helen Weston, University College London, University of London

Manet's "Le Déjeuner sur l'herbe," edited by Paul Hayes Tucker, University of Massachusetts, Boston

Picasso's "Les Demoiselles d'Avignon," edited by Christopher Green, Courtauld Institute of Art, University of London

JACQUES-LOUIS DAVID'S *MARAT*

Edited by

William Vaughan   Helen Weston

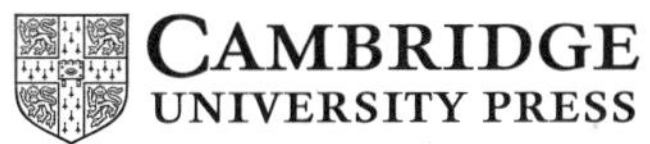

PUBLISHED BY THE PRESS SYNDICATE OF THE UNIVERSITY OF CAMBRIDGE
The Pitt Building, Trumpington Street, Cambridge, CB2 1RP, United Kingdom

CAMBRIDGE UNIVERSITY PRESS
The Edinburgh Building, Cambridge CB2 2RU, UK http://www.cup.cam.ac.uk
40 West 20th Street, New York, NY 10011-4211, USA   http://www.cup.org
10 Stamford Road, Oakleigh, Melbourne 3166, Australia

First published 2000

Printed in the United States of America

Typeface Bembo 11/13 pt.   *System* QuarkXPress® [GH]

*A catalog record for this book is available from
the British Library*

Library of Congress Cataloging-in-Publication Data

Jacques-Louis David's "Marat" / edited by William Vaughan, Helen
  Weston.
        p.   cm. – (Masterpieces of Western painting)
    Includes bibliographical references and index.
    ISBN 0-521-56337-2 (hardback). – ISBN 0-521-56524-3 (pbk.)
    1. David, Jacques Louis, 1748–1825.   Death of Marat.   2. Marat,
  Jean Paul, 1743–1793 – Portraits.   3. David, Jacques Louis,
  1748–1825 – Criticism and interpretation.   I. Vaughan, William,
  1943–   . II. Weston, Helen. III. Series.
  ND1329.D38A64   1999
  759.4 – dc21   98-43887
                                                           CIP

ISBN 0 521 56337 2 hardback
ISBN 0 521 56524 3 paperback

CONTENTS

ILLUSTRATIONS

ACKNOWLEDGEMENTS

We would like to thank all the authors in this volume for their willingness to contribute and their patience with our requests during the preparation stages of the text. With one exception, all essays were commissioned specifically for this volume in the hope of providing six very different ways of approaching David's *Marat*.

Postgraduate students in the Department of History of Art at University College London were more than willing to hear and respond to some of these essays during 1996 and 1997. We would like to thank Satish Padiyar in this respect and, in particular, Louise Govier, who read and commented helpfully on early drafts of two of the essays. We are also grateful to the third-year undergraduate seminar group of 1993 who worked with Helen Weston on an exhibition – *Re-presenting the Assassination of Marat* – displayed in the Strang Print Room at University College London, which provided much of the stimulus for this study. For that occasion we were indebted to Philippe Bordes and the cooperation of the Musée de la Révolution Française at Vizille for the loan of material and to the British Museum for access to the prints in the Chèvremont Marat collection and the staff of the Strang. These individuals and organizations have continued to be valuable resources in the preparation of the present volume.

For the infrared reflectography work, we are greatly indebted to Christina Masschelein-Curry (IRPA), Freya Maes (Musée royaux des Beaux-Arts, Belgium), and, in particular, to Frederick Laan from the same museum, who gave generously of his time in providing help and information. For help in gathering technical material we would like to thank Catherine Hassall (UCL), Inge Fiedler (Art Institute of Chicago), Leslie Carlyle (Canadian Conservation Institute), Mark Leonard (J. Paul Getty Museum), Jo Kirby (National Gallery, London), Molly March, Geraldine Guillaume Chavannes, Sarah Walden, Zahira Veliz, and Carol Blackett Ord. Arnt Fredheim also gave invaluable help in providing access to pictures not on public display in the Munch-museet in Oslo, for which we are most grateful.

Finally, we would like to thank Beatrice Rehl, Fine Arts Editor at Cambridge University Press, for inviting us to produce this volume and for her consideration, advice, and encouragement as work progressed on it.

William Vaughan and Helen Weston
London
April 1999

CONTRIBUTORS

THOMAS GRETTON is senior lecturer in the History of Art Department, University College London. Trained as a historian, he has published on nineteenth-century English and French art and history and is a specialist in the history of printmaking. He is the author of a forthcoming book on J. G. Posada.

TONY HALLIDAY is a part-time lecturer in the history of art at London University. He is the author of a forthcoming book on portraiture in late eighteenth- and early nineteenth-century France. He has also written articles in connection with the Paris Salons of the Revolution and on Mantegna and the antique.

WILLIAM VAUGHAN is professor of the history of art at Birkbeck College, University of London. He is the author of *Romantic Art* and *German Romantic Painting* and has published articles on the relationship between the French Revolution and British culture.

LIBBY SHELDON is co-director of the Painting Analysis Unit in the History of Art Department, University College London. Her publications include an article on Pre-Raphaelite techniques. She lectures on the methods and materials of painters at UCL.

HELEN WESTON is senior lecturer in the History of Art Department, University College London. She has published articles on David and his contemporaries – Girodet, Prud'hon, and women artists of the period. She is the author of a forthcoming book on Prud'hon.

DAVID LOMAS is lecturer in the Department of Art History and Archaeology at the University of Manchester. His publications include an article on Picasso's *Les Demoiselles d'Avignon* and physical anthropology, a revised version of which is published by Cambridge University Press in this series. He is the author of a forthcoming book on surrealism, psychoanalysis, and subjectivity.

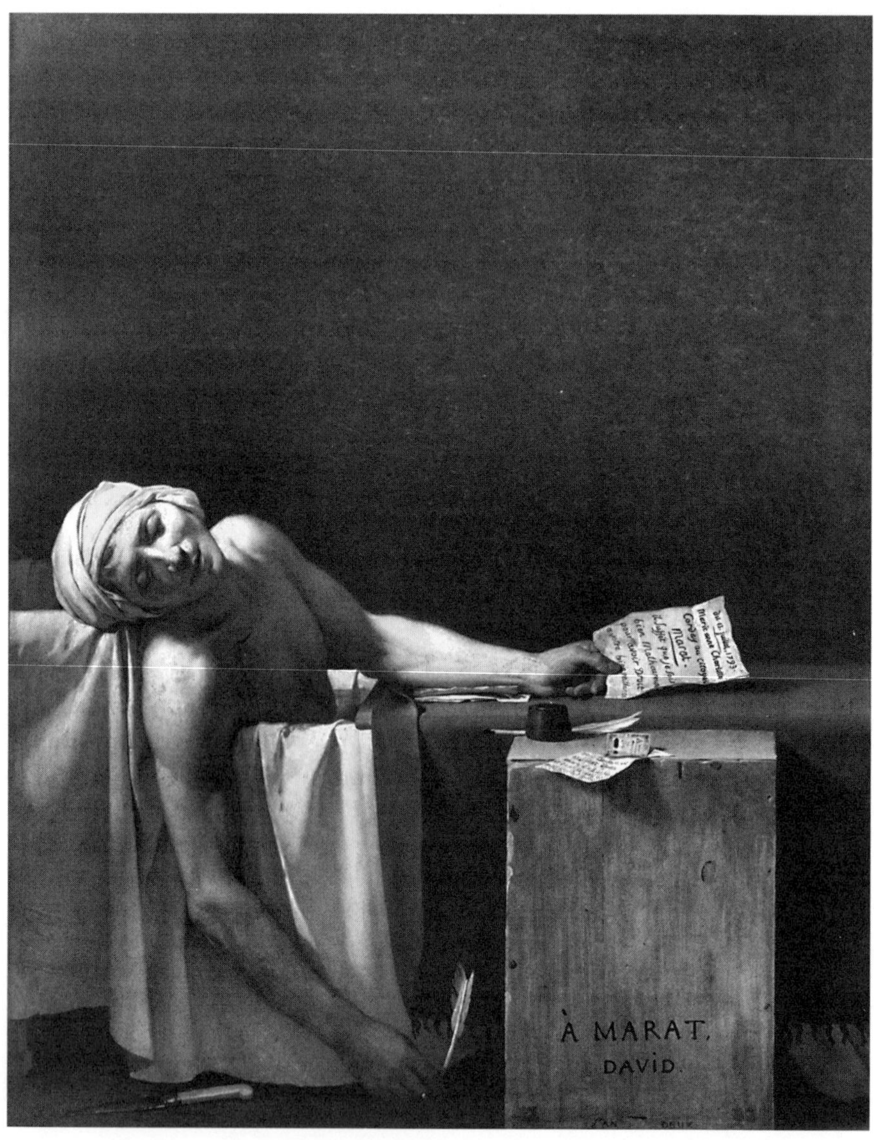

Figure 1. Jacques-Louis David, *Marat à son dernier soupir (The Death of Marat)*, 1793, oil on canvas, 165 × 128 cm. Musées royaux des Beaux-Arts, Brussels. (Copyright IRPA, Musées royaux des Beaux-Arts, Brussels.)

INTRODUCTION

THE DIVINE MARAT (BAUDELAIRE)

The *divine* Marat, one arm hanging out of the bath, its hand still loosely holding on to its last quill, and his chest pierced by the *sacrilegious* wound, has just breathed his last. On the green desk in front of him, his other hand still holds the treacherous letter: 'Citizen, it is enough that I am really miserable to have a right to your benevolence.' The bath water is red with blood, the paper is blood-stained; on the ground lies a large kitchen knife soaked in blood; on a wretched packing case, which constituted the working furniture for the tireless journalist we read: 'À Marat, David'. All the details are historical and real, as in a novel by Balzac; the drama is there, alive in all its pitiful horror, and by a strange stroke of brilliance, which makes this David's masterpiece and one of the great treasures of modern art, there is nothing trivial or ignoble about it. What is most astonishing in this exceptional poem is the fact that it is painted extremely quickly, and when one considers the beauty of its design, it is all the more bewildering. It is the bread of the strong and the triumph of the spiritual; as cruel as nature, this picture has the heady scent of idealism. What has become of that ugliness that Death has so swiftly erased with the tip of its wing? Marat can henceforth challenge Apollo; Death has kissed him with loving lips and he rests in the peace of his transformation. There is in this work something both tender and poignant, a soul hovers in the chilled air of this room, on these cold walls, around the cold and funereal bath. May we have your permission, politicians of all parties, even you, ferocious liberals of 1845, to give way to emotion before David's masterpiece? This painting was a gift to a tearful nation, and our own tears are not dangerous.[1]

We may no longer weep in front of this picture. We may need more help in understanding it than those people in the 1840s who first read Baudelaire's appraisal. But for us, too, David's *Marat* is an unforgettable work (Fig. 1). It depicts a murdered man at the last moment of his life with such graphic starkness that it communicates both the fascination and the horror of a detailed, eyewitness account. At the same time the picture is so carefully designed and painted that it strikes us, as well, with its beauty.

Such effects are intentional. The picture was painted by the artist to commemorate a personal hero who was assassinated during the period of mounting political crisis following 1789. As the artist himself said, he wished it to move the French people and to spur them to patriotic action. It is in every sense a political painting.

THE HISTORY OF THE PICTURE and the event it commemorates are extensively documented. We are in little doubt about why and for whom the picture was painted. It is a fascinating and highly important historical document. Yet this does not altogether explain the hold that it has exerted on later generations. Indeed, the historical circumstances of its origins were for a time a threat to its very existence. Because of political changes *Marat* was displayed in public for only a couple of years. After that it went into hiding – like many of the radicals who had been colleagues of its subject. It did not reemerge until after the artist's death. Since that time – and particularly since it was put on permanent public display in Brussels in 1893 – it has become a kind of icon of the French Revolution. It is a sign of the painting's importance that it is frequently used on the jacket of books covering the period, both from a political and from a cultural and artistic point of view. Furthermore, it has become a work that fascinates those who have no particular interest in the period it comes from. The shock of the picture has worked – like some of those shocking moments in twentieth-century film (for example, the nurse in the *Battleship Potemkin,* or the razor and the eye in *Un Chien Andalou*) – both on other artists and on spectators in general. It is one of those images that fascinates simultaneously by its horror and its beauty. It can be approached from many angles. In this book we have brought together studies by contemporary scholars that look at the painting from a range of perspectives using current practices.

THE EVENT

On 13 July 1793 Jean-Paul Marat, a deputy of the Montagnard faction and an extreme populist journalist, was attacked and murdered by Charlotte Corday, a Girondin sympathiser from Caen, who hated everything for which Marat stood.[2] It was a suffocatingly hot July; indeed, the heat was one of the factors that aggravated Marat's illness: he suffered from a severe skin complaint that caused him to seek relief through immersion in the bath with a vinegar-soaked cloth wound around his head like a turban. He was, not surprisingly, forced to abandon plans to be present at the 14 July Festival of Liberty on the Champ de Mars, and likewise to take his seat at the National Convention. Corday's carefully laid plans to assassinate Marat in one of these public spaces on that day were therefore thwarted. She had spent weeks working toward this goal, ever since she had heard the emotional speeches in Caen of Charles-Jean-Marie Barbaroux de Marseille, former Girondin deputy for the department of the Bouches-du-Rhône to the National Convention. He singled out Marat as the real enemy of the French nation and incited the people of Normandy to march on Paris and deliver it from such monstrous creatures. Armed with letters from Barbaroux, in connection with their common friend, Mlle de Forbin, to deliver in Paris to one of Barbaroux's former colleagues and fellow deputy, Lauze Deperret, Charlotte Corday arrived in Paris on 11 July with this as her ostensible mission. She booked herself into a cheap hotel, learned of Marat's indisposition, and realised that she would have to kill him at his home. She spent the next day with Deperret and then turned to her real objective on the following day – 13 July.

Meanwhile, on 12 July Jacques-Louis David, a prominent Jacobin, indeed president of its club for a month in the summer of 1793, deputy to the Convention and powerful member of the Committee of Public Instruction, was visiting his friend, Marat, where he found him working in his bath. He was clearly affected by Marat's diseased appearance and by the austerity in which the journalist worked.

> The day before Marat's death, the Jacobins sent Maure and me to get news of him; I found him in a state which stunned me. Beside him was a wooden box on which there was an inkwell and paper, and with his hand out of the bath, he was writing his final thoughts for the deliverance of his people.[3]

In her hotel room that evening Corday wrote a speech to the French people, *L'Adresse aux Français,* explaining her motives, her intention in destroying 'the savage beast fattened on the blood of Frenchmen', and her hopes for France's peace after Marat's death. She meant her speech to be found and read, so she attached it, together with her baptism certificate, to the dress she would wear to visit Marat. She rose early on 13 July and bought a newspaper. She read with fury of the guillotining to take place that day of nine men from Orléans who were accused of plotting against a Jacobin official. As the shops began to open in the Palais Egalité, Corday made her way to a cutler's and bought a kitchen knife with a six-inch blade and ebony black handle and two rings for hanging it from a shelf or cook's waist (David paints it white-handled, with no rings). She then hailed a carriage and asked to be taken to Marat's apartment.

Marat lived at 30 rue des Cordeliers, where he had installed a printing press for distributing his newspaper, *L'Ami du Peuple.* He shared the apartment with Simonne Evrard, his common-law wife who appears to have paid most of the bills, and her sister, Catherine, and a cook. It was a modest apartment; the walls were covered with paper with an illusionistic design of columns, which David clearly chose to ignore for his painting. Arriving at the building, Corday rang a bell and asked to see Marat but was refused entry by the concierge. An hour later she returned and managed to reach Marat's apartment but was refused entry this time by Catherine and Simonne Evrard. Returning to her hotel Corday wrote Marat a letter promising to give information about the Girondins in Caen and appealing to Marat's sense of patriotism. She sent it by the *petite poste.* Later that afternoon she wrote a second letter which she carried with her – the one that David adapted for his painting and placed in Marat's hand.[4] She changed her dress and transferred the *Adresse aux Français* and baptism certificate to it, tied green ribbons on her black hat, called another carriage, and returned to Marat's residence at about 7.30 P.M. On her arrival two men, employed in connection with Marat's newspaper, were being admitted into the apartment and Corday seized her chance to get a foot in the door and plead with Simonne to be admitted to Marat's room. On overhearing this exchange Marat agreed to see the citizeness from Caen. He was seated in a sabot-shaped hipbath (these could be hired quite cheaply) in a small room adjoining his bedroom. According to some accounts, he wore an old dressing gown over his shoulders, which David again chose not to represent. Around his head was some white cloth soaked in vinegar. Across the bath was a wooden board that Marat used as a writing surface. On the wall behind was a shelf with a pair of pistols and a map of France beneath it. Many of these details would emerge in contemporary prints recording the incident and in later nineteenth-century paintings, but David eliminated all evidence of decoration and personal possessions except the objects needed by Marat for his work as a journalist.

Marat himself was weak, immersed to the waist in water, naked beneath the dressing gown, but he was nevertheless busy with paperwork. His skin was badly marked with what was referred to at the time as a 'leprous' condition, presumably some sort of psoriasis. Corday gave him news of the uprisings in Caen and the names of the Girondists responsible – at which point he assured her, according to her own testimony, that they would be guillotined in a few days. Enraged but emboldened by this, Corday drew the knife from her clothing and plunged it hard into Marat's chest, withdrew it, and flung it away from her. Marat called out to Simonne – 'à moi, à moi, ma chère amie, je me meurs!' – these supposedly being his final dying words.

Chaos ensued as Simonne and the other women tried to lift Marat onto his bed and stop the bleeding, and the men forced Corday to the ground, tied her hands, and shouted at her. A doctor pronounced that it had been a clean blow and death instantaneous, the knife reaching between the first and second ribs, through the lung and into the heart, producing torrents of blood. A policeman questioned Corday at length in one room while the unpleasant business of embalming Marat's corpse began in the bedroom. Four deputies were sent for to interrogate the prisoner, the main spokesman being the former Capucine monk, François Chabot, and they brought pressure to bear to make Corday compromise other Girondins who they presumed had plotted with her against the friend of the people. She named no one and was taken to the Abbaye prison for further questioning.

The following day, by which time news of Marat's death had reached the Convention, Guirault, member of the deputation to the Convention from Marat's Section, turned to David; 'there is yet one more painting for you to do'. Another deputy, Audouin, begged David, 'Return Marat to us whole again' – which reveals an interesting faith in the power of the image to create a likeness so believable that the subject's actual presence might be felt.

In the following days attempts were made to convince people that it was possible for art forms to keep their friend alive. A death mask of Marat appeared at the window of his apartment, later to be replaced by a bust. Marat's body meanwhile was fast disintegrating, his head and shoulders turning green, and David was compelled to relinquish his initial plans for the funeral procession, in which he had wanted to exhibit Marat's body seated upright, as he had seen him the day before his death, working away for the sake of the people. Instead, he adopted the same form as the one he had used for displaying the body of another martyr, Le Peletier de Saint-Fargeau; a recumbent figure with the chest wound visible on the unwrapped upper torso (Fig. 4).

In all respects, however, the orchestration of Le Peletier's funeral had been much simpler than Marat's would prove to be. Le Peletier had died in the cold winter month of January, and the smell of rotting, diseased flesh was not a problem then. In the intense heat of July, Marat's corpse had to be accompanied by a sprinkling of heavy perfumes in order to overcome the stench. Le Peletier's allegiances had been straightforward. Marat, however, was claimed by disparate groups and there were therefore competing contenders for control over the arrangements. Robespierre wanted nothing to do with the cult of Marat or of any individual, which, for David, as one of Robespierre's allies, was potentially embarrassing. In the end it was the Sections of Paris that took responsibility for the funeral.

An oil sketch in the Musée Carnavalet, attributed to an artist by the name of Fougea and dating from the following year, gives an

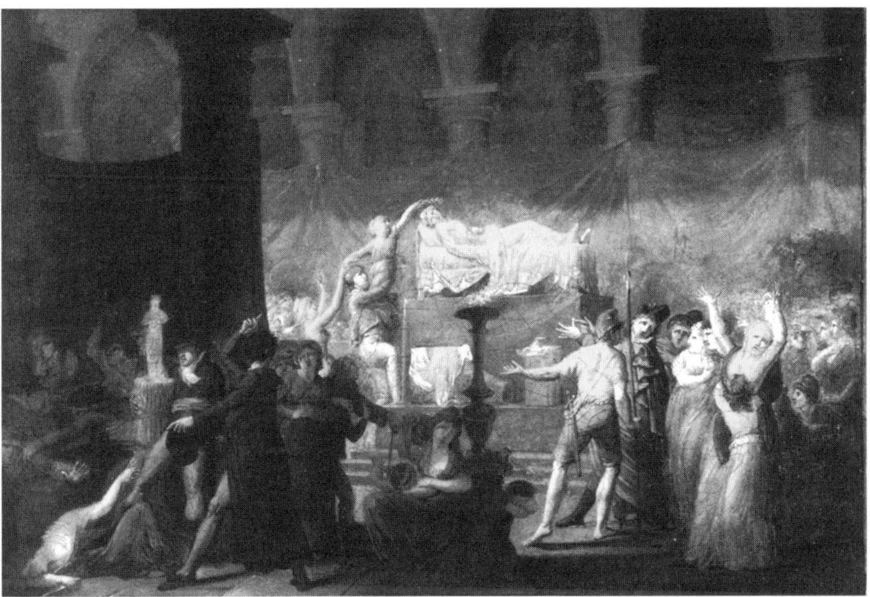

Figure 2. Fougea (attrib.), *The Funeral of Marat in the former Cordeliers Church,* 1794, oil on canvas, 59 × 73 cm. Musée Carnavalet, Paris. (Photothèque des Musées de la Ville de Paris.)

idea of the sort of scenes in the Church of the Cordeliers where Marat lay in state (Fig. 2). Significantly, the body was within reach of the mourning people, not just of their representatives, as was the case with Le Peletier. Also evident is the presence of wailing, keening women hugging their children and feeding their babies in the foreground. Marat's arm hangs down by his side as in David's painting, and the effects or attributes of the martyr – bath and blood-stained sheet, upended box, inkwell, papers and quill – are all there in reference and deference to David's painting. But Fougea's work could hardly be further removed from David's. Fougea's painting presents a compression of a diachronic sequence; it includes on the left-hand side the capture of Corday and her supposed conspirators, as well as the funeral ceremony of several days later. By contrast, David's painting represents a single moment of suspense. It makes no attempt to tell the story or describe the scene of Marat's assassination or to include any of the other characters who had been present. The first is a cluttered genre scene, a confused narrative; David's is a laconic transparent work, a history painting and an icon whose power to fascinate has hardly diminished since the day of its first exhibition.

THE DRAMATIS PERSONAE

The creation of David's *Marat* involved three people most directly: the victim represented in the picture, the assassin who precipitated the event it commemorated, and the painter.

JEAN-PAUL MARAT – THE VICTIM

Marat never produced the autobiography that he had wanted to write, but there is a diary that enables us to follow his early years. He was born in Switzerland in 1743 and was a sickly child but later proved to be a brilliant student. He spent the years 1762–5 in Paris studying medicine, followed by a ten-year period in England and Scotland practising as a doctor. It was here that he started his career as a writer, with a number of essays that were expanded into a book, on the nature of the human soul, followed by successful publications on electricity and optics, and the more famous *The Chains of Slavery* of 1774.[5] The influence of Descartes and Jean-Jacques Rousseau is tangible in these writings.

Back in Paris in 1776 he was, ironically, appointed the following year as doctor to the troops in the household of the king's brother, the Comte d'Artois. This position lasted only until 1782, when the first of his serious bouts of illness, together with financial difficulties resulting from constant persecution from the Science Academy, caused him to leave this employ. On recovery he vowed to devote himself thereafter to serving the cause of liberty. In *L'Offrande à la patrie* (Feb. 1789), he addressed the French people on the imminent elections for the Estates General and on the tone and language adopted by the king's letter of convocation, of which he disapproved, but most of all on the duties of the people's representatives and the misery of the people.

From then on Marat styled himself as the champion of the freedom of the press and of the cause of the people. He cultivated a lifestyle of austerity, truth, and virtue, and he gloried in rudeness as a sign of his integrity and refusal to please. Polite manners he viewed as a form of corruption. He constantly offered to die, to sacrifice himself rather than compromise his principles.

In September 1789 Marat started publishing *L'Ami du Peuple,* first called *Le Publiciste,* in which he noted from the start his intention to expose conspiracies, traitors, and plots and to warn the people of danger from whatever source. He called himself 'the eye of the people' and 'dénonciateur patriote', but 'l'ami du peuple' is the name that for many, including David, was synonymous with Marat. His life was one of self-imposed austerity and untiring devotion to the people's welfare. Much of the time he was persecuted by the authorities for his forthright attacks on government policies and, not surprisingly, had to work clandestinely, even literally underground, in a basement from which he emerged only after the overthrow of the monarchy on 10 August 1792. This picture of Marat working underground by the light of a lantern would appear frequently in subsequent imagery.

Marat was elected as a Paris deputy to the National Convention on 9 September 1792, sitting with Danton, Robespierre, and David, among others, and from this date he and his newspaper became the target of attack from the Brissotins, more generally known as Girondins. They believed Marat to have been responsible for inciting the sans-culottes to massacre Girondins held in Paris prisons in September. They also accused him of wanting to become a dictator. On 12 April 1793 they eventually obtained a decree from the National Convention to have Marat brought to trial before the revolutionary tribunal. This was a fatal mistake on their part. Marat was able to defend himself against all charges and was acquitted and carried in triumph from the courthouse on 23 April 1793. This victory would constitute one of the subjects of the famous painting competition of the Year II (1794). In the next weeks Marat's health deteriorated and alarming reports were given in the newspapers. It was understood that he did not have long to live. That his life and death would not, however, be allowed to follow their natural course, and that 'the friend of the people' would be assassinated by a young woman, supporter of the Girondin faction, could never have been foreseen.

MARIE-ANNE CHARLOTTE CORDAY – THE ASSASSIN

Like David, Charlotte Corday (Marie to her friends) had been well educated, especially in the literature of the ancient world, and she had a particular interest in Plutarch's *Lives.* Her education had been formed by nuns of the royal abbey at Caen until the convents were closed down in 1791. She also made reference during her trial and elsewhere to the writings of Abbé Raynal and to the political writings of Jean-Jacques Rousseau. She was born in Normandy in 1768 and lived in Caen at the time of the outbreak of the Revolution. Caen was a stronghold of Girondin supporters who had chosen to leave Paris as their moderate views became less and less acceptable from spring 1793 onwards. Since April, Corday had been planning to assassinate Marat, whom she regarded as the real enemy of the French, because he had been responsible for denouncing in the late May and early June issues of his newspaper the many Girondins whom he had branded as traitors – 'unmitigated royalists' who had wanted to 'annihilate liberty by treason and re-establish despotism by civil war'.[6] If she could eliminate Marat, Corday believed she could bring peace back to France.

Like David, she too had a strong sense of the theatrical, in her case stemming perhaps from the fact that her ancestor was Pierre Corneille, whose plays explored the value of patriotism over and above the passions of the human heart. In his play *Cinna,* for example, she found an expression of ambition and zeal similar to her own and an image of a bloodthirsty tiger in Rome, which, for many Girondins at this time, characterised Marat in Paris.[7]

Corday never married, and her unmarried status at the age of nearly twenty-five was held against her at her trial. Jacobin attitudes toward women – and these were endorsed by Marat – insisted that certainly by this age a woman should have married and should be producing little patriots to fight for their country. Corday was a virgin at this time, as ascertained shortly after her death.[8] Her attractive appearance was also manipulated to count against her at her trial, especially since the moderate press, certain poets (including André Chénier), and some sympathetic engravers had begun to show her in a positive light, as the obedient daughter writing to her father from prison, for example, or as a supremely calm and poised woman who displayed utter conviction in the rightness of her act.

Corday never swayed from her belief in herself and indeed spent some of her time in prison constructing the kind of image she wished posterity to have of her. She posed for a portrait of herself by the painter Jean-Jacques Hauer. Her trial took place on 17 July. She was condemned to the guillotine and executed that same day. The myth of her angelic beauty and power to enlist supporters to her cause through her innocence and serenity continued at the scaffold. When her head was held up to the crowd it was slapped on one cheek, which apparently caused the other cheek to blush. The legend of Charlotte Corday persisted intermittently throughout the nineteenth century, but it was considerably promoted by Jules Michelet in the mid–nineteenth century, and she became the subject of countless paintings (especially popular at the 1880 Paris Salon), sculptures, plays, poems, and prints, the study of which is beyond the brief of this book.[9]

JACQUES-LOUIS DAVID – THE PAINTER

David held a number of public positions during the early 1790s. He was one of the major orchestrators of the numerous Paris festivals, from the pantheonization of Voltaire in July 1791 to the Festival of the Republic One and Indivisible in July 1793 and the Festival of the Supreme Being in summer 1794. He also led a petition to restructure the Académie Royale de Peinture along more democratic lines, with the eventual outcome being its abolition in August 1793. And he was officially appointed to paint the posthumous portraits of three martyrs of the Revolution: the regicide, Le Peletier de Saint-Fargeau; the defender of the sans-culottes, Jean-Paul Marat; and the young republican boy fighting in the Vendée, Joseph Bara.

In 1791, for the *Société des Amis de la Constitution,* later to become the Jacobin Club, he had agreed to paint a huge canvas (26 feet long) of *The Oath of the Tennis Court.* In the Versailles tennis court members of the Third Estate, with a few defectors from the nobility and the clergy, had come together in an emergency meeting in June 1789 to ensure fairer representation of the people of France. David produced a finely detailed finished pen-and-wash drawing for this commission and started work on the canvas. By 1801, however, political events had overtaken it and the work was left unfinished. It is possible that he was still working on it in the summer of 1793, however. In the first half of 1792 David had experimented in a series of drawings for a portrait of King Louis XVI as a father, pointing out to his son, the dauphin, the articles of the new Constitution. But by 10 August 1792 the king was suspended, the monarchy overthrown, and a National Convention had replaced the Assembly. David would later deny any attempt to produce a portrait of the king.

David was elected deputy for Paris to the National Convention in September and sat with Marat, Danton, Robespierre, and other Jacobins. By the time he finished the painting of Marat the new revolutionary calendar had been brought into action to replace the Gregorian calendar. The Republic dated from September 1792, shortly after the collapse of the monarchy and the imprisonment of the royal family. In October 1793 France was therefore in year II of the Republic. Careful use of this calendar change is made in David's portrait of Marat.

In January 1793 David voted for the death of the king. He also produced his first martyr portrait in honour of Le Peletier de Saint-Fargeau, a former member of the nobility, who had been killed by one of the king's guards for casting his vote for the king's death. It was as a pendant to this portrait that David painted *Marat* the following July through October, intending both paintings to hang behind the speaker's rostrum in the hall of the National Convention, as inspiration to the representatives of the people assembled there and, by extension, to the entire French people. David's antipathy toward the queen, Marie-Antoinette, would also be made transparent in his drawing of her, believed to have been done as she passed under the window of his apartment in the Louvre, on her way to the guillotine on 16 October 1793 (25 vendémiaire, An II). In a wholly unflattering pen-and-ink drawing he represented the former queen without her wig, teeth, or any of the usual regal attire. Later this same day *Marat at his last breath* made its first public appearance. It was exhibited, along with *Le Peletier on his Deathbed,* in the courtyard of the Louvre, for the benefit of the Section du Museum, in order that David's fellow citizens of this Section might pay civic honour to the two martyrs.[10]

In September 1793 David became a member of the powerful Committee of General Security, and in the following month he was on the Committee of Public Instruction. These committees had the responsibility for promoting social reform and for ordering trials, imprisonment, or death for antirevolutionaries. Maximilian

Robespierre was the guiding force behind the committees, and David admired him and willingly went along with his propagandistic policies. At this date Robespierre appreciated what Marat represented for the people, yet his instinct was not to honour individuals during their lifetime but to use their deaths for rooting out anti-republican forces and for exalting the abstract notions of Virtue, Liberty, People.

For some time David had been campaigning for the reform of the 'despotic' Académie Royale de Peinture along more democratic lines. He had also been instrumental in bringing about structural and organisational reforms for the Salon since 1789 and in transforming the Louvre into the Central Museum of the Arts with its revolutionary programme of reforms. On 8 August 1793 David called for the total abolition of the Academy, 'last refuge of all aristocracies', as he labelled it, in a speech that is impressive for its passionate appeal: 'in the name of humanity, in the name of justice, for the love of art, and especially for your love of youth, let us destroy these sinister Academies, which can no longer survive under the reign of liberty'.[11] All academies were closed down on 14 August 1793.

On 14 October David announced the completion of his painting to the National Convention and asked for permission to display it first to his colleagues in the courtyard of the Louvre for two weeks before giving it to the Convention. David's colleagues' reactions, in which they pay respect to David's patriotism, are recorded:

> The expressed horror . . . permeates the whole canvas, which proves that the forceful and skillful touch of the artist would not have been sufficient in itself; it needed that ardent love of country that impassions the artist. . . . it is difficult to look on it [the *Marat*] for any length of time, its effect is so powerful.[12]

David eventually presented *Marat* to the Convention on 14 November, praising Marat's virtues and calling for the friend of the people to be given the honours of the Pantheon. In May 1794 the National Convention decreed that copies of the painting be reproduced by the Gobelin factory under David's supervision. By this time David had been at work for several months on his portrait of Joseph Bara. He was in charge of choreographing the public funerary ceremonies of Bara and another young martyr, Viala. He was also working on a curtain design representing *The Triumph of the*

French People, in which the procession of martyrs following the people's chariot is suddenly interrupted by the figure of Marat, who leaps out toward the spectator to reveal his wound and appeals for vengeance. The Bara portrait would be left in a state of uncertain finish by the time of Robespierre's fall in July 1794, and the drop curtain was never produced in finished form. They represent David's last activities under the Terror. With the fall of Robespierre David underwent a spell in prison, and after his release at the end of 1794, he went to stay with his wife's sister, Madame Sériziat, in Saint-Ouen in order to recover from an illness. He stayed there until October, with another period in prison from late May to early August. On 26 October 1795 the Convention agreed to a general amnesty for crimes under the Terror and David recovered his freedom and returned to Paris.

THE LOOK OF THE PICTURE

Although simple, the picture has been arranged with the utmost care. It is possible to read it as a set of two-dimensional rhythms. Despite the high relief suggested by the raking light, the picture has very little depth. It is almost like a frieze. Both the box and the bath are severely rectilinear and are parallel with the edges of the picture. They provide a rigorous structure against which the curves and diagonals of the dying Marat are set. All these curves and diagonals suggest collapse; they are sloping and sagging downwards, as are the pen that Marat is holding and the scattered pieces of paper. The head has rolled over the farthest. Although it is the focus of the picture, the face is also the hardest object to read. The tilt it is given cleverly performs two functions. It both indicates that Marat's death is near and prevents us from observing his features properly. For Marat's face was disfigured with the skin disease that caused him to spend so much time in the bath in which he has been assassinated. David has managed to prevent us from reading the distorted nature of his hero's features while avoiding an obvious idealisation that would have destroyed the picture's sense of actuality.

IT IS POSSIBLE to find a precedent for David's treatment of his theme in the depiction of martyred saints. In this sense the picture fits within a 'genre' of religious painting and that of other heroes who died for a noble cause. Within that genre, however, the picture stands out for its great originality. It has an unusual simplicity and starkness. This can be related to contemporary aesthetic interests. David was painting at a time when many artists were inspired by a return to classicism to explore new and radically simplified ways of designing pictures, sculptures, buildings, and other artifacts. This artistic climate probably helped David to formulate the extreme directness of the work. Yet the formula remains his own, and was in fact worked out by him on the canvas, as evidenced by a number of 'pentimenti' in the design. He was making changes to its details as he painted. The rhythm of shapes does not conform to any traditional compositional pattern – such as that of the 'Golden Section', which was much used by classical artists to communicate a sense of harmony. He seems instead to have chosen intervals that emphasise emptiness. The whole of the top half of the canvas is a dark, impenetrable space. The first object in the picture is Marat's head, which is placed exactly halfway down. This is the principle focus of the picture. It would be usual to have this focal point in or near the centre of the picture. Yet while David has made it halfway up the picture, he has also moved it across very far to the left. It is interesting to see from the one surviving supposedly preparatory compositional study (Fig. 17) that David has increased the extremeness of this position in the finished picture.

Although the picture appears to be very clear and 'real', it contains a subtle spatial ambiguity. Looking at Marat's head, we might imagine that we are on a level with it. It is exactly halfway up the picture, which is where one normally expects 'eye level' to be when looking at a picture unless some clear indication to the contrary is given within the picture itself. The head is turned toward us 'flat on', which would fit in with a central viewing point. Yet if we follow the diagonals of the edges of the box and the plank across the bath we see that they lead to a vanishing point high on the right side of the picture. They have been drawn as though we were looking down on the scene rather than directly at it, something that we might expect to do if we were standing in a room and looking down on someone in a bath. The lean of the shoulders toward us disguises the discrepancy between the two spatial systems. This discrepancy is not in any way due to ineptness. It is deliberately planned to make us simultaneously look down on

Marat and straight at him – to pity him yet respect him. It also enhances the strange sense of separateness that the head has from the rest of the picture, making it all the more hypnotic and doubtless reminding contemporaries of the many guillotined heads that were falling with increasing alacrity by autumn 1793.

In keeping with his training as a historical painter, David has made colour strictly subordinate to form. Colour is used in this painting to articulate shapes, and it echoes them in its simplicity. There is in fact a very restricted use of colour. Whites and browns predominate, the white sheets echoing the paleness of the body, the dark brown of the background providing a murky obscurity beyond the event. The green of the cloth (an unusual colour for David) gives a restful tone, as well as providing a background to throw the foreground wooden box into starker relief. This low-key series of tones makes the small touches of blood red all the more telling.

We can see how carefully David has staged his picture to make it seem compelling and 'authentic'. It has often been described as though it were a faithful record of what happened. Baudelaire, for example, said that it was as 'real as a Balzac novel'.[13] In recent times the historian Edgar Wind has praised it as a 'remarkable piece of reportage'.[14] Yet as has already been indicated, the artist has in fact been extremely cavalier with the evidence. Beyond the fact that the picture shows Marat having been stabbed in his bath, it contains hardly a detail that corresponds either to the sequence of events or to the appearance of the place in which they occurred. Marat was certainly stabbed in his bath, but he didn't expire quietly in isolation. The bath he had been sitting in didn't look like the one David created. It was a conventional sabot-shaped one, as can be seen in other representations of the event. Marat was not reading the letter he is shown as holding when Corday came in to stab him. Nor was he writing at the moment when he was stabbed. The makeshift desk he used did not look like the crude box in the picture. Even the knife that Charlotte Corday used to murder Marat did not look like the one portrayed.

There is more than 'artistic license' in all these changes. For the truth of the matter is that David was not intending simply to show one specific moment in the story of Marat's death. He was presenting a picture that would simultaneously record the horror of martyrdom and present an image of his hero as 'l'ami du peuple'. David had seen Marat at work in his bath a day before the assassination, and the memory of that visit is the base on which this picture is built. What he has done, in effect, is to imagine the assassination as though it had taken place immediately after the moment that he himself had last seen Marat alive. From a psychological point of view, this was perhaps how David himself experienced the event. For the next time that he saw Marat after his visit, the politician was a corpse. He has united the personal with the public to give this commemoration a particular charge.

The picture was originally intended as a commemorative image. This practice was part of a deliberate campaign to use pictures of revolutionary martyrs to replace religious imagery. It was done quite literally at times; new images actually took the place in some churches of the old religious ones. From September 1793 to March 1794 there was a strong 'culte de Marat'. By the end of November more than fifty commemorative ceremonies for Marat had been held in Paris, usually including a bust of him as a central focus. Increasing unease was felt by Jacobin leaders about the scale of these ceremonies. On 14 November, after the Pantheonization of Marat, Robespierre made a plea for these activities to cease.[15]

Robespierre attempted to replace the cult of martyrs with that of the Supreme Being in 1794. Although his effort did not succeed — and Robespierre himself was soon to fall from power and be executed — this shift does mark the beginning of the process that caused David's *Marat* to be removed from public view early in 1795.

THE PICTURE'S HISTORY AND RECEPTION

From the time of its first exhibition, the *Marat* has been perceived as a striking and disturbing work. The first published account appeared as a result of the exhibition of it together with the *Le Peletier* at the Louvre in October 1793: 'Although these two pictures are conceived each in their own way in the best possible terms, artists especially admire the picture of Marat. Indeed it is difficult to look at it for very long, so terrible is its effect'.[16]

Since the *Le Peletier* was destroyed in 1826 it is impossible to say whether it, too, might have enjoyed a subsequent history similar to that of *Marat.* However, important though it clearly was as a work (and included by David together with the *Marat* as his two most significant works), it did not contain the elements of shock and *verismo* that the *Marat* does, so it may not have occupied quite such a central position. It may have been those very elements that caused the artists, when they first saw the two, to prefer the *Marat*. Certainly the commentator's remark about the terribleness of the effect of this work has persisted and has been a key feature of the picture's fascination ever since.

The challenging nature of the picture has also been maintained by the continued controvertiality of its subject. Marat was long reviled after his death by both conservatives and liberals as a monster and an inciter of the rabble to barbaric deeds.[17] It was Marat, remarked Mme de Stael, 'whom posterity will perhaps remember in order to attach to one man the crimes of an epoch'.[18]

Even after the first Republic began to be rehabilitated in the 1840s, Marat remained condemned as a monster. Jules Michelet, in his classic study, used Marat's physical repulsiveness to enhance repugnance: 'from what swamp has come this shocking creature?' he asked.[19] Not surprisingly, Michelet exalts Corday's character and beauty in his work.

However, in the 1860s, when republican sympathies were beginning to revive, Marat began to be seen by some in a more sympathetic light. Alfred Bougeart, in *Marat, l'ami du peuple,* considered that Marat had been a check on unlicensed authority and felt that he would have saved the Revolution had he lived.[20] Such views were echoed by Engels in 1884, and from this time onwards Marat became a communist hero, eventually becoming widely celebrated as such in Soviet Russia.[21]

In recent years the divided view of Marat has continued. Following the staging of Peter Weiss's *Marat/Sade,* he became a cause celebre in the 1960s, and has continued to act as a bone of contention between left and right since that time. As Ian Germani observed in 1992, 'As long as the issues which divided France during the Revolution continue to divide us today, Marat must necessarily retain his symbolic identity, a figure of revulsion to some, of heroism to others'.[22]

It is difficult to gauge quite how the divided fortunes of Marat have affected responses to David's picture. It certainly doesn't seem to have diminished respect for the painting, though it has affected interpretations. On one hand, right-wing and liberal admirers of the work have tended to emphasise how the human dimensions of the drama 'transcend' the precise political circumstances of its origins. Left-wing supporters, on the other hand, have tended to see the work as the ultimate authentic revolutionary painting, in which personal and public commitment merge into one.

Since the picture remained concealed from 1795 until after David's death, there was no comment about it at the time that Marat was being most thoroughly vilified. However, when it did emerge at the sale of the contents of David's studio it was still regarded as too inflammatory an image to be sold. Nevertheless, the picture attracted attention because of its stark realism and modernity. Stendhal saw the work and wrote in its praise. His experience of the *Marat* seems to have informed his attack on the classicists in his *Salon* review of 1827.[23] In this he accused the classicists of imitating an imitation in modelling themselves on Greek art. David, he said, by contrast, modelled his art on nature. It was a similar sentiment that caused Delacroix to call David the 'father of the modern school'.[24] Delacroix was in fact recognising a tradition of which he was a part. For the two modern artists who were Delacroix's immediate forebears — Gros and Gericault — had developed a form of tragic modernity that some believed to be based on David. It was Gros — the artist who had preserved the *Marat* after David had fled to Brussels — who had taken up the challenge of David's *Marat* during the Napoleonic period with a work like the *Plague at Jaffa,* and Gericault who had taken this dimension further with his own modern disaster picture, the *Raft of the Medusa.*

Marat's next public appearance in Paris took place, interestingly, a couple of years before the 1848 Revolution. It was shown in 1846 at the Bazar Bonne-Nouvelle as part of a small exhibition of the works of David and Ingres. It would seem that the show had been designed as a vindication of the classical tradition. Yet the response that it caused had the opposite effect. Once again critics dwelt on the modernity of David's realism and the failure of academicians to follow his bold lead. This exhibition is memorable for precipitating the most famous description of the picture, that by Baudelaire already quoted at the beginning of this introduction.

This quote became the 'classic formulation' of the picture, both because of Baudelaire's status as a poet and critic, and because of the sheer beauty of his phrases. His obsession with the conflict of the real and the ideal relates perhaps most closely to his own metaphysical self-questioning. Moreover, Baudelaire's description sealed the reputation of the picture as one of quite unusual interest and complexity, and few commentators since that time have been able to avoid seeing a spiritual as well as a realistic dimension in it. Only a year later Alphonse Esquiros described it as a 'pietà jacobine' in his history of the Montagnards of 1847.[25]

The canonical status of the *Marat* received a further boost in 1855 when it was described in E. J. Delécluze's *Louis David, son école et son temps*. A former pupil of David, Delécluze had assiduously followed the works of his master during his career as an art critic and journalist. Now near the end of his life, he published what was to become the standard biography of David. In it Delécluze made clear that he regarded the *Marat* as David's principal work even if not technically his 'masterpiece':

> Likewise the *Marat,* if it is not exactly the artist's masterpiece, must be seen as the first of his works to reveal the power and originality of his talent. He had seen and felt what he painted and it was a moment of enlightenment that made him envisage his art from a completely new point of view.[26]

Delécluze's treatment is important because it places David squarely within the realist camp. Interestingly his book appeared in the same year that Courbet challenged the artistic authorities responsible for the selection of works for the French section of the Exposition Universelle with his 'Pavilion du réalisme'.

The rising reputation of realist art – together with the softening of attitudes to Marat himself – meant that the status of David's painting was no longer in doubt. However, the work was soon to become embroiled in a controversy of another kind. In 1860 Jacques-Louis Jules David, the artist's grandson, acquired *Marat* from his aunt. At the same time he made a gift of one of the copies of *Marat* also in his possession to Prince Napoleon, who placed it in his gallery at the Palais-Royale. Despite the fact that J. L. Jules David made clear the status of the two works in a publication in 1867,[27] claims were made that the Palais-Royale version was in fact the original. This was maintained in particular by the dealer Durand-Ruel, who acquired the version and sold it as an original

David in 1885. A dispute arose and in 1889 Louis David's widow was obliged to take the matter to court, where – despite some disagreements among the experts – the authenticity of her *Marat* was upheld. This unpleasantness may have cost France the work, for in 1893 Mme David bequeathed it to the Musées royaux des Beaux-Arts in Brussels, in recognition of the reception that city had afforded David when he had gone into exile in 1815.

In the nineteenth century David's 'progressive' realism was seen to be in conflict with his classical idealism. However, in the twentieth century opinions changed as the classical revival in the late eighteenth century came to be seen as a radical movement in itself. The starkness of *Marat* now began to be read as a sign of stylistic modernity. This interpretation also led to a reintroduction of the political debate around the image. For political radicals, the stark neoclassical manner was to be read as the visual analogue of republicanism. This position was summarized by Arnold Hauser in his magisterial *Social History of Art*. Writing about David's *Horatii* he said:

> If it is admissible to interpret pure artistic form sociologically, then here is a case in point. This clarity, this uncompromising rigour, this sharpness of expression, has its origins in the republican civic virtues; form is here really only the vehicle, the means to an end.[28]

Hauser's views were countered by those who wished to see neoclassicism in apolitical terms as a pure artistic movement that had the seeds of modernism in it. For some the extreme formal simplicity of the *Marat* was seen as a kind of protominimalism. In the most extensive and detailed exploration of the neoclassical minimalist style, *Transformations in Late Eighteenth Century Art*, Robert Rosenblum wrote of David's pictures as 'sequences of reformatory manifestoes that attempt consecutive purifications of his earlier styles'.[29] In this teleology the *Marat* is still one step away from the final statement of Davidian flatness, the *Sabines* of 1799.

Like much art historical formal analysis, Rosenblum's reading was supported by the concept of modernism as 'pure' pictorialism, the idea promoted by Clement Greenberg so powerfully in the art world in the 1950s and 1960s.

However, there was another dimension to Rosenblum's study. While subscribing to the Greenbergian view of the pictorial rigour

of the late eighteenth century as the harbinger of modernist mini-
malism in the mid–twentieth century, he was also aware of the revolution in iconographical studies brought about by Erwin Panofsky
and other art historians associated with the Warburg Institute. This
approach had been applied most effectively by Lorenz Eitner in his
pioneering article 'The Open Window and the Storm-Tossed
Boat',[30] in which he demonstrated the rich resources that could be
tapped by investigating the art of the late eighteenth and early
nineteenth century in terms of themes. In parallel with his minimalist account of neoclassicism, Rosenblum therefore included a
treatment of certain dominant themes of the period. He discussed
Marat in this context as an example of the vogue for the *exemplum
virtutis,* the spartan portrayal of heroic deaths.

As the high tide of modernism began to recede in the 1970s, the
thematic approach to David's work became increasingly popular.
Marat began to be interpreted again in terms of the psychological
and the political. Anita Brookner's 1980 study represented the psychological at its most extreme and personal. Even David's political
activism was read by her as a sign of psychic disturbance:

> His very activity – incessant between 1789 and 1794 – implies
> that he was affected or even dominated by 'la grande Peur', the
> paranoia of the revolutionaries, who saw themselves menaced by
> danger from without: royal plots, foreign troops, armed brigands,
> the legendary phantoms of delusion.[31]

For Brookner the historical was subservient to the psychological. But at the same time that she was working, historians in France
were providing a greatly enhanced view of the historical detail of
the artist's life and milieu that emphasised how important it was to
read his work in a precise social and political context. The result of
these researches can be seen in Antoine Schnapper's monograph,
published in Paris in the same year as Brookner's was in London.

When talking of *Marat,* Schnapper measures the painting against
the known facts of the assassination, dispelling the myth that it was
some kind of 'authentic' record. Schnapper is careful to emphasise
how the *Marat* must be read in terms of the power politics of the
Jacobins at this time, rather than as a symptom of the artist's state of
mind. However, he is not prepared to evaluate the picture's aesthetic properties in political terms and returns for this part of his

analysis to Baudelaire's characterisation of it as a dialogue between the real and the ideal.

It was left to Thomas Crow to locate the *Marat* within a precise political position. Crow had taken up the mantle of Marxist interpreters following the revolution in the understanding of the social history of art initiated by T. J. Clark and others in the 1970s. Most memorable in this new vein is the use made by N. Hadjinicolaou of *Marat* in *Art History and Class Struggle,*[32] the trenchant study that sought to move art history away from the connoisseurian world of authorship and the analysis of personal style and toward the accounting for the nature of pictures in terms of the social situation in which they emerged. Hadjinicolaou pointed to the frequent style changes in David's portraits to argue that their real point of reference was the sociopolitical situation in which they were created. The starkness of *Marat* becomes in these circumstances the appropriate mode of engagement with revolutionary France, just as the fussy detail of later portraits addressed the bourgeois world of Brussels in which David eked out his last days. Crow brought the conflict between the two approaches out into the open in a review of Anita Brookner's book in *Art History.* Here he used evidence provided by Schnapper to launch the view of *Marat* as a piece of carefully orchestrated Jacobin propaganda, the Marat cult that the Jacobins were then trying to manage and turn to their advantage:

> David's pacified, domesticated image of the dying Marat, his transformation into a beatific icon of all that was rebarbative in the man and inflammatory in the circumstances of his death, must be understood in terms of the complex of demands that occasioned the cult as a whole.[33]

David painted with passion – but it was passion with a purpose: 'Yes, David was personally committed to Marat in an impassioned way; he took it all seriously. But it was passion put to work, disciplined and engaged productively with a determined task'.[34]

Crow heralded the moment when the social dimensions of art could be given a new reality through the detailed exploration of a particular circumstance. Although generally sympathetic with the underlying premises of Hauser and other earlier Marxist historians, he did not share their concern about relating broad stylistic development to social movements.

However, this suspicion about using stylistic categories as historical entities does not imply an overall distrust of visual analysis, or even of the exploration of such analysis within the context of the personal situation of the artist. T. J. Clark himself has always maintained the presence of the visual in his analyses. In an important article published in 1994 he uses his formidable skills to return to the *Marat* as the starting point for modernism. He sees in David a combination of both political and pictorial commitment, a total sense of purposefulness with an 'all-or-nothing sense of the real'.[35]

Clark is still arguing with a sense of political purpose. He is reconnecting *Marat* here with the Marxist critical tradition that equates the modern with committed realism rather than with formal purity. In doing so he is moving back to a premodernist position, although he is handling it with a new sophistication and a thoroughly up-to-date sense of the minutiae of French revolutionary politics.

Meanwhile, others have moved toward a more postmodernist integration of the social with subjective psychologising, informed increasingly by the perceptions afforded by gender studies. In his more recent writings Crow has moved in this direction. In his recent study of French art of the revolutionary period, *Emulation,* he brings these resources to bear on *Marat.* The critic who censured Brookner in 1981 for peddling 'psycho-history' has now himself become a psychohistorian, albeit of a different hue. Following the lead of gender studies – and using the often-noted resemblance of Marat's pose to that of the statue of the *Borghese Hermaphrodite*[36] – he explores *Marat* as androgynous, a figure that combines the passive female with the muscular male. Delving into the depths of the artist's postulated psyche Crow also proposes a secret artistic history for the picture, reaching back to 'La Déposition du Croix' (Deposition of Christ from the Cross) by David's pupil Girodet. Above all, he uses the picture to assert the presence of a private world that most viewers cannot discern:

> David's *Marat* enters the unstable territory of a true androgyny, but buries that engagement so deeply and privately in the working process that few of its viewers, then or since, can have seen that quality as anything more than an elusive suggestion.[37]

The shift in Crow's mode of interpretation over the last decade is an indication of the changing nature of art historical studies today. There are many approaches now being practised, each capable of providing its own reflections and insights, as readers will find in the following chapters.

APPROACHING *MARAT A SON DERNIER SOUPIR* IN SIX DIFFERENT WAYS

The importance of Charles Baudelaire's poetic critique of David's image has been much commented upon. It is constantly quoted for its ability to find through its poetic language a literary equivalent to the emotional power of the image. We have found it sufficiently moving to quote it in full at the beginning of this introduction.

The different approaches in this book to David's *Marat* begin with the chapter by Tom Gretton, a cultural historian of eighteenth- and nineteenth-century France. Gretton throws light on some of the complex meanings of 'the People', 'Jacobin rule', and 'martyrdom', and he brings his findings as a historian to his interpretation of the image and to his understanding of the way in which this representation of *Marat* 'makes history as well as being made by it'. His chapter is followed by Tony Halliday's, which considers the painting in its secular context and in its relation to posthumous portraiture in late-eighteenth-century France and in public and private spheres. William Vaughan explores the image's pictorial qualities in a European framework and in relation to history painters of the period, especially those interested in the representation of fear and the irrational. This chapter is followed by Libby Sheldon's analysis of the picture's physical components, the methods and materials used by David in relation to the practise of other artists at the time. Helen Weston's study derives from the work of historians and art historians writing women's history, as she examines the absence of Corday but the evocation of her moral character in David's image. The collection closes with a psychoanalytical approach by David Lomas, who looks at later nineteenth- and twentieth-century reworkings of David's painting and considers the issues of martyrdom and sacrifice as they are staged by artists, writers, and filmmakers.

There is some difficulty in translating David's title, *Marat à son dernier soupir,* into English: 'Marat at his last breath' or 'Marat breathing his last' come close. Marat is represented by David at the point of dying, coming to rest at the end of the last breath, but not having fully expired. This title draws attention to the moment of the final dying breath, and the image represents Marat displaying his dying words – or his supposed dying words. The composition, however, suggests stasis already achieved.

We are accustomed, as indeed were art specialists in the eighteenth century, to seeing large-scale history paintings that represent the dying words of ancient heroes and philosophers. David, and Poussin most notably before him, had already painted such subjects. And indeed, as William Vaughan explains, this painting fits to some extent into the category of history painting, as practised by European artists in the latter half of the eighteenth century. However, Marat was a contemporary figure who had been ignominiously stabbed, not in battle but with a kitchen knife, by a female political opponent, while in a bathtub. Could David really put an image of the utterance of Marat's last words on a par with those of ancient heroes such as Socrates bidding farewell to his disciples, Eudamidas writing his final will and testament (Fig. 3), or Germanicus on his deathbed surrounded by loyal soldiers and family? Was the painting targeting the same kind of audiences as those who would have seen history paintings in the major public exhibition spaces of European cities?

The fact that the painting now hangs in a national museum and is acknowledged as a key work in the history of European art, much praised for its beauty and clarity, does not mean that it was conceived as such or that it functioned as such when first put on display – as Tony Halliday's chapter makes clear – or that it was received in this way at that time, or that it has been perceived as such for most of the time ever since. Vaughan addresses the need to articulate the work's qualities and to locate it in relation to its contemporary European paintings; he also explores the question of why the painting has come to occupy such a significant place in our cultural history.

Elizabeth Sheldon approaches this painting from the position of the picture analyst, and her chapter gives us new insights into the range of techniques available to and deployed by David, and into the practice in his studio during the later years of the eighteenth century. By examining, through infrared reflectography, the work lying beneath the surface of the image as we see it, she has been able to indicate some of the changes that David made as he went along. The importance of this approach lies both in informing us

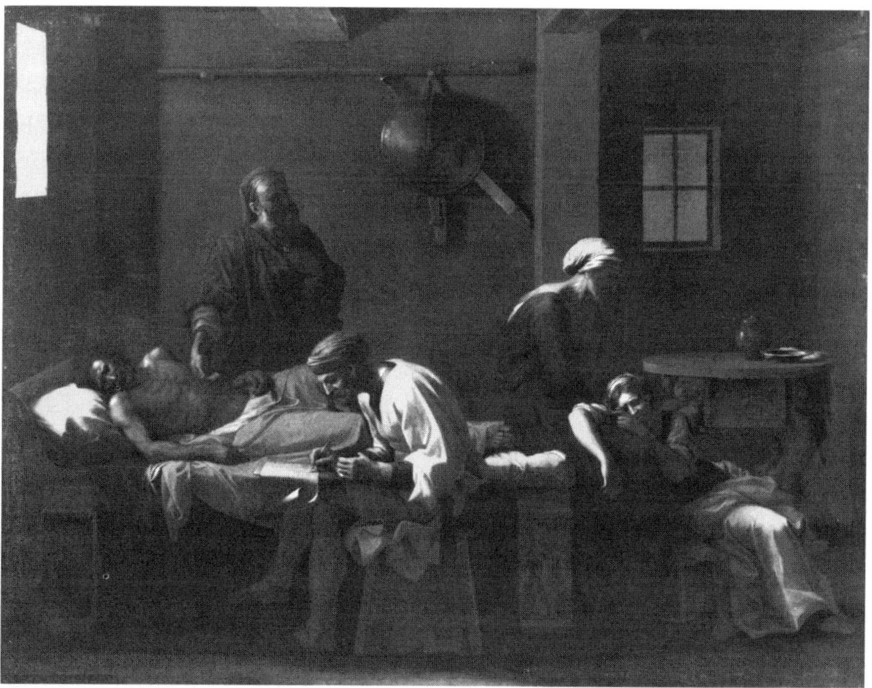

Figure 3. Nicolas Poussin, *The Testament of Eudamidas,* c. 1645–50, oil on canvas, 110.5 × 138.5 cm. Den Kongelige Maleri-og Skulptursamling, Statens Museum for Kunst, Copenhagen. (Photo: Hans Petersen.)

more accurately about David's working methods at this point in his career and in revealing the subtle modifications of meaning that then appear as we become aware of the final resolution of problems in the finished painting of *Marat à son dernier soupir.*

The grim circumstances of Marat's assassination clearly presented David with a number of problems. How was he to avoid the absurd and the ridiculous? How could he avoid making Marat look pathetic and disease-ridden? How could he raise the image above the level of a domestic genre scene or a piece of melodrama? Obviously, all his training in France and Italy as a history painter, as a portraitist, and as the current pageant-master of the Republic would have to be invoked to find solutions and ensure the desired interaction between icon and public in the immediate aftermath of the picture's production.

As a modern historian Thomas Gretton has approached this painting with a view to understanding the political moment when the crime was committed and when the picture was released to the people of Paris. In particular, his chapter explores the complex relationship between the powerful, radical group of Jacobins, to which David belonged; the popular movement in Paris that operated through its clubs and forty-eight Parisian Sections; and the self-styled 'ami du peuple', the 'friend of the people' that was Jean-Paul Marat and whom the Jacobins and certain Paris Sections both needed to appropriate to their own causes. Gretton indicates how crucial it was to the Jacobins for them to be seen as the obvious group to represent the People and the People's friend, and how David, as one of their number, was the obvious man to do it.[38]

In his speech to the Convention on 24 brumaire, l'an II (14 November 1793), David sees himself as answering the call of the People: 'The people wanted their friend back, its sad voice could be heard, it prompted me to paint, it wished to see again the features of its faithful friend . . . I heard the voice of the people, I obeyed'.[39]

But the notion of the 'People', as Gretton explains, had many meanings, which were constantly shifting. How, he asks, was David, as one of the Jacobin ruling elite, to represent that notion in the summer of 1793?

That David had no control over later reactions to or appropriations of his creation in the nineteenth and twentieth centuries goes without saying. In the last chapter of this book David Lomas examines these later appropriations and the free 'play of identifications' between the image, the artist, and the beholder that is invited by David's painting. Lomas explores the psychodynamics of David's painting in relation to reworkings of it by Munch and Picasso at the end of the nineteenth and in the early twentieth centuries, respectively. Drawing on the work of Freud, J. Laplanche, and J-B. Pontalis, Lomas views these later reworkings of Munch and Picasso as phantasmic scenarios, as staged tableaux in which the subject – possibly the artist himself – appears as actor in the unfolding of the drama.

Many of the chapters in this book raise the question of the representation of martyrdom and the need to transfer power from the assassin to the martyr/victim. In this respect Gretton discusses the place of the sword in *Le Peletier de Saint-Fargeau* (Fig. 4) as it invites the beholder to seize it, and the green fold draped over Marat's bath, in similar terms. The martyr continues to address the people. Weston's chapter invites the beholder to refuse to see self-sacrifice in Marat's death, but to acknowledge Corday's agency; paradoxically through David's attempts to twist Corday's words and eliminate her presence. She argues that David has, through his careful selection and deselection of certain words and letters, disallowed any positive, feminine, or virtuous force to drive Corday's act, and instead invested the victim with muscular power, purity of form, and magnanimity of action. Lomas argues for the possibility of a masochistic positioning of the artist/subject in relation to David's image, whereby the artist, not the painting's subject, might take the place of the Christ-like, submissive, sacrificial victim.

One of David's objectives was to produce an image of Marat that would stand in for the real man and convince the People that their friend was still with them. In this sense the painting also takes its place in other eighteenth-century traditions, those of the posthumous portrait or of the portraits of the great men of France. Tony Halliday's chapter calls for a consideration of the painting in its secular context and explores its relation to the contemporary practice of producing public memorials to national heroes and the illustrious dead with the aim of providing examples to potential successors. Drawing on the work of Mona Ozouf and J. Habermas, Halliday problematises the notion of the public sphere in relation to private grief and to eighteenth-century understandings of public and private, which, for republican France of 1793, stemmed ultimately from ancient Greece and Rome.

It is the hope of the contributors and editors that in the different approaches to David's *Marat à son dernier soupir* presented in this collection, readers will find fresh cause for thought and stimulus for further exploration of this endlessly fascinating and challenging image.

NOTES

1. Le *divin* Marat, un bras pendant hors de la baignoire et retenant mollement sa dernière plume, la poitrine percée de la blessure *sacrilège,* vient de rendre le dernier soupir. Sur le pupitre vert placé

devant lui sa main tient encore la lettre perfide: «Citoyen, it suffit que je sois bien malheureuse pour avoir droit à votre bienveillance.» L'eau de la baignoire est rougie de sang, le papier est sanglant; à terre gît un grand couteau de cuisine trempé de sang; sur un misérable support de planches qui composait le mobilier de travail de l'infatigable journaliste, on lit: «A Marat, David.» Tous ces détails. Sont historiques et réels, comme un roman de Balzac; le drame est là, vivant dans toute sa lamentable horreur, et par un tour de force étrange qui fait de cette peinture le chef-d'oeuvre de David et une des grands curiosités de l'art moderne, elle n'a rien de trivial ni d'ignoble. Ce qu'il y a de plus étonnant dans ce poème inaccoutumé, c'est qu'il est peint avec une rapidité extrême, et quand on songe à la beauté du dessin, il y a là de quoi confondre l'esprit. Ceci est le pain des forts et le triomphe du spiritualisme; Cruel comme la nature, ce tableau a tout le parfum de l'idéal. Quelle était donc cette laideur que la sainte Mort a si vite effacée du bout de son aile? Marat peut désormais défier l'Apollon, la mort vient de le baiser de ses lèvres amoureuses, et il repose dans le calme de sa métamorphose. Il y a dans cette oeuvre quelque chose de tendre et de poignant à la fois; dans l'air froid de cette chambre, sur ces murs froids, autour de cette froide et funèbre baginoire, une âme voltige. Nous permettrez-vous, politiques de tous les partis, et vous-même, farouches libéraux de 1845, de nous attendrir devant le chef d'oeuvre de David? Cette peinture était un don à la patrie éplorée, et nos larmes ne sont pas dangereuses.

Baudelaire, Charles, 'Le Musée classique du Bazar Bonne-Nouvelle', *Le Corsaire-Satan*, 21 January 1846; reprinted in *Oeuvres complètes* (Paris: Gallimard, Pléiade edition, 1976), 2:410.

2. For definitions of all political terms used, see the glossary provided at the end of the book.

3. *Le Moniteur Universel*, 18 July 1793, no. 199, 151–2.

4. The letter, together with its envelope, is kept in the Archives Nationales (côte W277, dossier 82, pièce 11). The police officer, Guellard, noted on it that its delivery to Marat had not been necessary since Corday had managed to get to see him at about 7.30 in the evening.

5. The full title is *The Chains of Slavery: a work wherein the clandestine and villainous attempts of princes to ruin liberty are pointed out, and the dreadful scenes of despotism disposed, to which is prefixed an address to the electors of Great Britain, in order to draw their timely attention to the choice of proper representatives in the Parliament.* It bore the motto that Marat had adopted from Rousseau – *Vitam impendere vero* – loosely translated as 'to lead a life wholly dependent

on seeking truth', and this would become the motto frequently attached to Marat in prints and monuments dedicated to his memory.

6. See the minutes of 2 June 1793 in *Le Moniteur Universel,* 5 June 1793, for the Convention's decree calling for the arrest of those whom Marat had named in his paper *Le Publiciste.*

7.

CINNA

Amis, leur ai-je dit, voici le jour heureux

Qui doit conclure enfin nos desseins généreux,

Le ciel entre nos mains a mis le sort de Rome,

Si l'on doit le nom d'homme à qui n'a rien d'humain,

A ce tigre altéré de tout le sang romain.

[Friends, I said, this is the happy day

Which should see the conclusion of all our great plans,

Heaven has placed the destiny of Rome in our hands,

If one must call a man that which is not human

This tiger gorged on the blood of all Rome.]

8. There is in fact no official document to support the story that Corday's body was examined to verify her virginity or otherwise, but a number of reports give a certain credence to the story, in particular that of Docteur Cabanis, 'La vraie Charlotte Corday, IV: l'Autopsie de Charlotte Corday', in *Le Cabinet secret de l'Histoire,* 2e série (Paris: A. Charles, 1897), 177–81. See Michael Marrinan, 'Texts and Contexts of an Assassination', *Arts Magazine* (April 1980): 158–75, n. 34.

9. For an excellent account of the imagery and various texts in connection with the case of Charlotte Corday, see Marrinan, 158–75.

10. The paintings were somehow arranged on sarcophagi in the courtyard of the Louvre, but just exactly how is not clear.

11. '[A]u nom de l'humanité, au nom de la justice, pour l'amour de l'art, et surtout par votre amour pour la jeunesse, anéantissons les trop funestes Académies, qui ne peuvent plus subsiter sous un régime libre'. Text given in J. L. Jules David, *Le peintre Louis David* (Paris: Victor Havard, 1880), 1: 127 ff.

12. *Journal de Paris,* 22 October 1793, no. 295, 1188.

13. See note 1.

14. Edgar Wind, 'The Revolution of History Painting', *Journal of the Warburg and Courtauld Institute* 2 (1938): 118.

15. 'Et moi aussi j'ai défendu Marat contre ses ennemis; mais après avoir fait son apothéose patriotique, il est inutile d'entendre tous les jours son éloge funèbre et des discours ampoulés sur le même sujet'. J.-Cl. Bonnet, ed., *La mort de Marat* (Paris: Flammarion, 1986), 58.

16. 'Quoique ces deux tableaux soient chacun dans leur genre ce que l'on peut concevoir de mieux, les artistes admirent plus particulièrement le tableau de Marat. Il est effectivement difficile d'en soutenir longtemps la vue, tant l'effet en est terrible'. René Verbraeken *Jacques-Louis David jugé par ses contemporains et par la postérité* (Paris: Léonce Laget, 1973), 71.

17. I. Germani, *Jean-Paul Marat: Hero and Anti-Hero of the French Revolution* (Lewiston, N.Y.: Edwin Mellen Press, 1992).

18. Germaine de Stael, *Considérations sur les principaux événements de la Révolution Française* (London: Baldwin, Cradock & Joy, 1818), 2: 51.

19. Jules Michelet, *Histoire de la Révolution Française* (1847; reprint, Paris: Gallimard, Pléiade edition, 1939), 2: 350.

20. A. Bougeart, *Marat, l'ami du peuple,* 2 vols. (Paris: Eugène Didier, 1865).

21. Germani, 237.

22. Germani, 252.

23. Stendhal, 'Des beaux-arts et du caractère français', *Salon de 1827.* See Verbraeken, 127.

24. Verbraeken, 43.

25. A. Esquiros, *Histoire des Montagnards* (Paris: Victor Lecou, 1847), 1: 152.

26. 'Aussi le *Marat,* s'il n'est pas précisément le chef-d'oeuvre du maître, doit-il être regardé comme le premier ouvrage de sa main où percent toute la puissance et l'originalité de son talent. Il avait vu, il avait senti ce qu'il a peint, et ce fut un trait de lumière qui lui fit envisager son art sous un point de vue tout nouveau.' E. J. Delécluze, *Louis David, son école et son temps* (1855; reprint edited by J.-P. Mouilleseaux (Paris: Editions Macula, 1983), 405–6.

27. J. L. Jules David, *David,* 1: 251.

28. Arnold Hauser, *Rococo, Classicism and Romanticism,* vol. 3 of *The Social History of Art* (London: Routledge, 1961), 137. First published in 1951.

29. Robert Rosenblum, *Transformations in Late Eighteenth Century Art* (Princeton: Princeton University Press, 1967), 182.

30. Lorenz Eitner, 'The Open Window and the Storm-Tossed Boat', *Art Bulletin* 37 (1955): 281–90.

31. Anita Brookner, *Jacques-Louis David* (London: Chatto and Windus, 1980), 109.

32. N. Hadjinicolaou, *Art History and Class Struggle,* trans. Louise Asmal (London: Pluto Press, 1978), 121.

33. Thomas Crow, 'Gross David, with the swoln cheek', *Art History* 5, no. 1 (March 1982): 113.

34. Ibid.

35. T. J. Clark, 'Painting in the Year Two', *Representations* 47 (Summer 1994): 13–63.

36. First noted by Polak. See B. H. Polak, 'De Invloed van Einige Monu-

menten der Ondheid op Het Classicisme van David, Ingres en Delacroix', *Nederlandsch Kunsthistorisch Jaarboek* (1949): 289.

37. Thomas Crow, *Emulation: Making Artists for Revolutionary France* (New Haven and London: Yale University Press, 1995), 169.

38. T. J. Clark has also noted: 'Marat was too important, and too volatile, a political sign to let one's enemies make use of; . . . The category people had to have *something* be its sign. Among the signifying possibilities on offer in 1793, "Marat" seemed one of the best available. At least in him the category was personified'. Clark, 27.

39. 'Le peuple redemandoit son ami, sa voix désolée se faisait entendre, il provoquoit mon art, il vouloit voir les traits de son ami fidèle . . . J'ai entendu la voix du peuple, j'ai obéi'. Cited in Daniel Wildenstein and Guy Wildenstein, *Documents complémentaires au Catalogue de l'oeuvre de Louis David,* no. 674. (Paris: Fondation Wildenstein, 1973), 674.

MARAT, *L'AMI DU PEUPLE*, DAVID

LOVE AND DISCIPLINE IN THE SUMMER OF '93

This chapter brings together four different topics: the painting *Marat à son dernier soupir,* the painter-politician Jacques-Louis David, the journalist-politician Jean-Paul Marat, and an idea, 'l'ami du peuple'.[1] The argument starts with the painting, and moves from there to the predicament of David and the position of Marat in the summer of 1793. It explores the historical resonance of the idea of the 'ami du peuple' and its relevance to the way in which David's political associates were trying to rule France. It closes by returning to the painting and reconsidering the evidence that emerged from its examination.

It is impossible for any historian to approach Jacques-Louis David's painting *Marat à son dernier soupir* without a range of knowledge and expertise, without enthusiasms and aversions. Historians of death, of religion, of disease, of the cutlery or packaging industries, would all have their own agendas. So, too, would the historians of journalism and the huge and quarrelsome crowd of historians of the Jacobin Revolution and of the popular agitation in Paris that accompanied it. All historians, whatever their agenda, work by examining documents. My agenda has two items: I want to use the painting to study the relationship between the Jacobins and the popular movement in Paris in the summer of 1793, and I want to use the relationship between the Jacobins and the popular movement to study the painting. So for me this painting is both a document (a resource for a study whose object is located somewhere else) and a monument (a thing-to-be-studied).[2]

To pursue either enquiry I must look at the painting. There I see simplicity and clarity of form. The colour range is limited, and there are few areas of saturated colour; complementary colours are not obviously juxtaposed to intensify what variation there is: one imagines that red blood spilled on green cloth, for example, would have made quite a splash. The tonal range is broader than the colour range, but it functions mostly to separate background and other inessential picture areas from the main focus of attention, rather than to differentiate forms or actions within that focus. The composition is highly ordered. Horizontals and verticals dominate; most of the key forms are displayed parallel with the picture plane. All represented objects are displayed in the bottom half of the painting and pushed into the foreground of the picture space. The edge of the picture cuts off the foot of the bath, the end of the draped structure behind Marat's head, and the bottom of the packing case. The compression of pictorial elements inevitably creates a void in the upper half of the picture, and in the middle and rear ground. This space is occupied by a surface which is differentiated both on the small scale, with a dappled texture, and on the large scale; it is most luminous in the top right-hand corner and darkest in the middle of the left-hand side, behind the white headdress of the man. This passage of paint – brushy, diagonal in its tonal gradation, loose and formless, refusing to indicate a location such as 'bath-room' – is quite unlike the precise and contrasty gridded arrangement of pigment in the bottom half of the canvas.

Here, objects are presented with the sharpest clarity. I see a noticeably small number of distinct things in the picture: a recumbent unclothed man wearing a turban; the bath in which he lies, indicated as such by a glimpse of bloodstained water; mended sheets draping the bath and the structure at its head; bridging the bath a wide board; on this a fringed green cloth, turned back at the near left corner to reveal the board's rounded edge; indistinguishable papers under the man's left forearm; a legible letter held still in the fingers of his left hand; a quill pen slipping from the relaxing grasp of his right hand, which rests on the floor between the viewer and the draped side of the bath; an upended packing case to the man's right, between the viewer and the bath; on top of this another quill, an inkwell, *assignats,* and a letter; on the floor in front of the bath a bone-handled knife such as one might use to prepare meat for cooking, with traces of blood on its blade; boldly lettered on the side of the packing case facing the viewer the words À MARAT, DAVID, and, in smaller and more cursive capitals on the lower edge of the box, L'AN – DEUX.[3]

That list of things seen was compiled as the result of a combination of naive looking and trained looking: I can articulate my observation of the composition and the manipulation of colour, space, and plane as a result of an extended informal training, and I can say naively 'that is a kitchen knife' because for a moment I am prepared to ignore the problem of how it is that David and I can agree that a particular arrangement of pigments bound in oil smeared on a flat surface is indeed a kitchen knife, set aside the problem of the relationship between 'seeing' a knife and 'reading' a pictorial sign for a knife.

Reading and writing have an important presence in this painting. The presence of the letters makes us consider the place of text as object. The packing case, in its flat assertion of the picture plane, resembles a dedicatory letter from David to Marat, as it were pasted onto the canvas: we are here encouraged to imagine object as text. From Charlotte Corday's letter we understand that visual messages may be both clear and obscure, that ambiguity and irony are among the painter's resources. Indeed, the picture is as full of signs as it is of objects, but whereas the objects in the image are distinct and unambiguous, the signs are not so clear to us now; some of them may never have been either distinct or unambiguous.

In the months before David painted *Marat,* he had painted another portrait of a martyred member of the Convention, Le Peletier de Saint-Fargeau, who had voted for the death of the king. He was assassinated on 20 January 1793, the night before the king's execution, by Pâris, a member of Louis XVI's guard.[4] The painting was probably destroyed after 1826 by Le Peletier's daughter in repudiation of his actions, but a drawing, and a fragment of an engraving, survive (Fig. 4). The image shows a dripping sword suspended above Le Peletier's chest as he lies on his funereal couch. That sword seems to me to signify two distinguishable sets of things. First, and most obviously, it is a 'portrait' of the weapon with which Le Peletier was murdered. Together with the gaping wound below the left ribs, it signifies the narrative that has led to this display of mortal remains. The sword skewers a sheet of paper on which we

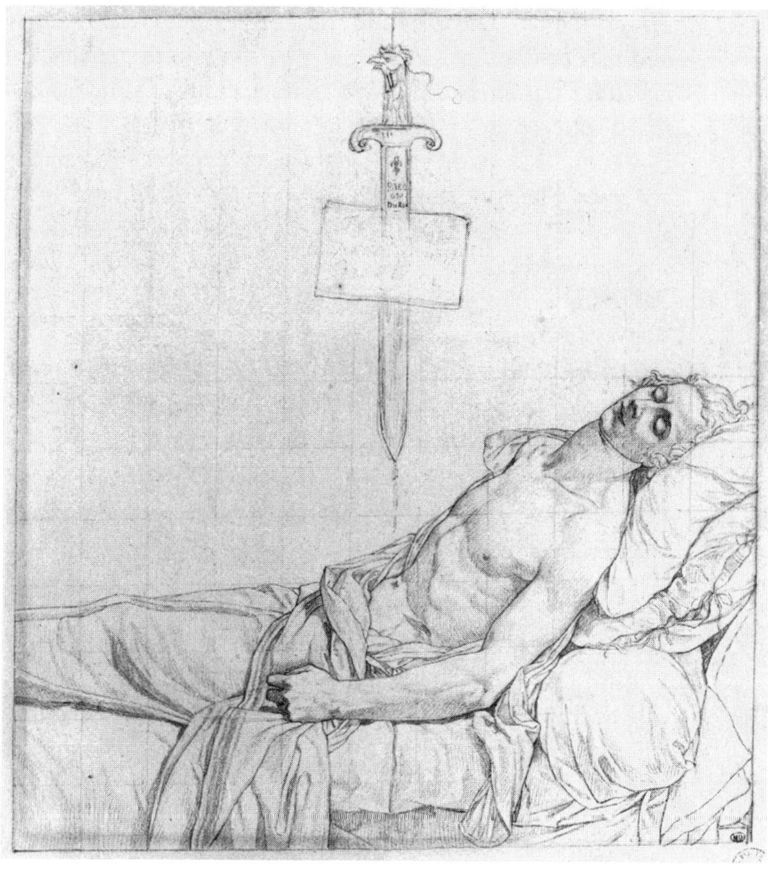

Figure 4. Anatole Devosge, after David, *Le Peletier de Saint-Fargeau on his Deathbed*, 1793, charcoal drawing, 38 × 33 cm. Musée des Beaux-Arts, Dijon. (Photo: Musée des Beaux-Arts de Dijon.)

may read the words 'je vote [pour] la mort du tyran'.[5] This reinforces the narrative, as an emblem of cause and effect. Commentators at the time noticed that the weapon, suspended by a hair, made direct reference to the sword of Damocles, telling us that the political arrangements for which Le Peletier gave his life remained under threat.[6] A second sort of meaning is generated partly as I consider the painting, and the cult of Le Peletier, in terms of the concept of the martyr; and partly as I think of the painting in connection with the use of raised swords in David's painting of 1784, *The Oath of the*

Horatii (Fig. 5). The sword in the *Le Peletier,* in which Roman, royal, and patriotic features coexist, is, like those in the *Horatii,* a distinctly classical weapon, and thus has connotations of stoic political virtue: the connotation of the sword's form is that it is Le Peletier's as much as his assassin's. The depiction happens to be reportorially accurate. The king's guards had recently been kitted out with just such swords, but it is not an adequate explanation for its commanding presence in the picture space to say, 'oh, but the sword was like that', since it was certainly never *there* like that, nor did it ever skewer that slogan thus.

In his painting of Le Peletier, David represents a martyrdom, a transfigured murder. A murder is a negation, of life and of the principles which that life embodies. A murder represented as a martyrdom negates the death that is its instance, so some of the sword's symbolic force, like that of the martyred body, comes from its contextual status as the negation of Pâris's act. But a martyrdom also transfers power from the killer to the victim. Thus I can not help seeing the raised sword, in symbiosis with the republican pledge, as in some sense embodying the transfer of power from murderer to victim, just as the swords in the *Horatii* embody the transfer of power from father to sons. The sword in the *Le Peletier* is, as it were, offered to the viewer to take up, in extension of the martyr's last wish to see the death of tyranny. The painting is thus both a representation of a negation and a representation of the negation of that negation.

CLEARLY THE KNIFE in *Marat à son dernier soupir* is not a symbol of the same order or resonance. But can that resonance be felt elsewhere perhaps? Look at the green cloth. Marat's elbow has turned it back from the board it covered. As it falls from the edge of the board, the form of the folded cloth makes a blade shape which echoes that of the knife discarded at the edge of the picture space. The fringed edge of the cloth for a moment seems to repeat the ripples and drips of blood running from the wound and splashed on the sheets; the knife-form points directly at Marat's writing hand, armed as it still is with its quill pen.[7] Political virtue, political discourse, and stabbing blades, so closely associated in *The Oath of the Horatii* and the *Le Peletier,* are, it seems, also centrally inscribed in the *Marat.* Or they are if we care to see the fold-form of the

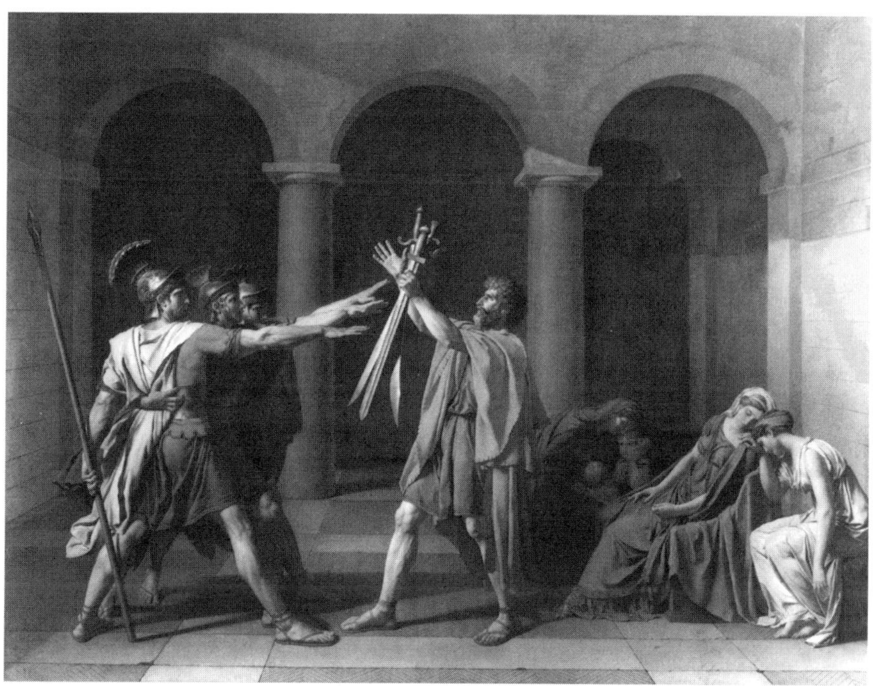

Figure 5. Jacques-Louis David, *The Oath of the Horatii,* 1785, oil on canvas, 330 × 425 cm. Musée du Louvre, Paris. (Photo: Réunion des musées nationaux.)

cloth as a dripping blade aimed at the journalist's writing hand, and cutting at the sheets lining the bath, which are marked not by Marat's pen but by his blood. This is to give the cloth blade a single meaning; but I see it as having the same sort of double meaning as the sword in the *Le Peletier,* growing out of his hand and his writing, its spirit made manifest in the moment of his death.

To see the painting as an image of clear and distinct things is to see it as an illustration, as a report of Corday's historical intervention, not as an intervention in its own right, even though *Marat à son dernier soupir* is evidently much more than a monumental snapshot.[8] It is, however, necessary to understand images produced in a period as doing something other than 'illustrating' or 'reflecting' it. I believe that representations in some sense make reality. A picture such as the *Marat* makes history, as well as being made by it. The same goes, of course, for any signifying practice, for the clothes

Charlotte Corday wore to visit Marat, and for those he did not wear to receive her. David's signifying practice as a painter may produce evidence which offers the historian more to work on, in that the images he made include dress codes, allusions to the whole of the history of art, legible games with the relationship between representation and reality, the closure of depiction and the openness of symbolization, and the luxury of retrospection. Thus, for example, Corday's choice of domestic knife rather than dagger, which may not have been significant to her, can become so to the painter or the viewer; the banal blade, a cause unworthy of its effect, is marginalised as an object, a compositional decision that is itself of considerable symbolic interest. Nonetheless, in the fold of cloth one may see the violence that knife and sword symbolise reinscribed at the centre of the image, so that a second signifying point is to be felt, even if not exactly seen.

At the moment this is merely a visual game: one might just as well see the fold as like a blade of grass. To give what I see some solidity, we need to ask what function, what effect, a symbol of violence both represented and repressed, both marginalised and inscribed at the centre of this martyr-portrait might have had in 1793, that would be missing from 'like a blade of grass'. This entails a discussion of David's tactical predicament in the summer and fall of 1793 in the traumatic and violent aftermath of the execution of Louis XVI, which split the revolutionary leadership in Paris, helped to stir up a widespread civil war, and intensified the war against foreign invaders. It also entails a discussion of the cultural context in which Marat made his claim to be *l'ami du peuple*. The political difficulties of the Jacobins' alliance with the People's friend, and the representation of that alliance which emerged from David's studio as *Marat à son dernier soupir*, must be understood with reference to the struggles over the idea of the People, and the realities of popular unrest, in eighteenth-century Paris.[9]

Marat came to prominence in revolutionary Paris as the owner, editor, and writer of a daily opinion-sheet, founded in September 1789, whose most famous title was *L'Ami du Peuple*. Within a few months he had become a key figure in the radical fringe of the Revolution: forever denouncing plots, treachery, and corruption, forever calling for their rooting out through the use of summary force; before the summer of 1792 he was violently and dismissively hostile to the dominant tendency in the National Assembly, and thus frequently subject to judicial harassment. *L'Ami du Peuple* was among the most important and influential of the newspapers and periodical pamphlets through which revolutionary events and debates were represented, and around which political tendencies and cliques crystallised. Other foci of organisation were to be found in salons, in the political clubs, of which the Jacobins and the Feuillants are the most famous, and also in the various informal sittings together of politicians in the successive debating chambers of the Constituent and Legislative Assemblies, and of the Convention: the Plaine and the Montagne, the left and the right. These all provided resources for the political elite, but from the summer of 1792 to the spring of 1794 the course of the Revolution, particularly in Paris, was vitally affected by new forms of popular mobilisation and informal organisation.

Something like 'dual sovereignty' emerged in Paris between summer '92 and winter '93–'94. The reasons for this were various: the prestige of the revolutionary Commune de Paris after 10 August 1792; the ability of the forty-eight Parisian Sections, working with the popular clubs, to mobilise men and women to put intense pressure on the legislators; and the ability of a small group of journalist-politicians to represent the political force and articulate the political will of 'the people'. Despite some expressed misgivings and hostility, it had served the Jacobins well to insist, in 1792 and the first half of 1793, on the sovereignty of the People, to nurture some of the claims of this second centre of power. It enabled the alliance between the cliques around Danton and around Robespierre to unseat the Girondins from their control over the course of the Revolution and of the war. Nevertheless, in the second half of 1793 the People became an increasingly troublesome idea for the Jacobins, once they had used the political muscle supplied by the clubs and Sections to win command of the Revolution.

There were certainly intense and intractable conflicts of economic interest between the bourgeois, property-owning, and respectable Jacobins and the artisan and petty-bourgeois radicals of the sans-culotte movement; there was also an enormous cultural gulf between the rational (educative, moralizing, and disciplinary) politics of Robespierre or Saint-Just and the carnivalesque (violent, excessive, or obscene) politics of Marat, Hébert, or Jacques Roux.[10]

There was also a purely political struggle: the Jacobins had come to power using the support of the Parisian popular movement, articulated by journalist-politicians such as Marat. Once in power, however, the Jacobins urgently needed to face the problem of this embryonic dual sovereignty: the Revolution might survive by becoming more 'professional' or by becoming more 'popular', but the particular dynamic confrontation and symbiosis between the two forms of political power could not itself survive for long. From now on, any 'popular' threat of violence against politicians in power must be aimed primarily at the Jacobins.

By the spring of 1794, the civil war in the west and the war against the coalition of foreign powers were going well, and the Jacobins felt secure enough to use the Terror to liquidate the leaders of the popular movement. Prominent among these were journalists such as Hébert (writer-publisher of the 'veritable' *Père Duchesne,* and a member of the Convention) and Jacques Roux, the *enragé* who briefly continued Marat's daily pamphlet after his assassination. The Jacobins had indeed begun to move against the most extreme *enragé* journals in September 1793.[11] However, for eighteen months, from August 1792, circumstances gave the organised People of Paris, and with them, their self-appointed and (for the time being) acclaimed spokespersons such as Marat, a sort of sovereignty, which the Jacobin politicians had little power to disavow or disallow. The Commune de Paris, which took the credit for the establishment of the Republic through the armed mass action against the Tuileries Palace on 10 August 1792, still had prestige and independence of movement. The Sections could mobilise huge groups of demonstrators, who through their armed lobbying coerced the Convention to adopt measures for which it had little enthusiasm. The Convention, led by the group of Jacobins around Robespierre, resisted many of the 'popular' demands both about the application of revolutionary justice and about maximum price levels, but particularly in the summer and fall of 1793 the Revolution's leaders were to a considerable extent the prisoners of the political will of the popular movement, and so they were forced to find ways of making virtues out of necessities.

It was as a key member of the Committee of Public Instruction that David forged a role for himself as 'pageant-master to the Revolution'.[12] He designed and organised collective representations of the new relationship between the populace, the sovereign Assembly, and the various legitimizing abstractions (the Nation, the People, France, Liberty, Equality, Fraternity, etc.) in a succession of *fêtes* and other republican ceremonies and installations. A key part of the Jacobin experience of power was the use of spectacles and festivities for disciplining men and women. On 14 September 1793 David was made a member of the Committee of General Security, one of the Convention's two key executive committees, the other being the more famous and powerful Committee of Public Safety. The Committee of General Security had responsibility for coordinating and to an extent administering the 'revolutionary' judicial system, soon to be systematised and labelled the 'Terror'. It is difficult to date the beginning of the Terror, but the events of late May and early June 1793, when the Girondin leaders were swept from power in a series of Parisian insurrections and were then, in defiance of the Constitution, tried and executed, marks the moment when terror became a central aspect of political life, an indispensable tool of rule, in France. So when he painted the *Marat,* David's political position concerning extralegal violence against legislators could not be the same as when he had painted the *Le Peletier,* and his attitude toward the *ami du peuple* was both very urgent and already contradictory.

In the summer of 1793 Robespierre's supporters had a firmer grasp of the reins of power in Paris than any other group largely because they were prepared to use the weapon of terror, and because they were able to cooperate, with distaste and distrust, with the popular Parisian movement. So in the martyr-portrait of the popular and terror-promoting journalist, the stakes were high. David had to produce a public image that would grant official legitimacy to Marat as a popular hero and martyr. The image could not overtly reject the popular pressure for violence that Marat had done so much to articulate and finally to legitimise, since the Jacobins continued to need the pressure in order to justify, and the violence in order to maintain, their hold on power. The Jacobins also urgently needed to extend their bureaucratic control over all aspects of revolutionary violence; thus the image had to demobilise Marat's supporters, rather than mobilise them, which an image exhorting to revenge, even to steadfastness, would have done.[13] By the summer of 1793 the Jacobins wanted the People to keep quiet, or rather, they needed them to speak when they were spoken to, and otherwise to be content to be spoken for. David's painting hushes Marat, tones him down, confines him in a shallow and gridded space, and speaks to him as it speaks for him: 'à Marat, David'.

À MARAT, DAVID.' In the death-head drawing that David made of Marat, which was quickly turned into an engraving by Copia, the four corners of the image are ruled off from the picture space, and the following text is inserted clockwise from top left: À MARAT/L'AMI/DU PEUPLE/DAVID (Fig. 6). The most obviously 'correct' reading of these words ('à Marat, l'ami du peuple, David') is available as a Z-track decipherment, but so are other phrases: a clockwise reading begins by giving us a simple votive 'à Marat l'ami David', but this leaves the reader with the implication 'David du peuple'.[14] The spatial distribution of the names also permits 'l'ami du peuple', lying between them, to apply to both Marat and David. The freedom of these seven words from the normal constraints of syntax is emphasised by the fact that those in the bottom two corners are the same way up as those in the top two: an orderly text set diagonally in the four corners of a rectangle would properly be wrapped round the image, and thus be inverted at the bottom of the sheet.[15]

The clear inscription but ambiguous signification of 'l'ami du peuple' in David's drawing makes its absence in the painting remarkable, and turns it into something that needs to be explained.[16] So what did it mean to be the 'ami du peuple' in 1793, and who could make that claim? In the ancien régime the answer had once been clear: the people owe the king a duty of obedience and respectful love (Louis XV promoted himself with the sobriquet 'le bien-aimé'), and the king owes the people a duty of love along with a duty to command. The etymology of 'ami' (friend) and 'aimé' (loved/beloved) being inseparable, the claim to be the *ami du peuple* can be voiced only by the sovereign. During the years of the Revolution 'le souverain' became a site of intense and articulate struggle: sometimes it meant the elected assembly, sometimes the people represented in that assembly, sometimes simply the people.[17] So the claim to be the People's friend was not sanitised, emptied of its political force, when the king was killed. Far from it; in a situation of dual sovereignty, no claim could be more powerful. Marat made it, and the success of his claim was based in part on the way

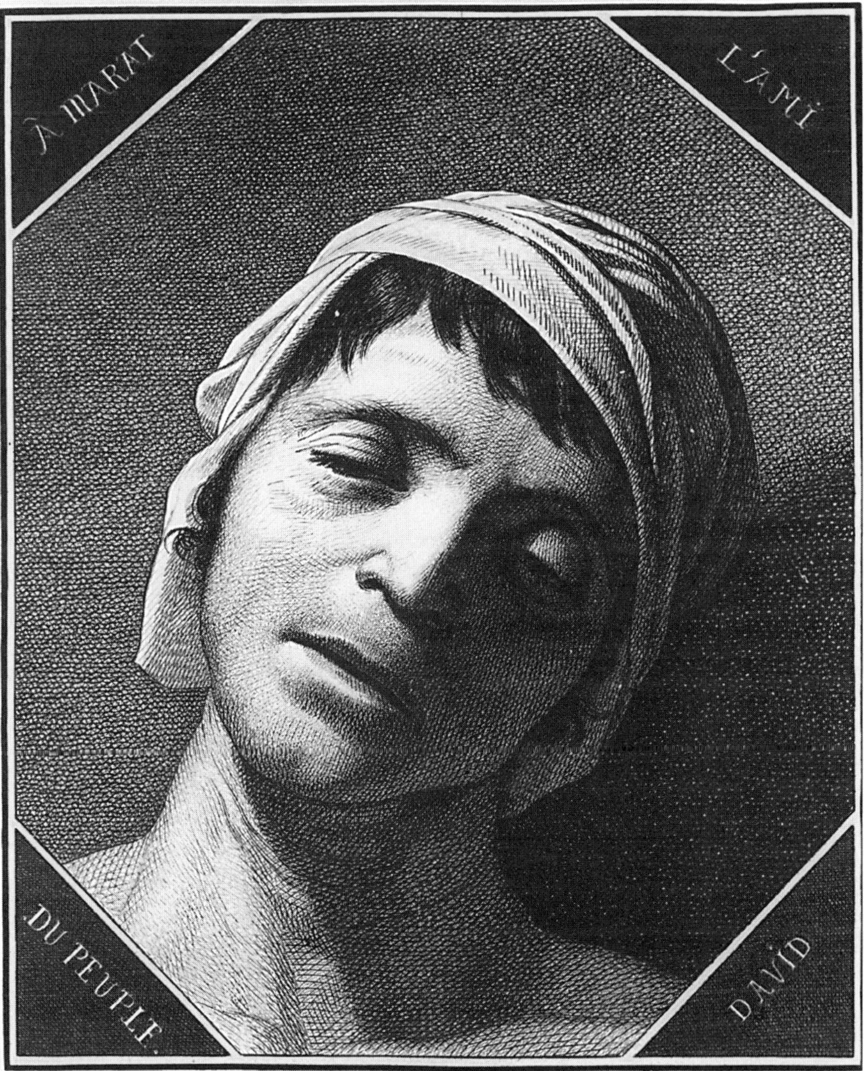

Figure 6. Jacques-Louis Copia, after David, *Posthumous Portrait of Marat*, 1793, pen and ink and charcoal, 27.7 × 21.5 cm. Private collection, London. (Photo: author.)

he replaced paternal 'friendship' with fraternal 'solidarity'; but the deputies in the Convention were bound to make it too; and for most of them the contradictions between the paternal and fraternal friendship were less easy to resolve than they were for Marat.

'Peuple', the People, was an idea with several meanings and connotations in eighteenth-century France. It was a way of naming the population of France without dividing it up into Estates, Corporations, or lineages. Only the king was above all such belongings; thus the name of king required a name for the other term of the relationship from which his power and his legitimacy flowed. 'Subject' named individuals in that relationship, but the king was only a king because he embodied a collectivity: 'the People' named this. As part of his loving relationship to the People, the king owed it a duty of violent repression; without the firm (read 'lethal') paternal hand of the king, the People would quickly fall into murderous and miserable anarchy.[18] This group, which would otherwise be unruly, was not thought of as all French men and women, but as only a section of them, in particular those otherwise excluded from secure social locations in the ancien régime. Thus in the language of eighteenth-century absolutist paternalism, the People are both the transcendental collectivity and the particular group which cannot look after its own interests, those who have nothing but a call on an unstable kin structure, a shifting neighbourly solidarity, or a recourse to violence with which to confront hardship and bad luck; nothing, that is, except the love of the king.

This ancien régime ideology of paternal love and discipline had never functioned very perfectly, and by the second half of the eighteenth century it was under great pressure from various positions. Perhaps the best known of them is what has been called the growth of a bourgeois public sphere, a sense that the business of ruling and being ruled is open to public scrutiny and debate, and that not only the king, but 'public opinion' is legitimately able to identify a public interest.[19] However, as Arlette Farge has brilliantly established in recent essays, the public sphere was not only a bourgeois space, the People not only a legitimating abstraction in that space. Her work establishes clearly the vigour of a developed discourse among the poor and unruly concerning public affairs, and the intimate connection of that discourse with a language, and an acting out, of violence.[20] Farge shows how the idea of the popular as used by eighteenth-century policemen and by those they observed and interrogated indicates a relationship between disorder and subordination, between poverty and wealth, between the threat of violence and the fear of violence (from both sides of the relationship), between anonymous solidarities and the individuating eye of the law: 'popular' was a way of acting and speaking that could be of use to men, women, and children on the streets of Paris, just as it was an idea available to cultural reformers to put such people in their place.[21]

I have suggested that the paternalist monarchical conception of the People entailed a contradictory pair of ideas: the People as the generality of subjects, and the People as the target of disciplinary authority. This contradictory coupling was modified, but in no sense transcended, as part of the fundamental cultural evolution in which the bourgeois public sphere emerged. When men and women who felt empowered to intervene (in the first place, by speaking and writing) in this emerging 'public sphere' claimed to speak to the king, and to their fellow inhabitants of the public space, they claimed to speak for one or more of a number of powerful abstractions. The Nation, Reason, the People, are among the more important of these. In this emerging discourse the People is the name given to all those who are members of the polity: this is the sense in which it is used in the political discourse of the American revolutionaries. The coupling of subjecthood and peoplehood is undone in this modification: the legitimacy of subjection has ever since been contested.

The position of the disorderly People in the new discourse was significantly unclear. The Jacobin leaders saw them primarily as the targets of education, rather than of lethal force; but lethality as an inevitable instrument of rule had by no means gone away. Who then should be the target of terror? Violence and the discourse of violence had in a real sense constituted the People old-style. In Jacobin discourse, violence could not constitute the People in this way: the public sphere made such a relation impossible. Instead, violence defined the boundaries of the People: if the rulers of France put a man or a woman in the discursive or actual realm of violence, it was to show that they were excluded from the People.

Ancien régime authorities had always dealt with the threat or the reality of popular violence by a combination of concessions and repression: the concession in order to return the street to its normal life, the repression to reassert authority in the aftermath of disorder.[22] The thousands of armed representatives of the Sections who intimidated and in some respects imposed their will on the Convention through the summer of 1793 were not in essence treated by the revolutionary authorities in a different way than that in which the pre-Revolutionary authorities had treated *their* troublemakers, and beneath the rhetoric of solidarity and unity there was inevitably fear, distaste, and incomprehension. Of course, the patriot crowds of 1793 were organised on a very different basis from the sociabilities that had produced ancien régime disaffection and tumult, and of course the availability to them of the discourse of the *peuple-souverain,* as well as the behaviours and discourse of the *peuple-resistant,* transformed the relationship between speech and action in the sans-culotte popular movement, but it by no means transformed the political and cultural relationship between the People and their rulers.

David was one of those rulers. In the late summer of 1793 the balance of power in Paris and France meant that it was still impossible to reject or criticise the policies of the popular movement. Resistance, delay, and administrative action against those calling most clearly for an extension of revolutionary violence were the only weapons available to the coteries around Robespierre and Danton. In these circumstances, in this extraordinary tense and deadly three- or four-cornered fight between the internal and external enemies of the Republic, the factions in the Convention, and the popular forces mobilised in Paris, how should the *ami du peuple* be represented?

We have seen David ambivalently associate 'l'ami du peuple' both with Marat and with himself, the fellow Conventionnel, the administrator of police action and public instruction, in the posthumous portrait drawing. In the painting, many papers are displayed on Marat's makeshift writing surfaces. There would have been space and excuse to include Marat's journal as an attribute even in this 'realistic' image.[23] Failing that, it would have been easy to expand the inscription on the box to name Marat as the People's friend, but David has suppressed any such reference. Nonetheless, *Marat à son dernier soupir* seems to me to articulate a range of the meanings of *l'ami du peuple,* while it denies others. The letter sending the

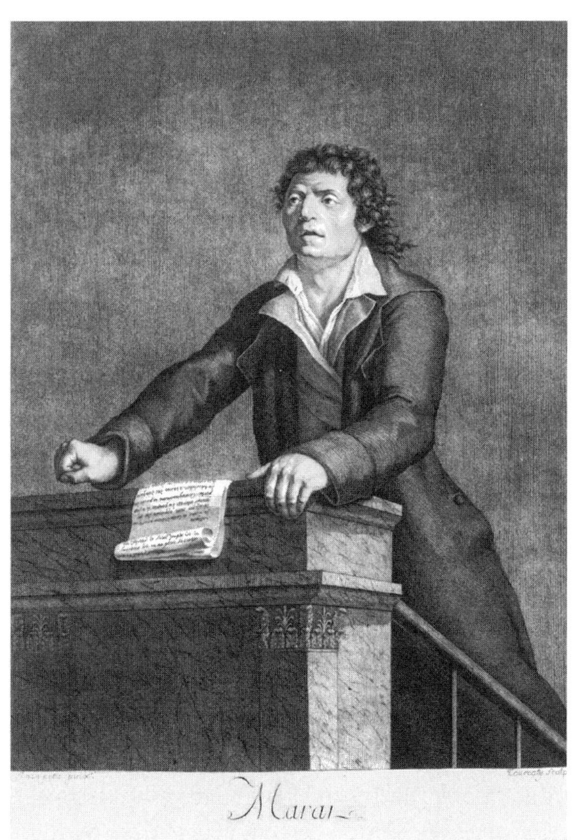

Figure 7. Tourcaty, after Simon Petit, *Marat (at the tribune of the Convention),* engraving, 43 × 30 cm. British Museum, Department of Prints and Drawings, Chèvremont Marat Collection, London. (Copyright The British Museum.)

assignats to a needy family implies a paternal (rather than fraternal) relationship between the *ami* and the *peuple,* and the suggestion of the orator's tribune in the geometry of the packing case and the names of the two members of the Convention inscribed oratorically upon it implies, through this public declaration of friendship, that the *ami du peuple* is a position in the public sphere: one widely circulated image of Marat has him making a speech at such a box-shaped tribune in the Convention (Fig. 7).[24] However, the solidarity of the anonymous crowd, disorder, unauthorised speech, and violence are all formally or anecdotally negated in David's image. The painting is evidently orderly, all horizontals and verticals, all planes parallel with the picture surface, and it is devoid of movement: not a ripple in the reddening bathwater, not a suggestion of a delivered blow or a departing assassin. Marat is individuated and shown in solitude, both of which remove him from the *peuple:* he is shown in a domestic situation and an undefined space, located neither in nature (as Bara was to be) nor in a mythic space (as Le Peletier had been), but in a banal bath. David represents Marat-as-the-People stilled, arranged, mapped out. The painting is thus made of claims both asserted and denied, contradictions held in suspension. The image celebrates the nature of Marat's death, but not by celebrating his life. His representation imposes silence and order. These qualities apply both to Marat and to the *peuple,* which is inscribed in the painting only as a legitimating abstraction, not as a noisy and disorderly presence.

The first four years of the Revolution had seen an extraordinary growth in the public sphere, in the aspects of social and political life discussed in it, in the number of speakers and actors it could accommodate. Marat, as journalist, as the friend of the people, as Conventionnel, well represented this dynamic enlargement. Despite this profound change, *Marat à son dernier soupir* depicts him alone in a confined and rigidly organised space; if this is the public space of the people, how extraordinarily shallow it is. Violence is here represented as negating Marat's place in public, whereas in truth the glorification of violence had permitted Marat to force open the discursive space of the 'People' and to make a relationship between people and politicians that could not be reduced to the conventions and corruptions of parliamentary representation on the one hand, and to the paternalistic discipline and mercy of absolutist authority on the other.

MARAT HAD LIVED his unruly relation with the Parisian crowd intensely and successfully as a key aspect of his power. Charlotte Corday, in a premeditated and principled act, negated his position in a second's knife thrust, at the same time fulfilling his prophecies of treacherous plots and acting out his own repeated calls for direct action against conspirators. Murders turned into martyrdoms affirm the values embodied by the victim, and they show as worthless and futile the killer's attempts to negate those values: martyrdoms negate negations. But the way that *Marat à son dernier soupir* negates the negation is not through a reaffirmation of the values that were attacked in the murder, since the attack precisely endorsed those values: the exaltation of political violence, the personalisation of political conflict, and the fascination with political conspiracy. Charlotte Corday's actions were perfectly congruent with Marat's rhetoric, and an inscription of the futility of the one entailed an inscription of the futility of the other. To resolve this problem, but not this problem alone, the painting has to transform the values Marat embodied into their own opposites.

So I have to approach *Marat à son dernier soupir* as a painting in which key elements are both present and absent, both represented and repressed. A most obvious instance of this is Corday herself. However, Marat's twin positions as representative politician and as turbulent popular champion are also both inscribed and denied. So is the relation of violence to Marat's authority; likewise that of Marat's violent and unruly discourse to the rational discourse, yet rule through violence, of the Committees of Public Safety and General Security. We come back to the fold of cloth which in my eyes both is and is not a knife blade. In as much as it is present as a suspended weapon, I can give it the same double status as the sword in the *Le Peletier,* a sign both of the crime and of its transcendence. Maybe we can now identify the reasons for its absence, its insertion as a thing repressed, and understand why the sword that grows from Marat's pen should be inscribed, in the most literal way possible, as something that is not there. There seem to me to be a host of reasons why Corday's knife could not be represented centrally in the image as Pâris's sword had been: Helen Weston discusses some of them, to do with the gendering of political discourse and of direct public action alike, in this book. There are besides clear reasons to see the fold of cloth as a significant form; reasons to do with the paradoxes of Marat's claim to be the People's friend, with the oppressive successes of popular agitation, with the bureaucratisation of governmental violence that was soon to be named the Terror, and with the symbolic inscription of the relationship between discourse and violence.

One may see the whole of the tragic dilemma of the Jacobin leadership of the Revolution from the summer of 1793 to the summer of 1794 in terms of the relationship between text and violence. Political discourse in the form of declarations of rights, constitutions, journalism, and David's festivals, which arranged the populace of Paris in a legible symbolic order and processed these human messages through Paris, all commend text and textuality as the proper medium of the Revolution. Yet external circumstances, and their own fears and ambitions, had forced the Jacobins into the arbitrary truncation of discourse via the guillotine. If they could defeat treachery, silence dissent and end disorder, capture and discipline the friendship of the People, and dissimulate the violence on which rule relies, the Jacobin Republic could survive and could return its politics to the world of discourse. The painting projects these ambitions onto the dying Marat, and offers this resolution, not as Marat's last gasp, but as his last wish for the beloved People, his *dernier soupir.*

NOTES

1. This is an interpretative piece of writing; it relies primarily on modern secondary sources. On David, the 1989 exhibition catalogue from the Louvre, *J.-L. David, 1748–1825,* edited by A. Schnapper (Paris, Réunion des musées nationeaux); also R. Michel, ed., *David contre David: actes du colloque organisé au musée du Louvre [. . .] décembre 1989* (Paris: La documentation française, 1993). On Marat, the essays in J.-Cl. Bonnet, ed., *La Mort de Marat* (Paris: Flammarion, 1986), and L. Gottschalk, *Jean Paul Marat: A Study in Radicalism* (London: Allen & Unwin, 1927). For revolutionary journalism, J. Popkin, *Revolutionary News: The Press in France 1789–1799* (Durham, N.C.: Duke University Press, 1990), and R. Darnton and D. Roche, *Revolution in Print* (Berkeley: University of California Press, 1989). Students wanting a place to start looking for historical background may try D. Sutherland, *France 1789–1815: Revolution and Counter-revolution* (London: Fontana, 1985), though one of the lessons I have learned again from working on the painting is that it is hard to tell background from foreground.

2. M. Foucault, *The Archaeology of Knowledge,* trans. A. M. Sheridan Smith (London: Tavistock, 1972), 6–7; originally published as *L'Archaéologie du savoir* (Paris: Gallimard, 1969).

3. On the two sides of the lower edge of the box can be seen the figures 17 and 93, smeared and partly obliterated. The date was changed to 'l'an deux' in October 1793.

4. See Robert Simon, 'David's Martyr-Portrait of Le Peletier de Saint Fargeau and the Conundrums of Revolutionary Representation', *Art History* 14, no. 4 (1991): 459–87; D. Hunter, 'Swordplay: Jacques-Louis David's Painting of Le Peletier de Saint-Fargeau on His Deathbed', in *Representing the French Revolution: Literature, Historiography and Art,* ed. J. A. W. Heffernan (Hanover, N.H.: Dartmouth College, 1992), 161–91;

T. J. Clark, 'Painting in the Year Two', *Representations* 47 (Summer 1994): 13–63; and L. Johanneson, 'le Yo-Yo, David et Madame Tussaud: notices sur l'iconographie de la Révolution', in *L'Art et les Révolutions,* ed. R. Rosenblum et al. (Strasbourg: Société alsacienne pour le dévelopement de l'histoire de l'art, 1992), 35–83.

5. 'I vote [for] the death of the tyrant'. D. J. Delécluze's sketch-note of the painting, made in 1826, transcribes the inscription with the 'pour'; but it is conventionally given in abbreviated form.

6. Hunter, 181. Hunter shows that the sword signifies both the threat to the citizen of arbitrary violence and the fact that the legislator is always faced with the responsibility for (then) his own actions, and with the mortal struggle to establish and maintain legitimacy.

7. Helen Weston pointed out the morphological similarity of the fringe to the drips of blood from the sword in the *Le Peletier:* this whole discussion owes a great deal to the combination of enthusiasm, perceptiveness, and lucidity with which she has initiated and responded to discussions about the painting.

8. There is of course good historical support for the 'reportorial illustration' view of the image: David had made a business visit to Marat in his bath the day before the murder and, probably the day after it, had returned to Marat's lodging to make a drawing (Fig. 6).

9. Tom Crow's celebrated review (*Art History* 5, no. 1 [March 1982]: 109–17) of A. Brookner, *Jacques-Louis David* (London: Chatto and Windus, 1980) sketches a politicised reading of David's *Marat* in terms of the predicament of the Jacobins in the summer of 1793; so does K. Herding in 'David's *Marat* als dernier appel à l'unité révolutionnaire', *Idea, Jahrbuch de Hamburger Kunsthalle* 2 (1983): 89–112. My reading is perhaps closer to Crow's. I read and assimilated Crow's remarks at the time; I encountered Herding's ideas (with Verena Bertmaring's indispensable help) as part of the documentation for the present chapter. More recently, T. J. Clark's discussion in *Representations* has related the techniques of representation in the *Marat* to the circumstances of its first presentation, in a search to find the originary moment of modernism. See also J. Rubin, 'Disorder/ Order: Revolutionary Art as Performative Representation' in *The Eighteenth Century,* vol. 30 (1989), 83–111.

10. R. Stalybrass and A. White, *The Politics and Poetics of Transgression* (Ithaca, N.Y.: Cornell University Press, 1990) offers an excellent introduction to the idea of the carnivalesque.

11. For a good general account of the successive exploiters of Marat's *L'Ami du Peuple,* see C. Bellanger et al., *Histoire générale de la presse française* (Paris: Presses universitaires de France, 1969), 1:405–518.

12. See D. Dowd, *Pageant-Master of the Republic: J-L David and the Revolution* (Lincoln, Nebr.: University of Nebraska Studies, 1948). The way in

which historians think about revolutionary festivals has been transformed by M. Ozouf, *La Fête révolutionnaire* (Paris: Gallimard, 1976).

13. The progressive suppression of the instrument of revolutionary violence in David's martyr portraits – the sword centrally evident in the *Le Peletier;* both present and absent, both marginal and central, in the *Marat;* entirely absent (so that even the other penetrating instrument, the phallus, is erased) in the *Bara* – may indicate the evolving nature of David's predicament as both a Jacobin politician and 'a man and a brother'.

14. Given that David was the leader of the *Commune populaire et républicaine des Arts* at this time, it is probably an implication that he would not have rejected.

15. Its companion piece, a death-head drawing of Le Peletier, is much simpler in its four-part inscription: M. LEPELLETIER/PREMIER/MARTYR/DE LA LIBERTE. That this text is not open to our word games is emphasised by the fact that it is wrapped around the image; thus the words in the two bottom corners appear upside down. See Schnapper, 1989, 220, fig. 70. [There was no standard spelling of Le Peletier's name: one word or two, one 'l' or two.]

16. The more so since the other half of the inscription survives, and in the *Le Peletier,* which hung as a pendant to the *Marat* in the Convention, there seems to have been both the valedictory dedication 'à Le Peletier David' and the slogan-text as an attribute of the 'sitter'.

17. F. Furet and M. Ozouf, *Dictionnaire critique de la Révolution française* (Paris: Flammarion, 1988) has several relevant articles: 'Souveraineté' and 'suffrage' are among the most useful. Note that the people-represented-in-the-Assembly excluded a very significant section of the people-of-the-streets: women, children, servants, and employed men without property.

18. G. Bollème, *Le peuple par écrit* (Paris: Seuil, 1986) examines 'le populaire' as a discursive phenomenon, particularly in the eighteenth and nineteenth centuries. G. Fritz, *l'Idée du peuple en France du XVIIe au XIXe siècle* (Strasbourg: Presses universitaires de Strasbourg, 1988) approaches the problem from a rather different position: parts 1 to 3 of his discussion have been important to the development of my ideas. Volume 20 of *Revue française de l'histoire de l'édition,* 1990, has a special number 'Peuple' with relevant contributions by D. Roche, A. Geffroy, A. M. Cocula, and others.

19. The key text here is J. Habermas, 'The Public Sphere', trans. by S. Lennox and F. Lennox, *New German Critique* 1, no. 3 (1974): 45–55; originally published in 1964. T. Crow, *Painters and Public Life in 18th-Century Paris* (New Haven and London: Yale University Press, 1985) uses a version of Habermas's conceptual framework; for a discussion of the impact of the idea on recent studies of the crisis of the ancien régime, see

B. Nathans, 'Habermas's "Public Sphere" in the Era of the French Revolution', *French Historical Studies* 16, no. 3 (1990): 620–45.

20. *La vie fragile: violence, pouvoirs et solidarités à Paris au XVIIIe siècle* (Paris: Hachette, 1986) and *Dire et mal dire: l'opinion publique au XVIIIe siècle* (Paris: Seuil, 1992).

21. R. Muchembled, *Culture populaire et culture des élites dans la France moderne XVe–XVIIIe siècles,* (Paris: Flammarion, 1978), English translation (Baton Rouge, La: Louisiana State University Press, 1985); P. Burke, *Popular Culture in Early Modern Europe* (London: Temple Smith, 1978).

22. S. Kaplan, *Bread, Politics and Political Economy in the Reign of Louis XV,* (The Hague: Martinus Nijhoff, 1982); F. Gauthier, G.-R. Ikni, eds., *La Guerre du blé au XVIIIe siècle* (Paris: Editions de la Passion, 1988).

23. In 1866, facsimile reproductions of two bloodstained copies of *L'Ami du Peuple* (nos. 506 and 678) marked by Marat's blood at the time of the assassination were published in Paris as *Le sang de Marat* by M. E. Bellot.

24. If I am right that the Tribune is here invoked, then both friendship and fatherhood are in play. The distinction between 'père du peuple' and 'ami du peuple' is an important one; the revolutionaries took the distinction over from the political vocabulary of the ancien régime and worked to insert it into their own discourse. All members of the Convention were called 'père du peuple'. In the terrible weeks before Thermidor, the woman who may have tried to kill Robespierre and the man who did try to kill Collot d'Herbois were guillotined dressed in the red cloak reserved for the execution of father-killers, or parricides. Charlotte Corday was similarly dressed for her execution.

DAVID'S *MARAT* AS POSTHUMOUS PORTRAIT

Interpretations of David's *Marat* have treated it as a history painting rather than a portrait. The search for religious prototypes in particular has preempted investigation of links with contemporary portraiture. Yet the quasi-Christian character of the Marat cult has itself been overemphasised, as research has shown.[1] It is surely time to consider David's painting in its secular context, particularly since it has obvious affinities with two types of portrait practice current in the late eighteenth century – the production of public memorials to national heroes as examples for their successors, and the commemoration of recent deaths in images designed to provide a focus for the expression of private grief. In his *Marat,* David brought together the emotional and social scope of these two types of posthumous portrait, fusing the hortatory with the sentimental, and the public with the private. The result was a portrait whose meaning was secured by the manner of its public exhibition. In this it resembled not only other representations of the martyrs of the Revolution, but also the effigies at the origin of European posthumous portraiture – the wax images of ancestors that had been brought out at noble funerals and other ceremonies in ancient Rome. The period during which David's painting played its intended role was brief. Its prolonged invisibility thereafter ensured that its ultimate reappearance would be in a very different context from that for which it had been painted – that of the public museum.

The bases for the traditional social interpretations of the French

Revolution have been extensively challenged in recent years. Partly as a consequence of this reevaluation, historians have sought new perspectives. In particular, they have investigated the political culture of the Revolution, using methods derived from cultural history and anthropology rather than traditional historiography. This approach emphasises those aspects of the Revolution that have proved most influential on the thought and behaviour of later generations.[2] One concept that was of fundamental and enduring importance for revolutionary culture was that of the public sphere and its relationship to the private. These are categories whose present form evolved in the late eighteenth century, and they still shape the way we think and feel about the world in which we live.[3] Eighteenth-century perceptions of public and private derived from classical antiquity, from ancient Greece and Rome. It was to these cultures in particular that French republicans looked for models for their own republican practice. This chapter engages specifically with the way in which one of the principal figures of the Jacobin dictatorship, Jacques-Louis David, attempted to transform the relationship of public to private in revolutionary society through his paintings.

DAVID'S *MARAT* AND THE *GRANDS HOMMES*

It is at first sight paradoxical that the two most important paintings completed by David while serving as a representative of the people, the *Le Peletier de Saint-Fargeau* and the *Marat,* should have been portraits rather than history paintings. In general, portraits were not highly regarded in the eighteenth century. They were still judged first and foremost as likenesses, and only exceptionally as works of art. Most portraits were privately commissioned, and this, too, contributed to the low reputation of portraiture as a genre. Commentators considered that artists' talents were more fittingly employed on the production of history paintings to serve the general interest than on portraits, which merely pandered to the private vanity of individual sitters.[4] There was one exception, however, to the general contempt in which the genre was held – the portrayal of the illustrious dead. In this department the portraitist was able to work, for once, in the public interest. It was known that in antiquity the likenesses of great men had been perpetuated in statues and medals, and David's own initial suggestion for a memorial to Le Peletier was for 'a heroic portrait in imitation of the statues which the Greeks erected to their great citizens'.[5] Images erected in honour of great men had long been held to be socially useful, because they provided future generations with an incentive to emulate their achievements, as in a famous anecdote of how an encounter with a statue of Alexander the Great had fired the ambitions of the youthful Julius Caesar.[6] It was to further such emulation among his comtemporaries that Quatremère de Quincy urged the conversion of the church of Sainte-Geneviève into a Panthéon in 1791. By dedicating the former church to the commemoration of dead national heroes, he wanted to create a site, as Mona Ozouf has observed, not merely for the recital of great deeds, but for their production.[7]

There was a precedent in contemporary France for the type of heroic statue that David at first proposed for Le Peletier. This was the series of figures of specifically French 'Grands Hommes' of the past, which had been inaugurated in 1774 by Louis XVI's Directeur des Bâtiments, d'Angiviller, and which continued in production throughout the revolutionary period and beyond. David's *Marat* shares a significant characteristic with the statues commissioned by d'Angiviller. Although the statues were intended to celebrate achievements in the public sphere, d'Angiviller stipulated that those to be so honoured should have been conspicuous for virtuous living and for self-denying devotion to the general good.[8] David's portrayal of Marat murdered while making a charitable gesture offers a similar characterisation of greatness, one that is reinforced by David's emphasis on the poverty and plainness of the dying man's surroundings.[9] In other respects, however, David's two 'martyr' portraits mark a radical departure from this tradition of portraying great men. In both paintings death itself and, more specifically, the manner of death were emphasised. Le Peletier was depicted on his deathbed; Marat, at his last breath. Such dwelling on the fact of death is foreign to the 'great men' tradition exemplified by the d'Angiviller project. The latter proclaimed to posterity that the immortal fame of great deeds could transcend individual mortality. Any attempt to invoke the spectator's sympathy with the transient agonies of dying, as in David's *Marat,* could only distract from that lesson. Indeed, Quatremère de Quincy specifically called for the exclusion of monuments with imagery suggestive of death in his proposals for the Panthéon.[10] Officially commissioned statues of 'great men' were rarely executed in the immediate aftermath of death. It was as though the emotions consequent on recent bereavement might interfere with the impartial evaluation of a public career if the recipients of such honours were chosen too hastily.

DAVID'S *MARAT* AND THE PRIVATE POSTHUMOUS PORTRAIT

There was another tradition of posthumous portraiture, one in which the fact of death and the grief to which it gave rise provided the occasion for the image's production. In commemorating Le Peletier and Marat with portraits executed shortly after their deaths, David followed a long-established custom that ultimately derived from ancient Rome. It contributed to a cult of family identity. According to the Roman author Pliny, wax likenesses were taken from the heads of noble Romans after death and painted. These likenesses were preserved in prominent positions in the family home, whence they were carried forth to attend, as it were, the funerals of their descendants.[11] Similar portraits were not uncommon in Renaissance Europe, where paintings, as well as modelled busts, perpetuated the appearance of the recently dead.[12]

It is likely that many sixteenth-, seventeenth-, and eighteenth-century portraits, which have since been assumed to represent the living, were produced to commemorate the dead. The posthumous status of images of 'great men' from the more or less distant past is generally self-evident, if only because of anachronisms in iconography and execution, but this is by no means true of private posthumous portraits. The latter were often commissioned in the immediate aftermath of the subject's death, which makes it difficult or impossible to identify them as posthumous in the absence of documentary evidence. Even if dated, they may well bear the year in which the subject died. It has been easy enough for later commentators to conclude that work on such portraits was merely interrupted by a sitter's death, when in reality it was occasioned by it. Given the terms in which portraits from the past are conventionally appraised in the twentieth century, scholars have been understandably reluctant to entertain the possibility that portraits were posthumous, and thereby to forgo the pleasure of interpreting them as records of personal communion or confrontation between artist and sitter. There is every indication, however, that the production of posthumous portraits for private consumption remained a significant branch of art at the time when David painted his *Marat*.[13]

It was not only the example set by the patriciate of ancient Rome that recommended posthumous portraiture to bereaved families in the eighteenth century. Mourning was increasingly regarded as a private activity, and posthumous portraits evidently played their part in the rituals of family mourning. They were objects of private contemplation. Unlike the individuals commemorated in the 'grands hommes' tradition, those depicted in posthumous portraits for family consumption were at least as likely to be women as men, and it was their private identity that was portrayed, sometimes to the exclusion of indications of external privilege. Thus, for example, the posthumous portrait of Madame Louise-Elisabeth de France, duchess of Parma (Madame Infante), which Adélaïde Labille-Guiard exhibited at the Salon of 1789, depicts the subject as an affectionate mother rather than as a royal princess (Fig. 8).[14] In this respect, it is in striking contrast with Labille-Guiard's portraits of Madame Infante's two surviving sisters, Mesdames Adélaïde and Victoire, to which it served as a pendant. These are replete with Bourbon symbolism − symbolism whose very absence in the *Madame Infante* points to the private status of this, as of other posthumous portraits, as a record of family bereavement. A further indication of the essentially private scope of such images is the way in which the portrait's posthumous status is merely hinted at by pictorial effects that were doubtless poignant enough for the bereaved, but whose significance might well have escaped a stranger's notice − a shadow cast on a wall, a shaded face in the midst of a sunny scene, the intensity with which a child is made to reach out to a loved one in reality already lost. It was evidently superfluous (if not tactless) to allude more directly to a subject's death in a work designed for her or his surviving family. Only exceptionally did a posthumous portrait like Labille-Guiard's *Madame Infante* appear at the Salon.[15] Of the two functions ascribed to posthumous portrait busts by Pliny − preservation as private mementoes in the recesses of the family home and display on public occasions such as funerals − these paintings perpetuated only the former.

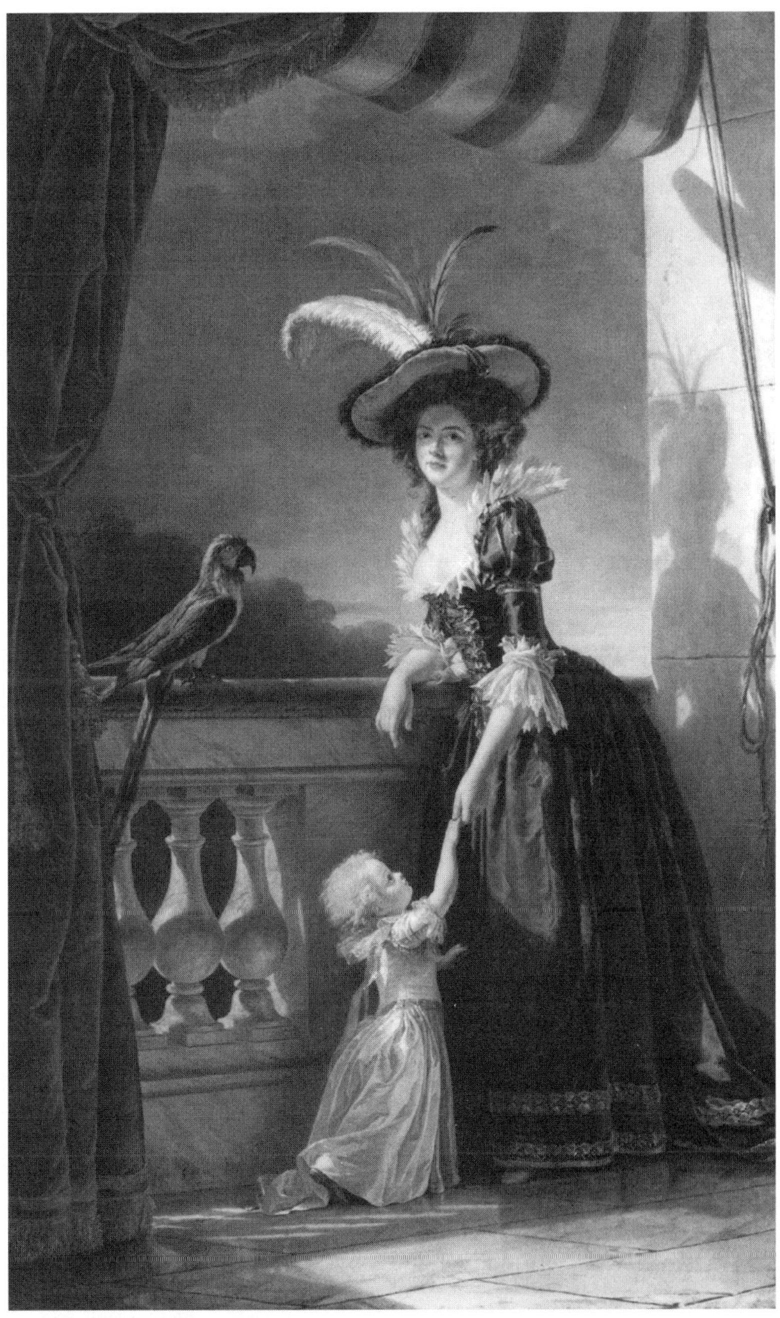

Figure 8. Adélaïde Labille-Guiard, *Portrait of Madame Louise-Elisabeth de France, Duchess of Parma (Madame Infante) with her Son,* 1788, oil on canvas, 272 × 160 cm. Musée national du château, Versailles. (Photo: Réunion des musées nationaux.)

Like private posthumous portraits, David's *Le Peletier* and *Marat* set out to awaken pity and a sense of loss in the spectator, and they employed similar means. In both paintings, pathos was enhanced by the depiction of homely domestic detail in the context of death — the crumpled bedclothes in the *Le Peletier,* the paraphernalia of disease and writing materials in the *Marat.* More specifically, the representation of an interrupted act of penning a final communication has a parallel in another portrait that Labille-Guiard had painted at about the same time as her *Madame Infante,* which also appears to be posthumous. This other painting portrays an unidentified woman in tears seated at a desk at which she writes a letter of farewell to her children (Fig. 9).[16] As in the David, so in the Labille-Guiard, the well-worn desk and the still life of writing implements suggest a domestic interior. Like David's *Marat,* this dead mother is made to reach out from beyond the tomb with a message for posterity. But this shared device serves only to emphasise the underlying difference between Labille-Guiard's characterisation of her subject and David's. The anonymous but affluent mother is concerned exclusively for the well-being of her own offspring, whereas Marat's final thoughts are revealed to have been for the poor and bereaved of the Republic. Though portrayed in the privacy of his bath, Marat is defined as a public man by the range of his emotional preoccupations. Another point of difference between the two portraits is in their treatment of death. In Labille-Guiard's painting the subject's demise is to be inferred only from discrete hints — a tear on the sitter's cheek, the handkerchief clutched in her hand, and, of course, the letter itself. David, in contrast, chose to depict Marat at his last breath, thereby perpetuating the memory of his agony. Marat had died a representative of the people, and his death was a significant moment in the history of the newborn Republic, one that required commemoration for generations yet unborn.

DAVID'S *MARAT* AND
THE ROMAN REPUBLICAN FUNERAL EFFIGIES

Whatever it owed to the tradition of private posthumous portraiture, David's *Marat* was intended as a memorial for the nation as a whole, not merely for the victim's immediate family. It provided a focus for the grief of individual citizens, but it was intended to realise its full meaning only as a participant in public life. Together

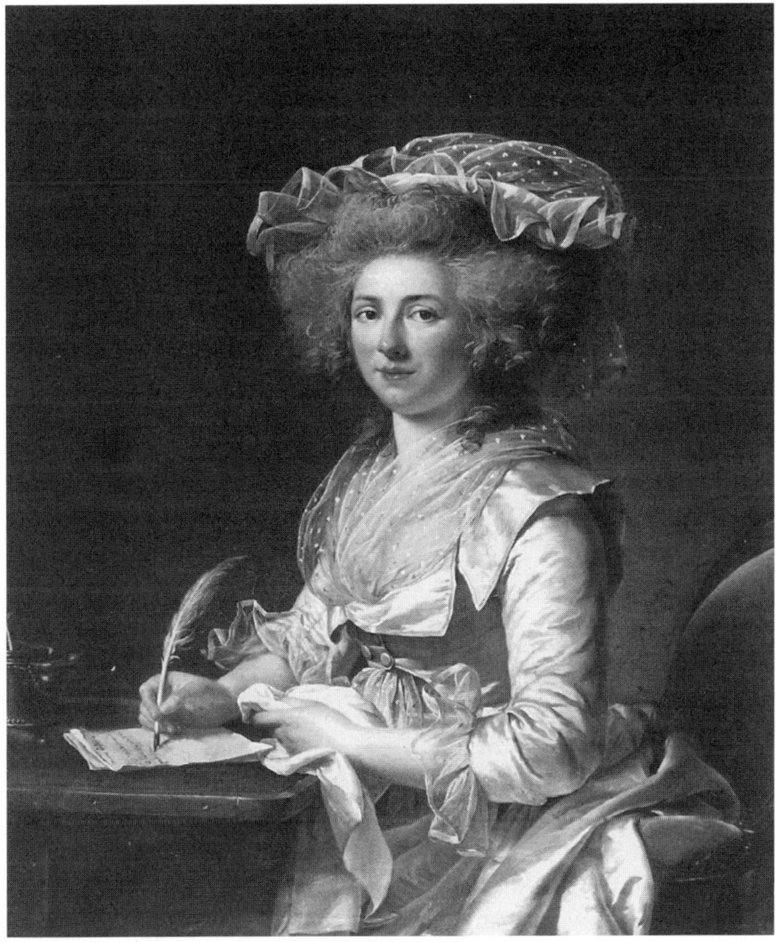

Figure 9. Adélaïde Labille-Guiard, *Portrait of an Unknown Woman*, n.d., oil on canvas, 87.3 × 78.7 cm. Musée des Beaux-Arts de Quimper. (Photo: Musée des Beaux Arts de Quimper, France.)

with the *Le Peletier*, it was destined for the National Assembly, a prop in the ongoing drama of the nation's self-determination. Unlike d'Angiviller's 'Grands Hommes', however, it was designed to exploit feelings of bereavement in the spectator – the sort of feelings associated with private posthumous portraits. The incorporation of elements drawn from an essentially private portrait tradition into a painting whose function was wholly public involved a certain strain. This is evident in the speech with which David presented his painting to the Convention, where the opening sentence awkwardly straddled the two spheres, attributing the language of bereaved *amitié* to an abstract and personified 'People'.[17] Such a dissolving of the private in the public is characteristic of Jacobin ideology, which sought to reduce the distinction of the private man from the citizen as much by politicising private feelings as by moralising politics.[18]

In the context of posthumous portraiture, the synthesis of private with public may well have appeared to David and his contemporaries as restitution rather than innovation. Pliny's is not the only surviving account of the Roman rituals that involved the display of posthumous likenesses. There is, in particular, an earlier and more detailed description where the same procedures are interpreted in a different social sense, as providing incentives to acts of virtuous self-sacrifice on behalf of the Republic rather than as affirmations of family identity; in other words, a similar function to that accorded to the display of the *Le Peletier* and the *Marat* by David and his contemporaries. This account appears in the Greek historian Polybius. Unlike Pliny, who wrote under the Roman Empire, Polybius had lived during the heyday of the Roman Republic, two hundred years previously. Through such writers as Machiavelli and Mably, the Greek historian's views played an important role in shaping modern ideas about how republican virtue had functioned in antiquity.[19] In particular, Polybius fuelled the belief that such virtue had declined when Rome ceased to be a republic. His account of Roman funerals is tailored to its context – an extended comparison between Carthaginian and Roman institutions, in the course of which he attributes Roman superiority in arms to the care with which a taste for valour was fostered in the young. According to Polybius, the funerary practices of the nobility were an important ingredient in this process. Unlike Pliny, Polybius emphasised the way in which the public display of posthumous portraits kept alive the memories of the deceased and their achievements as examples for subsequent generations of the nation as a whole, not merely for individual families. He described how posthumous busts were taken from their positions of honour in patrician houses to be donned as masks by actors at family funerals. Speeches were then addressed to these living simulacra of the dead in which the achievements of their originals were recalled and praised. In Polybius's view, this practice clothed the deeds of dead heroes with immortal lustre and provided an incentive to acts of courage and self-sacrifice in the living. As evidence of the cult's effectiveness, he cited instances of Roman patriotism – the propensity of noble Romans to lay down their own lives in single combat or even the lives of their sons for the good of the fatherland. His account concludes with a description of the valour of Horatius Cocles.[20] Thus the institution that for Pliny enshrined the exclusive esprit de corps of old families had previously been presented by Polybius as serving the interests of the *res publica* to the detriment and even to the potential extinction of lineal heredity.[21]

There is no direct evidence to connect David's *Le Peletier* and *Marat* with this passage in Polybius, but there can be no doubt that David was aware of and approved the conception of Roman virtue that it sets forth. Two of Polybius's three chosen instances of heroic self-denial – willingness to undertake single combat on behalf of the Republic and the willingness of those entrusted with high office to sacrifice their own sons' lives for the public good – furnished the subjects of the two history paintings that David had already painted on Roman republican subjects, the *Oath of the Horatii* (Fig. 5) and the *Brutus*. Retrospectively, these paintings were interpreted as prophetic calls for a return to the austere virtues of early Rome. Insofar as David's two posthumous portraits harnessed the emotive charge of a tradition of private portraiture to public ends, they could be viewed as attempts to restore a degenerate institution of the recent past to a condition of pristine republican virtue.[22]

The funerals of Le Peletier and Marat were modelled on Roman practice. Indeed, the arrangement of Marat's body for its display at the church of the Cordeliers incorporated elements apparently derived from a specific Roman funeral, that of Julius Caesar as described by Suetonius.[23] The texts connected with these ceremonies, whether programmes, speeches, or inscriptions, framed calls for acts of self-sacrifice, emulation, and revenge.[24] On later occasions, however, David's paintings were treated as substitutes for the dead, like the ancestral images brought out by the Romans to attend funerals and other public ceremonies. The painter's own behaviour toward his two portraits on these occasions had more in common with the way in which the Romans were reported to have treated funerary busts than with that in which eighteenth-century Frenchmen usually treated paintings. When he presented his *Le Peletier* and *Marat* to the Assembly on the 29 March 1793 and

14 November 1793, David delivered speeches intended to stir the blood with affirmations of national unity against a common enemy, like those spoken at the funerals.[25] When requesting the Assembly's permission to display the two posthumous portraits in the court-yard of the Louvre in a ceremony organised by the Muséum Section, he did so in language that equated the presence of his paintings with that of their subjects, a conflation of identities suggestive of Roman attitudes.[26] In a later speech to the Convention in which he announced plans for the commemoration of two more dead heroes, Bara and Viala, David called on Marat and Le Peletier to display their wounds – exhortations presumably addressed to his own paintings, by this time in place on the walls of the hall where he was speaking.[27]

DAVID'S *MARAT* AND WAX EFFIGIES

It was as substitutes for funeral effigies that the portraits of Le Peletier and Marat were displayed in the ceremony organised by the Muséum Section in the courtyard of the Louvre, where they appeared together with two sarcophagi, as Jean-Claude Bonnet has observed.[28]

The images of departed Romans had attended later family funerals as recipients of public addresses in common with the deceased, himself present either as a corpse or in effigy. The way in which the ceremony was conducted had thus tended to efface the distinction between the bodies of the deceased and their simulacra. Eighteenth-century waxwork displays also invited spectators to identify their exhibits as closely as possible with their human sub-jects. These commercial exhibitions of waxworks had affinities with the long-standing tradition of displaying waxwork effigies as part of the funeral ceremonies of royal and other public persons. Waxwork 'courts', in which figures of the great and powerful were grouped together, were exhibited from the late seventeenth cen-tury, and it was with such a group that the immigrant Swiss wax modeller Philippe Curtius, Madame Tussaud's uncle, scored his first success in Paris.[29]

Effigies played an important role in the rituals following the death of Marat. Before his body was put on public view in the Cordeliers on 15 July, a death mask had been displayed in the win-dow of his house, where it was later replaced by a bust.[30] Following

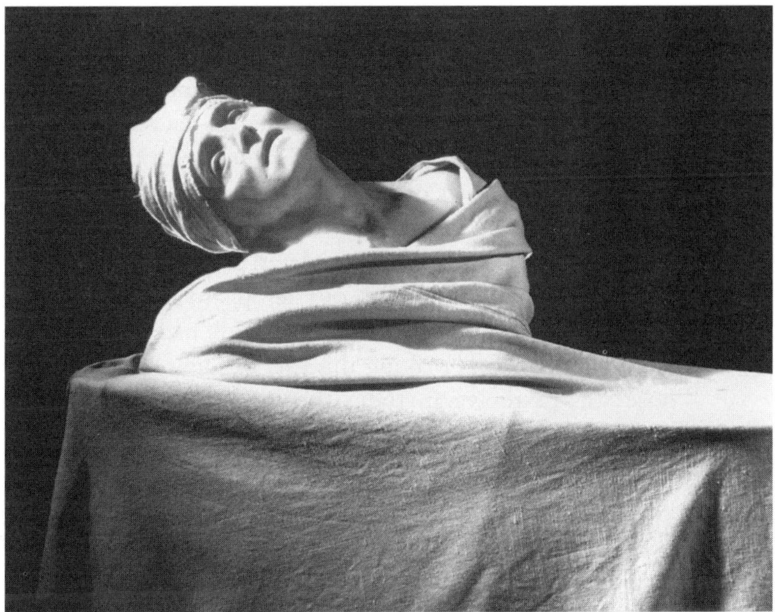

Figure 10. Philippe Curtius or Madame Tussaud, *The Death of Marat,* wax model. Madame Tussaud's, London. (Photo: Madame Tussaud's.)

his death, an effigy of his body appeared at commemorative ceremonies held at the church of Saint Eustache on 10 August and at the Bonne-Nouvelle Church on 18 August. If, as is likely, either the death mask exhibited in Marat's window or a bust deriving from it is identifiable with the likeness preserved at Madame Tussaud's (Fig. 10), it presumably formed the centrepiece of a tableau representing the assassination itself, which was already on show at Curtius's waxwork museum before Thermidor.[31] The bust at Madame Tussaud's is clearly similar in pose and features to the representation of the dead Marat in David's painting, and the relationship of the two images to each other has been debated, together with that of the painting to Curtius's waxwork tableau.[32]

The reception of wax images was governed by an aesthetic of imitation. As Annie Becq has observed, the traditional conception of art as imitation maintained a concrete relationship of resemblance with the object imitated in which value was held to consist. Such an aesthetic testified to a perception of use value in the work of art rather than exchange value.[33] Art that depended on the merits of imitation was viewed with increasing disfavour in late eighteenth-century France – this was one reason for the low opinion of portraiture expressed by critics and artists. Too great an emphasis on imitation was stigmatised as slavish by aesthetic theorists who considered it to be at variance with the status of a work of art as the product of independent genius.[34] It is thus surprising that David should have invited such close identification of his portrait of Marat with the person Marat, particularly since David himself expressed a low opinion of attempts to imitate reality exactly.[35] But it is clear that the efficacy of David's painting depended on its intended spectators making this sort of identification, since its purpose was to revive in them the virtues of the deceased and to inspire them with grief and the will to avenge Marat's death. It was essential for effective republican art to convince, as David himself made clear in a speech that he delivered in the Convention on the day following that on which he had presented his *Marat* to the same assembly:

> It is not only by charming the eyes that artistic monuments have attained their goal, but in penetrating the soul, in making a deep impression on the mind akin to that made by reality itself – it is then that deeds of heroism and of civic virtue, presented to the people's view, will electrify their souls and breed a passion for glory and devotion to the welfare of the fatherland.[36]

If this account of how art should operate is applied to David's own painting, it suggests that the identification of the latter with its subject was indeed intended to be as intimate as in the case of a wax effigy, but that it was meant to operate on a deeper level than that which could be achieved by an illusionistic likeness. How his painting might affect spectators for whom Marat's virtues and his death were no longer live issues was evidently not something that concerned the painter.

CONCLUSION

It was only for a brief period that David's two posthumous portraits remained on public display. As the government of the Republic increasingly sought to circumscribe rather than to encourage popular participation in the democratic process, the ideology that David's paintings had promoted was discarded. The Constitution of the Year Three, implemented in the autumn of 1795, rewrote the duties of the good republican as those of the good father and husband. Henceforth the citizen was expected to keep his heart at home. As an exhortation to be more outgoing, David's *Marat* was intolerably out of keeping with the new ideology and was soon banished from public view. It was literally invisible for the remainder of the painter's lifetime, and was to surface only intermittently before being placed permanently on public view in 1893 in the Brussels museum.[37] The case that David had ignored in the 1790s – the emotional indifference of a viewing public to the circumstances of the painting's production – turned out to be the precondition for its public exhibition.

The years during which David's painting was out of sight witnessed a transformation in the ways in which the types of portrait discussed here were regarded. What all these paintings and effigies had in common at the time of their production was their primary function. Whether they were designed for private or for public consumption, it was a person's death, and the desire of survivors to commemorate that person, that provided the reason for their existence, and the people who commissioned such images did not envisage them as 'working' in any other context than that of personal commemoration. The significance of such acts of commemoration has been occluded by time, except in the case of the *grands hommes* (where faith in the capacity of bronze and marble to defy the destructive power of time is a precondition of the tradition itself). The products of the other two versions of the Roman art of death have enjoyed strangely different critical fortunes. Repudiated by the bourgeoisie and excluded from its halls of fame after Thermidor, most images of Marat and the other martyrs of the French Republic were destroyed wholesale or relegated to sideshows on the boulevards, where likenesses of the martyrs of the Revolution and their Jacobin brethren figured prominently in waxwork museums. They were too faithful to the appearance of their models – too basely utilitarian – to be judged works of art at all. They pandered to that lowest of aesthetic appetites, the taste for a good likeness.[38]

Insofar as David's *Marat* fulfilled functions similar to those of the waxwork heads exhibited by Curtius, it stands at the end of a long tradition in European portraiture, rather than at the beginning – a tradition in which a portrait's significance depended first and foremost on that of its subject and intended placement, on its utility, in a word, rather than on its status as a work of art. What was innovative about the *Marat,* however, was its use of private means for public, universal ends. Insofar as it tried to harness the individual's private feelings to a public cause by deploying the pathos of private posthumous portraiture in an image designed to move a nation, it proved abortive. But by giving the stamp of universal currency to the private and particular language of personal bereavement, it performed the generalisation of feeling necessary for the transformation of the private portrait into a universal commodity, thereby foreshadowing the appearance of other posthumous portraits, such as those painted by Labille-Guiard, in the setting of the public art gallery.

NOTES

1. See F.-P. Bowman, 'Le "Sacré-Coeur" de Marat (1793)', in *Les Fêtes de la Révolution,* Colloque de Clermont-Ferrand (juin 1974), Actes receuillis et présentés par Jean Ehrard et Paul Viallaneix (Paris: Société des études robespierristes, 1977), 155–78. According to Bowman, the 'sacralisation' of Marat postdates the Revolution and appears initially in a polemical, counterrevolutionary context. The occasional appearance of Christ's name in the context of the 'martyr' cults of the Revolution indicates 'the humanisation of Jesus rather than the deification of Marat'. M. Ozouf, *Festivals and the French Revolution,* trans. A. Sheridan (Cambridge, Mass. and London: Harvard University Press, 1986), 266.

2. For the best and most approachable introduction to the issues raised by the political culture of the Revolution, see L. Hunt, *Politics, Culture and Class in the French Revolution* (reprint, London: Methuen & Company, 1986).

3. The fundamental text on the history of the public sphere is J. Habermas, *The Structural Transformations of the Public Sphere: An Inquiry into a Category of Bourgeois Society,* trans. T. Burger with the assistance of F. Lawrence (Cambridge, Mass. and London: Polity Press, 1989).

4. See J. Locquin, 'La lutte des critiques d'art contre les portraitistes au XVIIIe siècle', in *Mélanges offerts à M. Henri Lemonnier par la Société de l'Histoire de l'Art française, ses amis et ses élèves* (Nouvelles Archives de l'Art français, nouvelle période, quatrième série 7: 309–20). David concurred with the generally low estimate of both the genre and its practitioners. See the letter of 27 June 1800 (8 messidor an VIII), in which he refused a request from the citizen Verninac to exhibit his portrait of Verninac's wife (D. and G. Wildenstein, *Documents complémentaires au Catalogue de l'oeuvre de Louis David* [Paris: Fondation Wildenstein, 1973], no. 1350), and the objections he voiced to the allocation of a studio in the Louvre to

the patriotic portraitist Joseph Ducreux. See G. Lyon, *Joseph Ducreux Premier peintre de Marie-Antoinette (1735–1802), sa vie – son oeuvre* (Paris: La Nef de Paris, 1958), 96.

5. J. L. Jules David, *Le peintre Louis David (1748–1825), souvenirs et documents inédits* (Paris: Victor Havard, 1880), 1: 116. Cf. Wildenstein, no. 409. In his speech of 16 July 1793, David compared Marat with such ancient heroes as Arisides and Cato (Wildenstein, no. 466). As Bowman indicates, such comparisons were commonplace in the literature produced in the aftermath of Marat's death (Bowman, 159f).

6. Suetonius, *Caes.*, 7. On critical responses to portraits of *grands hommes,* see Loquin, 315–17. Robespierre considered the emulation provoked by the sight of live *grands hommes* at the Panhellenic games to have been of more consequence to the civic virtue of the Greeks than the spectacle of the games themselves. See his speech of 18 floréal an II (7 May 1794) in C. Mazauric, ed., *Robespierre. Ecrits* (Paris: Messidor, 1989), 325. On the cult of *grands hommes* and the tradition of éloges in eighteenth-century France, see J.-Cl. Bonnet, 'Naissance du Panthéon', *Poétique* 33 (1978), 46–65.

7. 'Le Panthéon. L'Ecole normale des morts', in *Les lieux de mémoire, I, La République,* ed. P. Nora (Paris: Gallimard, 1984), 150. Quatremère went so far as to propose the segregation of the tombs of those whose actions had earned them public recognition from those of private citizens whose careers had lacked that distinction. See *Gazette national, ou le Moniteur universel,* 13 April 1791 (Deuxième année de la liberté); reprinted in *Réimpression de l'ancien Moniteur* (Paris: 1847), 8: 109f.

8. Cited by G. Gramaccini, 'L'image de l'homme nouveau: exemples de la sculpture publique à la fin de l'Ancien Régime et â l'époque révolutionnaire', in *La Révolution française et l'Europe 1789–1799,* Exhibition catalogue (Paris: Grand Palais, 1989), 675. See also F. H. Dowley, 'D'Angiviller's *Grands Hommes* and the Significant Moment', *Art Bulletin* 39 (December 1957): 259–77, and A. McClellan, 'D'Angiviller's "Great Men" of France and the Politics of the Parlements', *Art History* 13 (June 1990): 175–92.

9. Like other deputies who addressed the Convention after their colleague's death, David stressed Marat's indigence as the consequence of rectitude and self-denial. See *Gazette national, ou le Moniteur universel,* 18 July 1973, L'an II de la République française, no. 199; reprinted in *Réimpression de l'ancien Moniteur* (Paris: 1847), 17: 152. He again drew attention to Marat's self-denial and charity in the speech with which he presented the finished painting to the Convention on 14 November 1793 (24 brumaire, l'an II). See Wildenstein, no. 674. The most famous commemoration of virtuous poverty and self-denying charity in French art was Poussin's *Testament of Eudamidas* (see Fig. 3). Several features of David's painting recall this work. Cf., for example, D. Johnson, *Jacques-Louis David. Art in Meta-*

morphosis (Princeton: Princeton University Press, 1993), 96. These similarities include the pose and expression of Marat himself and the austerity of the setting, particularly the form of the 'desk' and its alignment parallel to the picture plane. The illumination of Marat's face and the choice of an elevated light source also derive from the Poussin, where they presumably indicate that the last wishes of the dying man will be fulfilled by those he leaves behind. There is nothing to suggest that the lighting of David's painting should be interpreted in any other sense (e.g., as some quasi-Christian hint at personal salvation).

10. *Rapport sur l'édifice dit de Sainte-Geneviève, fait au Directoire du Département de Paris* (Paris: 1791), 31.

11. 'Semper . . . defuncto aliquo, totus aderat familiae eius, qui unquam fuerat, populus' (*NH,* 35:2). Pliny the Elder, *Natural History,* 35, 6.

12. See Lorne Campbell, *Renaissance Portraits. European Portrait Painting in the Fourteenth and Fifteenth and Sixteenth Centuries* (New Haven and London: Yale University Press, 1990), 190, and, most recently, Dominique Thiébaut, 'Un chef-d'oeuvre restauré. Le *portrait d'un vieillard et d'un jeune garçon* de Dominique Ghirlandaio (1449–1494)', *Revue du Louvre* 46 (June 1996): 42–53. The account in Pliny (or that in Polybius; see n. 20) is evidently the source for the practise as described by Vasari in his *Life of Verrocchio,* to judge from Vasari's account of the positions accorded to such portraits in Florence interiors (see Campbell, 190). If Vasari was aware of this connection, he did not mention it.

13. The question of posthumous portraits in eighteenth-century France is discussed more fully in my thesis, 'French Portraiture under the Directoire and the Consulat' (Ph.D. thesis, University of London, Courtauld Institute of Art, 1996), 49–53.

14. A.-M. Passez, *Adélaïde Labille-Guiard, 1749–1803. Biographie et catalogue raisonné de son oeuvre* (Paris: Arts et métiers graphique, 1973), no. 99. On mourning in eighteenth-century France, see McManners, *Death and the Enlightenment. Changing Attitudes towards Death among Christians and Unbelievers in Eighteenth-Century France* (Oxford and New York: Oxford University Press, 1981), 344, 463.

15. Madame Infante had died in 1759, and it was doubtless the lapse of almost thirty years between that event and the execution of the portrait that made its exhibition acceptable, the period of mourning having expired.

16. 'A mes enfants, je vous recommande à l'amité elle vous protégera', Passez, no. 94. It has hitherto been assumed that this work represents a living sitter and that it commemorates a mother's imminent abandonment of her children, but it is most improbable that such a dereliction of maternal duty would have been seen as a fit circumstance for celebration in an eighteenth-century portrait. Death, however, was a proper occasion for such commemoration.

17. 'Le peuple redemandoit son ami, sa voix désolée se faisait entendre, il provoquoit mon art, il voulait revoir les traits de son ami fidèle: David! saisis tes pinceaux, s'écria-t-il, venge notre ami, venge Marat. . . .' ['The people called again for its friend, its despairing voice made itself heard, it called upon my art, it wanted to see the features of its faithful friend once more: David! seize your brushes, it cried, avenge our friend, avenge Marat. . . .'] Speech of 14 November 1793 (24 brumaire l'an II), Wildenstein, no. 674.

18. M. Revault d'Allonnes, 'Rousseau et le jacobinisme. Pédagogie et politique', *Annales historiques de la Révolution française* 50 (1978): 595. According to a later statement by David, the equality of a republic transformed a vast population into a single family. Speech of 11 July 1794 (23 messidor an II), Wildenstein, no. 1096. On myths of the nation as family, see L. Hunt, *The Family Romance of the French Revolution* (London: Routledge, 1992).

19. See A. Momigliano, 'Polybius' Reappearance in Western Europe', in *Entretiens sur l'antiquité classique publiées* par Olivier Reverdin, XX. Polybe (Vandoeuvres-Geneva, 1974), 347–72; J. G. A. Pocock, *The Machiavellian Moment. Florentine Political Thought and the Atlantic Republican Tradition* (Princeton: Princeton University Press, 1975), 539.

20. Polybius 6: 52–4. Polybius's text was formerly interpreted as though it referred to the use of effigies in funeral celebrations, and not to live actors. See J. Kirchman, *De funeribus romanorum* (Lübeck: 1637), 245. Cf. Dom V. Thuillier, *Histoire de Polybe, nouvellement traduite du grec* (Paris: 1726–30), 6: 39f., probably following Casaubon). It is now understood that the latter are meant. See F. W. Walbank, *A Historical Commentary on Polybius* (Oxford: Clarendon, 1957), 1: 739.

21. In fact, the rite in question, the *ius imaginum,* was a privilege of the nobility, and as such was soon to be contested by Marius and the 'new men'. The way in which it is described by Polybius is thus evidence for the historian's sympathies with the older nobility, but this conclusion is by no means obvious from his text. Cf. C. Nicolet, 'Polybe et les institutions romaines' in *Entretiens . . .* (1974), 219, n. 3. Cf. Kirchman, 34.

22. See Polybius 6: 53f. The first Roman funeral oration is reported to have been delivered over the body of the same L. Junius Brutus portrayed in David's 1789 painting. Cf. entry by Jaucourt on 'Oraison funèbre', *Encyclopédie ou dictionnaire raisonné des sciences, des arts et des métiers* (Neufchâtel: Chez Briasson, 1765), 11: 550 A bust of Brutus was displayed in the Convention, together with David's posthumous martyr portraits. The difference of emphasis between Polybius's account and that of Pliny would not have surprised David. In his 11 July 1794 speech, he was to describe how patriotism was banished by despotism and virtue replaced by egoism, whereas in a republic all thoughts and deeds concerned the fatherland (Wildenstein, no. 1096).

23. Suetonius records that Caesar's body was carried from the site of his murder on a litter from which one arm dangled ('dependente brachio') (*Caes.*, 82). The body was subsequently exhibited to the people in a specially constructed 'temple', within which it lay on a bed, with the presumably bloodstained clothing in which he had died displayed on a trophy beside the head (Caes., 84). From the painting of the interior of the Cordeliers church with Marat's corpse on display (Fig. 2), it would appear that Marat's body was exhibited with one arm hanging down, as well as with a 'trophie' formed by his bath and makeshift desk, the sheets being draped over the former. As in Suetonius's description, so in the exhibition of Marat's body, the hanging arm was presumably intended to emphasise the suddenness and violence of the murder. The use of a similar pose in David's painting of the dying Marat perhaps derives from the way in which the body had been displayed at the Cordeliers.

24. According to Bowman, two themes dominate the literature produced in the aftermath of Marat's death: 'Marat doit vivre encore dans nos coeurs, et Marat demande vengeance' (Bowman, 173). Similar effects were looked for from Le Peletier's funeral. See M. J. Chénier's programme, *Convention nationale. Rapport fait à la Convention nationale, au nom des comités d'instruction publique et des inspecteurs* (Paris: 1793; l'an second de la République).

25. Wildenstein, nos. 427 and 647. Similar addresses were doubtless delivered at the ceremonies held to inaugurate the mass-produced plaster busts of Marat, which were distributed throughout the departments. See J.-Cl. Bonnet, 'Les formes de célébration', in *La Mort de Marat,* ed. J.-Cl. Bonnet (Paris: Flammarion, 1986), 114. Had David's paintings remained in the location for which they were designed, the debating chamber of the Convention, they would presumably have been harangued in this fashion on a regular basis.

26. David stated that he wanted to lend the paintings for exhibition so that Le Peletier and Marat 'puissent être l'un et l'autre présents en quelque sorte aux honneurs civiques qu'ils reçoivent de leurs concitoyens' (speech of 14 October 1793, Wildenstein, no. 601). David's language is very close to the terms in which Pliny had described the 'attendance' of ancestors at Roman funerals. See note 9. According to eyewitnesses, Marat's bath and other belongings were also on show (J. L. Jules David, 145f).

27. Speech of 11 July 1794 (23 messidor an II), Wildenstein, no. 1096.

28. See Bonnet, 'Les formes . . .', 114.

29. See J. Adhémar, 'Les Musées de cire en France, Curtius, le "Banquet Royal", les têtes coupées', *Gazette de Beaux-Arts* 92 (1978): 203–14.

30. Report in the *Gazette de France,* cited by J. Guilhaumou, 'La Mort de Marat à Paris', in Bonnet, ed., *La Mort de Marat, 54,* n. 26.

31. *Madame Tussaud's Memoirs and Reminiscences of France, forming an Abridged*

History of the Revolution, edited by Francis Hervé (London: 1838), 345–7. Cf. D. Bindman, *The Shadow of the Guillotine. Britain and the French Revolution* (London: British Museum Publications, 1989), 147, no. 127. Madame Tussaud claimed that she had been sent for to go to Marat's house following his murder 'for the purpose of taking a cast of his face' (*Memoirs,* 199, 340), and the likeness of Marat that was subsequently displayed in a touring exhibition in Great Britain was described as having been 'taken immediately after his Assassination, by order of the national Assembly'. See *Biographical and Descriptive Sketches of the Whole Length Composition Figures, and other works of Art, forming the unrivalled Exhibition of Madame Tussaud (Niece to the celebrated Curtius of Paris) and Artist to Her late Royal Highness Madame Elizabeth Sister to Louis XVIII* (Bristol: 1823), 36. There is no reason to doubt these assertions, although Madame Tussaud's reported memories of the Revolution are not always reliable. It is highly probable that the wax bust of Marat at Madame Tussaud's derives from an eighteenth-century original. The format of waxwork exhibitions is highly conservative (see Adhémar), and the process of reproduction has ensured that wax models often replicate distant ancestors. See E. Gratacre and L. Dru, 'Portraiture in the Cabinet de Cire de Curtius and Its Successor Madame Tussaud's Exhibition', in *La Ceroplastica nella scienza e nell'arte, Atti del Congresso internazionale, Firenze 3–7 giugno 1975* (Biblioteca della *Rivista di storia delle scienze medicale e naturali,* 20), (Florence: Olschki, 1977), 619. For another waxwork exhibit that represented Marat in hiding, see Adhémar, 213, n. 21.

32. There is insufficient evidence to confirm or refute Helen E. Hinman's suggestion that the composition of David's painting is based on that of Curtius's tableau ('Jacques-Louis David and Madame Tussaud', *GBA* 66 [sixième période, 1965]: 331–8). Hinman's hypothesis is vigourously rejected by J. R. Mantion ('Enveloppes à Marat', in Bonnet, ed., *La Mort de Marat,* 1986, 212). The suggestion that the composition of David's painting derives from a drawing recording his impressions at the site of the murder (K. E. Maison, 'Note on a Drawing by J.-L. David: "Marat Assassiné"', *GBA* 69 [sixième période, 1967]: 60) is untenable, if only because the drawing in question (private collection), like the final painting, represents a still breathing Marat who still holds his pen. The attribution of the drawing and its relationship to the painting are in any case problematic: see the entry in *Jacques-Louis David 1748–1825* (Paris: Editions de la Réunion des musées nationaux, 1989), 287, no. 120. If the Tussaud wax likeness is to be identified with the bust displayed in the window of Marat's house, it would clearly have priority over David's painting.

33. *Genèse de l'esthétique française moderne. De la raison classique à l'imagination crétrice 1680–1814,* (Pisa: Pacini, 1984), 1: 29.

34. See, for example, Claude-Henri Watelet and Pierre-Charles Levesque,

Dictionnaire des arts de peinture, sculpture et gravure (Paris: 1792), 5: 157, under 'Portrait' (article by Levesque). Such imitation was associated with portraiture and with the subservience of the artist to the will of the patron that portrait painting was held to involve. The critic Amaury Duval (Polyscope) stigmatised the portraitist's excessive emphasis on qualities of execution as a sign not merely of the artist's servility but of the degradation of art under despotism to the status of mere *luxe*. See *Décade*, 10 floral, an II (29 April 1794), 1: 7.

35. He did so on a visit to Curtius's waxwork display. See E. J. Delécluze, *Louis David, son école et son temps* (1855; reprint edited by J.-P. Mouilleseaux, (Paris: Editions Macula, 1983), 343, and cf. A. Becq, 'David: théries en perspective', in *David contre David. Actes du colloque organisé au musée du Louvre par le service culturel du 6 au 10 décembre 1989*, ed. R. Michel (Paris: Réunion des musées nationaux, 1993), 2: 671–99 for the interpretation of Delécluze's text and for a detailed treatment of David's theoretical approach to the issue of imitation in general.

36.

> Ce n'est pas seulement en charmant les yeaux, que les monuments des arts ont atteint le but, c'est en pénétrant l'âme, c'est en faisant sur l'esprit une impression profonde, semblable à la réalité; c'est alors que les traits d'héroisme, de vertus civiques, offerts aux regards du peuple, électriseront son âme, et feront germer en lui toutes les passions de la gloire, de dévouement pour le salut de la patrie.

Report on the nomination of a national Jury, made on behalf of the Committee of Public Instruction, 15 November 1793 (25 brumaire an II), Wildenstein, no. 677, cited and discussed by A. Becq, 671–99. In the speech delivered on the previous day, David had expressed the hope that the sight of Marat's image would foster the dead man's virtues in the souls of his colleagues: 'C'est à vous, mes collègues, que j'offre l'hommage de mes pinceaux; vos regards, en parcourant les traits livides et ensanglantés de Marat, vous rappelleront ses vertus, qui ne doivent jamais cesser d'être les vôtres' (Wildenstein, no. 674).

37. See *Jacques-Louis David 1748–1825*, 282, no. 118, for a summary of the painting's subsequent fortunes, together with bibliography.

38. See Delécluze and Tussaud. It is against the background of the popularity of such spectacles that the reiterated denial of aesthetic value of wax models by connoisseurs of high art must be seen. See A. Becq, 671–99, for other instances.

TERROR AND THE *TABULA RASA*

DAVID'S *MARAT* IN ITS PICTORIAL CONTEXT

THE LOOK OF A PICTURE

Every picture has a 'look'. With David's *Marat,* there is a starkness that produces a shock.

This effect is deliberate, and it is intended to engage us in the horror of a murder and enlist our sympathies. This approach is highly appropriate, as *Marat* was painted for the ceremony honouring the victim.

However there is more to it than that. David was able to give his *Marat* its particular starkness because of his experience with a manner of painting that had been evolving throughout Europe at the time, and which focussed on the production of dramatic spartan effects. He brought a lifetime's knowledge of picture making to the work. It is as much an expression of his expertise and ambitions as it is a record of a historical event.

In this chapter I intend to look at the ways in which this kind of painting developed and consider why it became so important in the 1790s. I will also look at the special position that the *Marat* occupies within this practice. For while some pictures do little more than reproduce the current vocabulary of forms, others challenge and change it through the need to make some statement that is beyond the reach of the formal possibilities available. David's *Marat* is one such work.

HISTORY AND FICTION:
MARAT AS A HISTORICAL DOCUMENT

Pictures need to be evaluated as carefully as texts when they are being used as historical evidence. The problem is that it is not always clear what kind of records they represent. Sometimes the necessary contextual information is very difficult to obtain. In the case of *Marat,* however, we have a lot of material to go on. Essentially it is a commemorative portrayal, intended to form a centrepiece at the funerary celebrations of the murdered leader. David's involvement was extremely personal. He was in a sense as much the commissioner as the creator of the work. He had personal vested interests at stake. As the dedication on the picture makes clear, he presented it very much as his own tribute to the fallen hero.

It is also possible to use contextual information to explore the picture's accuracy as a record. Its 'look' is so stark, and has such a sense of actuality about it, that one might think at first that it was a close record of what had actually happened. This sense is heightened by the knowledge that David had himself visited the victim shortly before the assassination, and had seen him at work in his bath. He had a better opportunity than most to make a faithful reconstruction of the scene.

Despite this, as has been seen in the introduction to this volume, *Marat* is almost pure invention. David was well aware of this. He knew he was constructing a fiction that bore little relationship to the facts of the case.

It is because of this inventiveness that I feel it is of central importance to pay attention to the pictorial form of the work. It functions because of David's consummate skill in constructing a certain type of rhetorical image. This skill relates to his training and ambitions as a painter of history. Not as a painter of history in the way we might understand the term now – as one who records events experienced – but as a painter of history as it was understood in the eighteenth century, as a painter who creates a heroic and idealised image out of the events of the past, one that deals with aesthetics and morality before it deals with reportage. From this point of view, it is instructive to see how far David's *Marat* differs from the many prints that were made of the assassination at the time. Each of these, of course, had its own propagandist point to make. But they were far more likely to include the actual reported details of the event because they were practising a genre that had reportage as its main objective.

There is nothing essentially dishonest about David's position. Every painter of history of the period knew that it was necessary to alter events when making a pictorial representation of them that would bring out their 'importance'. David would have known this from his training at the Academy. For contemporaries at large the point had been forcefully made in the *Discourses* of the president of the Royal Academy of Arts in London, Sir Joshua Reynolds. In his fourth discourse, when speaking of the 'Grand Style' necessary for the heroic portrayal of history, Reynolds talked of how historical characters should not be portrayed literally, because that might distract from the dignity and nobility that was necessary to convey their character or importance. He concluded this section by saying that history painting was really closer to literature than history, because it was interpreting the past imaginatively and poetically: 'I call this part of the art History Painting; it ought to be called Poetical, as in reality it is.'[1]

This point is worth reflecting on for a moment. History paintings are fictions, much in the way that historical romances or epic poems about the past are. Nowadays this point might not seem to carry as much weight as it once did. In our 'post-historical' age, we are critically aware of the arbitrariness of interpretation and the impossibility of recovering some single, objective 'truth' about the past. Because interpretation is so dependent upon personal position, it might seem that there is no fundamental difference between the multifarious narratives that can be told about the past under the guise of history, and the narratives of fictional writing. But there is a fundamental difference. Historical narratives, no matter who makes them or what purpose they are intended to serve, are always told with reference to events. Their plausibility is dependent upon the way we test them against our knowledge of these events. If our knowledge of these events changes, then the plausibility of historical narratives about them changes too. In the case of fiction, there is no such outside referent. The plausibility of the narrative in fiction depends upon an internal structure, a cohesion that has to do with our expectations of the genre that is being practised, rather than by reference to events outside.

Judged by these criteria, David's *Marat* is fiction, not history. He knew full well that the events he was relating in the painting did not happen as he showed them. His concern was not to show what had happened as closely as he could. His concern was to convey a certain set of ideas and emotions about the event that fitted in with his own personal beliefs and the position of the political faction that he supported.

Since this chapter is looking at the pictorial context of the work, I shall be reaching back into David's career, as well as looking at how his picture relates to the visual language prevalent at the time that it was made. I shall be focussing on three issues: David's ambitions as a history painter; the nature of the type of picture that the *Marat* is; and the position of the *Marat* in relation to the dominant pictorial mode of the period.

THE ROLE OF THE HISTORY PAINTER

Nowhere was the position of the history painter more jealously guarded and supported than in France. It was part of the cultural programme of France since the age of Louis XIV that there should be an academy that promoted the best kind of painting as a matter of national prestige. In the Academy students were trained in the practices of history painting. The best of them were encouraged to try for the coveted Prix de Rome, which would enable them to spend years in Rome perfecting their skills. Then, if successful, they would produce work that would lead to prestigious government commissions and election as a member of the Academy.

David was one of those who pursued this course. It was a difficult one, and he experienced many disappointments. A man of painful sensitivity, he suffered perhaps more than most from these setbacks. At one point (when he had failed to win the Prix de Rome for the third time), he attempted suicide. At another (when a student in Rome), he had a prolonged period of mental disorder.

The strains and difficulties of succeeding in this extremely challenging genre were exacerbated by the extent to which the successful history painter was dependent upon the support of both artistic and political authorities. Other kinds of painters – for example, still-life painters like Chardin or painters of scenes of modern life like Greuze – could rely on popular interest for their success. But history painting was an expensive and esoteric genre that appealed only to a minority and could be financed effectively only by direct government subsidy.

This situation created a particular problem for the painter of history in the later eighteenth century. For while these painters might see themselves as being on a level with the intellectuals in society, they were not able to express their views with the same level of independence as that constituency. Writers such as Rousseau, Voltaire, and Diderot could launch their critiques of society based upon Enlightenment principles confident of support via the sale of their works to a broadly based readership. They were persecuted to a degree by the government, it is true, but this did not deprive them of the means of continuing their careers.

At the time it was not expected that the history painter would show such independence. Certainly the authorities expected the painters to depict what they approved of. Furthermore, the authorities had the means of controlling the subject matter quite precisely. However, the increasingly popular practice of exhibition meant that historical works also were judged by a larger audience, much of which was influenced by the doctrines of the *philosophes*. Yet even the *philosophes* did not expect the history painter to share their independence of mind. Artists, after all, were not intellectuals, and they could not be expected to produce work with intellectual content without guidance. This was certainly the view taken by Diderot, who made significant interventions in the reception of art through his Salon reviews.

David first came to prominence at a time when these issues were reaching a head. He began his exhibiting career in the 1780s, after studying in Rome. The French Revolution provided him – as it did so many artisans and professionals – with unheard of opportunities. He became his own man. Elected a member of the National Convention in August 1793 (just at the time when he was working on *Marat*), he was a political as well as an artistic leader. He was able to abolish the Academy – a hated symbol of monarchical authority – and to instigate wide-ranging reforms in art education and state patronage. He also became the designer of revolutionary pageants and costumes. Never before had a visual artist assumed such authority. And yet such authority was what artists claimed a painter of history should have, as a man of intellectual and moral probity.

It is as a history painter of this new type that David operated in the revolutionary period when he painted *Marat*.

A QUESTION OF GENRE

Yet is *Marat* actually a history painting? It certainly refers to a historical event, as the title David gave it makes clear. But it is also a portrait of Marat, and the occasion for which it was painted was a commemorative one. From that point of view it would be fairer to see it as a commemorative portrait, as indeed is argued by Tony Halliday in another chapter in this book.

This might seem like a rather academic distinction. In a literal sense it is; for it is an argument about the way in which pictures were classified by academies in the eighteenth century. For the academies it was a matter of considerable importance in judging how effectively an artist had practised his profession. A heroic history painting would have to be treated one way, a portrait another, a modern life scene another, and so on.

The problem with David's *Marat* is that it doesn't fit neatly into any of the categories that were available. Instead it draws from a number of them to create what is in effect a new genre. In doing so David was very much of his time. There was a widespread call for pictures that could deal with the contemporary and individual in a manner that had all the gravitas of a public statement. Artists, too, were questioning the criteria that defined the different genres. David's pictorial innovativeness was part of the visual radicalism of the age.

While *Marat* is certainly a commemorative portrait, it is also a history painting. It is historical not just because it shows an event, but also because of the pictorial rhetoric that is used in it to present the situation. Through the teaching of the Academy, history painting had become strictly codified. Following the model developed by classical rhetoric for literature, the academies had developed a theory of the genres. Each type of art had its place in the hierarchy. At the top was the painting of religious, mythological, and historical work. Then came 'genre' – the depiction of everyday life. After that followed the depiction of the subhuman – the worlds of animals, plants, and minerals. The lower genres were seen as being 'simple' copies of nature – such as still-life painting, for example –

and requiring more mechanical than intellectual skills. The highest genre, history (comprising, of course, religion and allegory within it), was more about the narration of stories and the conveying of complex ideas. While it was held to necessitate the portrayal of the most ideal visual beauty, it also had to obey a strict set of conventions governing the way a story was to be narrated. Gestures and expressions were stipulated, so that emotions such as grief, surprise, joy, and anger could be shown unequivocally. There were rules controlling the action that were largely borrowed from classical drama. There had to be unities of time and space and action. There were also the particular constraints that visual representation brought with it. Because a painting could represent only one moment in a story, it was critical to choose the 'right' one, typically the moment of catharsis, that would sum up the whole essence of the story being told.

For painters in the later eighteenth century, historical art was the ideal. It took them back to the practice of the great masters of ancient Greece and Renaissance Italy. It was their kind of reform in an age full of reform and the desire to return back to first principles.

While presenting a visual ideal, the history painting was also essentially moral. It emulated the highest form of literature in emphasising the tragic. This is not the place to go into the question of why tragedy should be seen as the highest literary form, but it can at least be observed that tragedy is the point at which destiny and heroic action can be observed at its highest. It is the crisis and sense of loss that tragedy inevitably brings with it that enables the highest conception of humanity to be viewed dramatically.

In the later eighteenth century tragic forms of history painting abounded. The most telling was the *exemplum virtutis*. This was the portrayal of a hero sacrificing himself for some noble cause. It usually involved death, the ultimate sacrifice. Sometimes it was the 'good death', a virtuous man coming to his end and distributing wisdom and solace to those who surrounded him. But it could equally well be of a person making the decision that a moral prin ciple lay above personal interest and that the ultimate sacrifice was therefore necessary. The *Death of Socrates* was a common example of such an *exemplum virtutis*. It could also be a soldier dying for his country. Usually, in this case, it was a general or leader who was doing the dying.

David had plenty of historical precedents to draw on for both types of work. The most important was almost certainly that of the French painter Nicholas Poussin, who had painted *exempla virtutis* in a severe classical mode in the seventeenth century (Fig. 3). David had himself painted a heroic death in 1787, *The Death of Socrates*,[2] in which the Greek philosopher is shown voluntarily taking the hemlock that will lead to his death, discoursing abstractly while his companions and disciples are beside themselves with grief.

David presents Marat's death as if it were an *exemplum virtutis*. But it was difficult to make this portrayal fit with the facts of the assassination. Marat had to be shown dying not just as a victim, but also as a hero, making some kind of sacrifice. This is where the fiction of the letter comes in. According to the picture, Marat has just received a letter from Corday asking for help and has himself just finished a letter in which he is sending financial assistance. He is a victim, it is implied, of his own burning desire to help others. He died because he responded to Corday's plea for help. This is what makes the scene an *exemplum virtutis*.

However, we should not lose sight of the impact on David of another type of tragic painting. This is the portrayal of the martyr. Some have seen a reference in the work to the ultimate Christian martyr, Christ himself, as the picture appears to owe something to Michelangelo's famous *Pietà*.[3] David also had a great interest in the art of the Baroque, in which dramatic images of martyrs abound – frequently as part of Counter Reformation propaganda. He had made a study of the sensational renderings of martyrs using extremes of light and dark by Caravaggio and his followers. David himself had had a notable success with a religious painting – that of the plague saint *St. Roch* – when still in Rome.[4] In *Marat* he used the skill he had developed in handling dramatic contrasts of light and dark to develop a compassionate image. This martyrdom, however, is a secular one. There is no hope of personal salvation beyond. Perhaps that is why its darkness feels so bleak. There is no saviour about to break through to waft the soul of the departed up to heaven.

Because history painting was considered to be dealing in universal truths, it was held by the purists to be irrelevant exactly when such noble actions took place. According to official academic theory, it was better for actions to take place in antiquity, because such examples had stood the test of time and because the costume then was sufficiently generalised to enable abstract beauty and grandeur to be displayed at the same time.

It was at this point, however, that history painting and the *exemplum virtutis* ran into problems. For there remained the problem of relevance. However noble the events of the past, there was the question of how they could be made relevant to a modern audience, particularly an audience that was becoming progressively more secular and less schooled in classical lore. How, in fact, could the painter contribute to the project of the *philosophes,* if they resolutely turned their backs on the predicaments of contemporary life and society?

This dilemma is one of the points that makes history painting in the later eighteenth century so interesting. It was a genre committed to an ideal that needed to come down into the marketplace. If it did not do so, then it would run the risk of being irrelevant to the wider issues of the day. But if it made too many concessions to popular taste, then it would lose status and be unable to command more artistic authority.

There were no more important history painters, from this point of view, than the British. In retrospect, they did not cut a very fine figure. They had both the advantages and disadvantages of working in a 'liberal' regime. They were free of government interference, but they also received no official support. On the whole they could succeed only by convincing the market of their significance. The result was a series of brilliant 'sports', of one-off pictures that did something amazing but that were not followed up by anything of substance. For David, as for many of his contemporaries, the hero of this process was the American artist Benjamin West. West had studied in Rome in the 1760s and had subsequently settled in London. He eventually became president of the Royal Academy. But in his earlier, more iconoclastic days, he had made a mould-breaking innovation in history painting. He had depicted a modern subject with all the heroic dignity that it had been felt could only be achieved with a subject from ancient history. The subject is not one that we would nowadays be inclined to think of as the last word in heroism. It was the British general Wolfe dying at the moment of his victory over the French at Quebec in 1760 (Fig. 11). Nowadays we would see this struggle simply as a squabble between two imperialist countries seeking to wrest the booty of North America from each other's clammy grasp. But at the time Wolfe was a national hero in Britain, a saviour of the country. The problem for West in determining how to paint the death of this modern hero was how to preserve the dignity of high art while remaining true to the modern dress of the actual event. The result was a huge success at the time. Looking at the work, one might have a hard time figuring out why. For unlike David's *Marat,* this picture does not have any of the compelling urgency that can appeal beyond the bounds of a particular set of interests. However, we can at least see how West has made his picture obey the unities of history painting while clothing the figure in modern dress. The whole composition is a fabrication, bearing no relation whatsoever to the events that actually took place. Wolfe died away from the battle, almost alone apart from a couple of attendants. West has him surrounded by grieving officers (they each paid £100 to be included), with a Union Jack waving above his head, and Wolfe looking for all the world like the dead Christ. The battle is seen taking place in the background, and the dramatic continuity is brought about by a messenger running in from the left announcing the victory.

West's great achievement was to find a way of blending ideal form – poetic narrative (to give it its polite term) – with the sense of actuality brought about by such details as convincing portraiture and modern dress.

David himself did not attempt to paint modern history paintings before the outbreak of the French Revolution. It was that momentous event that both liberated him to try out this new genre and gave him a burning occasion to do so. His great modern celebratory work was never achieved. This was the *Oath of the Tennis Court,* which would have shown the moment of resolve that led to rebellion by the Estates General against monarchical authority. Thematically, it was the modern-day equivalent of his famous scene from Roman history, the *Oath of the Horatii.* The *Oath of the Tennis Court* was never completed because of the problems caused by changing political fortunes. The *Marat* was his one completed modern historical drama. Containing only one figure – as opposed to the hundreds in the *Oath of the Tennis Court* – it could be exe-

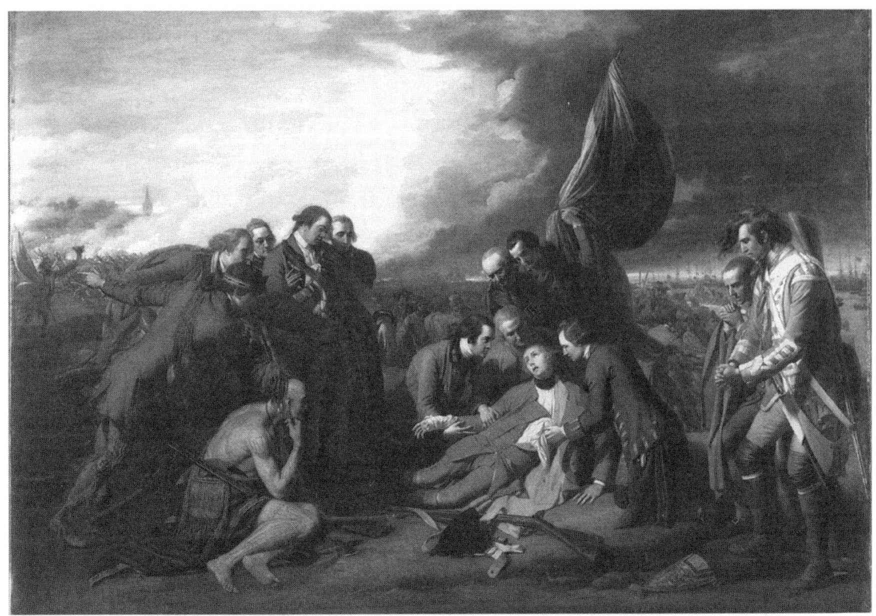

Figure 11. Benjamin West, *The Death of General Wolfe,* 1770, oil on canvas, 152.6 × 214.5 cm. National Gallery of Canada, Ottawa. (Photo: National Gallery of Canada.)

cuted swiftly and was therefore completed well before further political changes would have rendered it obsolete.

The result was a new kind of work, which might be called commemorative historical painting. As Tony Halliday has argued, this type emerged out of a new combination of the private and public spheres that answered the conflation of these domains as part of the social change brought about by revolution.

TOWARD THE *TABULA RASA*

Having considered what type of painting *Marat* is, I want to look more closely at its visual character.

There was a time when the history of art was primarily concerned with the look of things. The form that a work took – its style, colour, design, and composition – was held to be its most symptomatic characteristic. It was this form that summed up the work's essential importance and explained what it was that made it different from other pictures. A century ago this process became codified, in particular by the Swiss art historian Heinrich Wölfflin in his book *Principles of Art History*.[5] For Wölfflin the form a picture took was not an arbitrary matter. Rather, it was a revealing trait that told us about the person who made the work, the country that he (it was invariably he) came from, and the time in which he lived. The history of art, he declared, was the 'history of vision'.[6] Differences in pictorial form were caused by different ways of looking. By analysing them we could gain access to the character of individuals, countries, and times.

Since the days of Wölfflin, confidence has dwindled in using pictorial features as a diagnostic tool in this way. Art historians today take greater interest in the messages conveyed by pictures through themes and signs. Yet while the possibility of using pictorial form to trace a history of vision has largely disappeared, it should not be thought of as a matter of no importance. For pictures are deliberately made objects, and the forms they exhibit are the consequence of conscious decisions made by their creator (or creators). They are made to have this or that look primarily because their creators wanted them to have a particular effect, both to convey the picture's meaning and to accord with a wider set of pictorial interests. These wider interests will vary according to the nature of the maker and the culture within which he or she lived.

The presence of a particularly spartan pictorial style throughout the late eighteenth century has long been noted by art historians. It was a subject explored by Robert Rosenblum in his important early book *Transformations in Late Eighteenth Century Art* (1967). In a chapter entitled 'Towards the *Tabula Rasa*', Rosenblum looked at the way in which a remarkable pared-down style began to emerge at the end of the eighteenth century. This style could be seen not only in painting but also in sculpture, architecture, and all manner of design. Its origins could be traced to the classical revival, which began in the mid-century. But this revival in itself was not sufficient to explain the particularly tense and extreme simplification that took place in the last decade of the century.

That such a development took place is clear enough. But its significance is unclear. In the days when analysing style still formed a major activity for art historians, it was interpreted as a kind of harbinger of modernism, a dramatic pictorial breakthrough that reflected the sweeping social changes that had been brought about by the French Revolution. Historians like Sir Nikolaus Pevsner would point out how close some of the architectural designs of the period came to modern architecture of the early twentieth century. Marxist historians such as Arnold Hauser would claim that this radical style was the pictorial analogue of the revolutionary radicalism of the period.[7]

UNDOUBTEDLY THE DRAMATIC NATURE of events in the 1790s contributed to the inclination to use a starker, more striking visual language. But it would be a grave oversimplification to see this move as some kind of direct response to political events. Not all the artists involved in this pictorial radicalism were politically radical. John Flaxman, for example, the creator of the severely pared-down illustrations of Homer and Dante that David so admired, was staunchly conservative.

Rather than seeing this style as a harbinger of modernism, or as a direct reflection of revolutionary fervour, it is probably better to think of it in terms of the stated ideals of those who practised it. For it can be seen to grow directly out of artistic practices prevalent in the period. In former times this shared interest might have been described in near mystical terms, as a kind of 'spirit of the age', or Zeitgeist. But there is really no need to resort to metaphysics here. Shared interests of this kind can be accounted for usually in terms of more material connections.

There were three major factors that connected the artists who practised this spartan style. The first was a shared influence of art theory. The later eighteenth century is one of the great ages of art theory. This was itself a response to the Enlightenment interest in culture and learning and the idea that a more intellectual approach to criticism was effective. Books such as Johann Winckelmann's essay on the *Imitation of the Greeks in Painting and Sculpture* (1755) or Edmund Burke's treatise on the *Sublime* (1757) became international best sellers and were absorbed by artists of serious intention from Stockholm to Salerno. Equally important is the point that these books on art theory were being read by artists who were already united in their ideals about art by the academic system of training. This practice, which had begun in Italy in the sixteenth century, had led to the establishment of art academies on the Italian and French model throughout Europe. By the 1790s there was no country in Europe that did not have an academy modelled on this form. It was a central tenet of such academies that history painting was the highest type of art.

The second factor that linked these artists was the circulation of prints. Like the first, this dissemination depended upon a thriving publication trade. Printmaking and selling mushroomed in the later eighteenth century and became a thoroughly international trade. It not only made the images of the old masters more available than ever before but also gave unprecedented circulation to images of modern artists. Thus Goya, working in relative isolation in Spain, could become aware of the pared-down images of Flaxman almost as soon as they were published, or indeed of the dramatic paintings of David. In a curious way, the ubiquity of prints may have helped to enhance the impact of certain works. For the very process of printmaking strengthened the images in two ways. First, because the prints were largely black and white, it was the strength of the design and chiaroscuro that was known rather than the more elusive effects of colour. Second, because the works were conveyed via the interpretive skills of the engraver, nothing could be known about the actual painterly quality, the facture, of the original. All that came across was the design and overall effect. Thus British historical painters of the period could have an impact through the originality of their designs, even though their actual painting quality was rather mediocre. David, for example, was an enthusiastic admirer of Benjamin West because of the originality of this artist in introducing modern history painting (a point of particular importance in the case of the *Marat*). But when, in 1802, West finally came to Paris and exhibited some of his works there, David was quite appalled by what he saw. He dismissed West's work as a 'caricature of Rubens'.[8]

The third factor shared by these artists was the mecca to which they all turned: Rome. The late eighteenth century was the last period in which Rome was to be the leading international centre. The revival of interest in classicism had played into its hands, and all flocked to Rome if they could to complete their classical education. The French played a leading role there, because of the French academy at Rome, the place where the winners of the

Grand Prix came to complete their education. But there were artists of great originality from all over Europe there at that time and the place generated a real exchange of interests. For example, Rome is where David got to know the Swiss-German Henry Fuseli, whose remarkable proto-expressionist designs were to become an important stimulus and may well – it is argued here – have been critical for the formulation of the arresting effect of the *Marat*.

ROME, THE SUBLIME, AND HEROIC ART

Rome had begun to provide a focus for a classical revival in the 1750s. In the first instance the call for renewed simplicity led to rather tame pictures – such as those by Anton Raphael Mengs or David's own master Vien. But by the time that David arrived in Rome in 1774 a more dramatic form of classicism had become well established. Among the painters who practised it, probably the most influential at the time was the British artist Gavin Hamilton. Around 1760 he had produced a remarkable series of dramatic paintings of scenes from Homer's *Iliad*. Looking at these pictures now, we might see them as being little more than re-creations of the style of the great classical history painters of the seventeenth century, in particular Poussin. But at the time they attracted attention as they seemed to bring a new seriousness into painting. They were a starting point for a new kind of dramatic simplification that culminated in works such as David's *Marat* in the 1790s.

Hamilton's works were also important because they reestablished a claim for the visual artist: the right to deal with tragic and expressive subjects. According to strict classical theory, the visual arts were concerned with the production of beauty, and therefore could not engage in any kind of theme that produced distortions of extreme emotion, as this would interfere with the display of pure beauty. It was for this reason that Winckelmann had promoted the use of allegory in painting. His argument was that allegory could combine the intellectual with the display of pure beauty. Instead of displaying a distorting emotion, a figure could carry a symbol that would convey an idea. Not surprisingly, this dislocation of form and content did not catch on. Hamilton, and other practising artists, took the view that painting could encapsulate extreme emotion while not destroying its essential pictorial beauty. The question was how to do it.

It is here that another leading theoretical work of the day came to provide assistance. This was the treatise by the British statesman Edmund Burke, *A Philosophical Enquiry in the Origins of Our Ideas on the Sublime and Beautiful*. Essentially, Burke added a new aesthetic category that was capable of taking on board the expressive and the tragic. This was the Sublime. The concept of the Sublime in itself was far from new. It had already been a term used in late antiquity, when it was the subject of an important treatise by Longinus. But previously the Sublime had been seen as a kind of excessive beauty. Burke saw it as quite distinct from beauty. He claimed that they had different origins. Beauty was generated from our sense of love and attraction, the Sublime from our sense of aversion and fear.

It might seem strange to postulate an aesthetic category based upon fear. But in fact this fear was not just of 'nasty' things. It was of anything that went beyond the normal scope of human experience. It was fear of immensity, of darkness, of the unknown. Seen like this, it could become the harbinger of an awareness of the new and the great, of those things that drew us out of ourselves and toward new heights.

It was this inspiring view of the Sublime that was so attractive to people in the later eighteenth century. In a period of breathtaking and unprecedented political and economic change, the Sublime became a category of experience much drawn upon.

As a pensioner of the French Academy, David found himself at the centre of a turbulent artistic world that was promoting a new and more dramatic form of classicism, admiring the works of Michelangelo, and looking with awe at the gigantic remains of classical sculpture and architecture. By and large it was artists from Britain and northern Europe who were at the forefront of this more dramatic evolution, although French artists on the whole remained in the ascendancy technically. The opportunities that the French Academy offered for study made it a focus for artists of other countries as well, and David would certainly have come into contact with such fiery figures as the Swedish sculptor Sergel and the Swiss-German Fuseli. It is known that he met such people, though not how close his contact was with them.

In many ways, Fuseli was the most striking. A man of formidable intellectual gifts, he had come to painting after first pursuing a literary career. His knowledge of literature – both classical and modern – was incomparable, and he also had the closest acquaintance with art theory. Fuseli was in a perfect position to adapt Burke's literary treatise for the visual arts. Indeed, one might say that the whole of Fuseli's approach to the visual arts was syntactical. He simplified forms into monumental shapes with strong codified gestures. He also saw them largely as forms, having little time for colour and indeed being careless about the niceties of painting techniques. It was as designs, rather than as paintings, that his works primarily made their effect. Clearly there was nothing that Fuseli had to teach David about pictorial technique. But Fuseli and other northern artists could offer an exciting view of the artist as committed to displaying dramatic and important themes and, perhaps above all, to political commitment.

Fuseli was at that time very much a political artist. His sympathies were radical and reformist. Indeed, he had been forced into exile from his native Switzerland because of the part he had played in exposing corruption in the town council of his native Zurich. Inspired by the German Sturm und Drang movement, and by an Enlightenment faith in the perfectibility of man through the application of reason and morality, he was a vociferous opponent of oppression and a supporter of reform. When, in 1779, he finally left Rome, he designed the *Oath of the Rütlii* for the town hall of his native Zurich (Fig. 12).

This picture is a highly significant one in terms of the prevalent pictorial themes of the day. Depictions of oaths took on a new significance in a world of mounting seriousness. The taking of oaths implies the resolve to act, even if that action will lead to the loss of life. The cult of oath pictures had been initiated – as had so much else – by Gavin Hamilton with his *Oath of Brutus* in 1763–4.[9] Fuseli took the oath theme and gave it a modern context. His *Oath* was the one taken in 1291 by the representatives of the first Swiss Cantons to challenge the authority of the Hapsburgs. It was in fact the nucleus of the rebellion that led to the establishment of an independent Swiss Republic.

In Fuseli's work heroic simplicity was being given a new and positive role. David certainly knew the picture, and it has been shown that he used the central group of the three men swearing allegiance

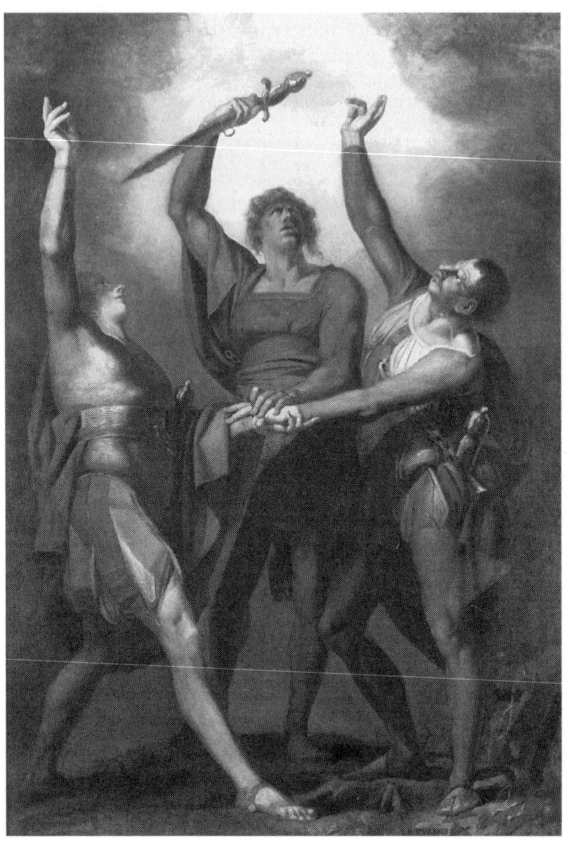

Figure 12. Henry Fuseli, *Oath of the Rütlii,* 1780, oil on canvas, 267 × 178 cm. Kunsthaus, Zurich (Leihgabe des Kantons Zurich). (Photo © 1998 by Kunsthaus Zurich.)

as a stimulus for his own central group in the *Oath of the Tennis Court* (Fig. 13), that representation of the critical oath scene that precipitated revolution in France. It was presumably also in his mind when he chose to paint an oath scene when given his first major commission by the French State, opting to depict the Oath of the Horatii.

While not wishing to overplay the significance of Fuseli's influence, I think one can say that his simplified, dramatic art, full of political commitment (in the 1770s at least), presented a challenge to David as he himself moved into a world of political action and the use of art for rhetorical and propaganda purposes.

From this point of view it is interesting to see that David went through some kind of crisis in his last years in Rome. This was precipitated partly by a fellow student who challenged authority and was subsequently dismissed from the Academy. David was deeply

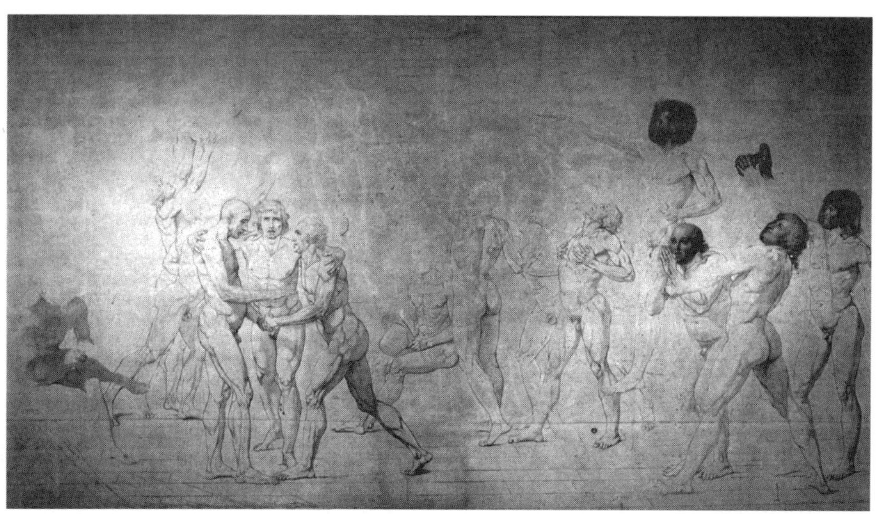

Figure 13. Jacques-Louis David, *The Oath of the Tennis Court* (fragment), 1791–2, oil on canvas, 358 × 648 cm. Musée national du château, Versailles. (Photo: Réunion des musées nationaux.)

disturbed as he felt himself hampered by the authoritarian regime of the Academy. A trip to Naples seemed to have provided him with relief. It also offered him an antidote to idealist art by bringing him closer to the 'realist' work of Caravaggio and his followers, which he saw there. The Caravaggesque use of dramatic shadow to heighten a sense of the real became a leading feature of David's history painting soon after. The adoption of this effect should not be underestimated. David was surrounded by pensioners of the French Academy (such as his rival Peyron) who were steeped in the ideal and often preceded him in treating heroic classical subjects. Yet none of them gave their works that arresting sense of actuality that David achieved through his espousal of the Caravaggesque. In a way one might say that Caravaggio provided David with a means of rivalling Fuseli without imitating him.

After Rome, Fuseli's and David's careers took increasingly divergent paths. While David became more engaged and political, Fuseli became less so. In the 1780s Fuseli – who had returned to settle in London – was part of a circle of radicals that included the publisher Joseph Johnston and such sympathisers of reform as Tom Paine, Mary Wollstonecraft, and William Blake. Soon after the outbreak of revolution in France, however, Fuseli trimmed his sails and became increasingly pessimistic and conservative. He joined the Royal Academy, despite having previously railed against academies on the grounds that they promoted mediocrity and hobbled genius. He was also foremost among those who criticised David as a 'man of blood' for having signed the death warrant of the French king.

Before Fuseli retreated to a position of 'safe' eccentricity, he did produce one puzzling and highly suggestive work, which became an international icon. This was his *Nightmare*. Fuseli first painted and exhibited the subject in 1781. He repeated the theme in 1791, in a tighter and more compelling format (Fig. 14). David must surely have known these works through engravings. In fact, a special French edition was published in Paris in 1784.[10] Furthermore, the *Nightmare* was sufficiently well known in France to be used repeatedly as a basis for satirical prints. One such print, which shows an aristocrat (unsurprisingly) having a nightmare about the outcome of the Revolution, was produced by Copia, the engraver who worked for David to produce a print of his commemorative head of Marat.[11] Fuseli's *Nightmare* pictures show him increasing his command of a dark, sublime manner. He moved in them from a public to a private world – the domain of dreams and fantasy. This bringing of a private world into public view might in itself have been of interest to David since he was seeking to bring together the public and private in his own revolutionary pictures.

Fuseli's work is also frankly sadoerotic. The 'victim' of the nightmare is a woman in white. She sprawls down to the floor over the bed and gives the impression of having been raped – something that is suggested, too, by the snorting tumescent image of the horse's head as it forces its way through the curtains behind. She could almost be out of a novel by de Sade.

Putting *Marat* and *The Nightmare* side by side, one can certainly find many associations between them. There is the general sense of darkness and fear, expressed in a rigid rectilinear structure. Then there are features that could almost seem like specific quotes – in particular the relation between the trailing arm of Fuseli's woman and that of the dying Marat. There might even have been a deliberate intention of appropriation – taking an internationally renowned image of fear of the irrational and transposing it into the commemoration of a dying hero. While David's picture admits starkness and fear, it also suggests tranquillity and resolve. Death here is a

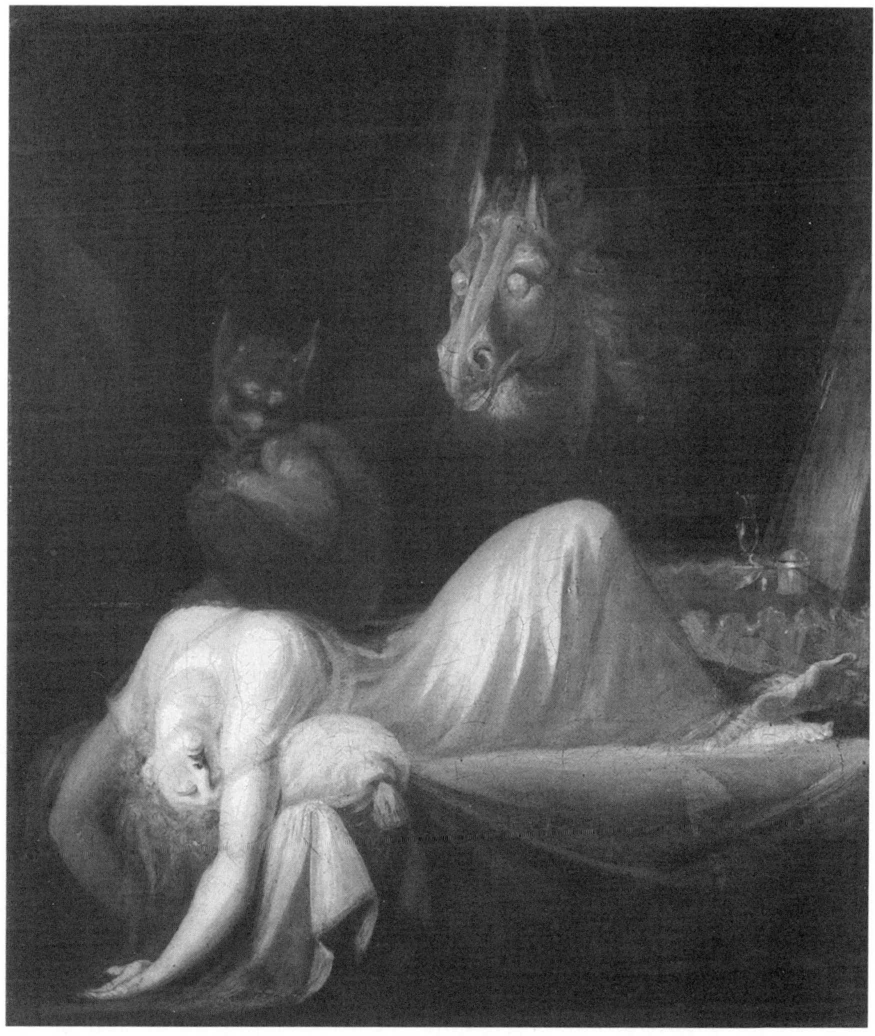

Figure 14. Henry Fuseli, *The Nightmare,* 1791, oil on canvas, 75.5 × 64 cm, Goethe Museum, Frankfurt am Main. (Photo © Ursula Edelmann.)

relcase, as well as being frightening. The assailants in Fuseli's picture – the homunculus and the horse – have no equivalents in that of David. For the woman has now ceased to be the victim. She has become the perpetrator of the crime, in the form of Charlotte Corday. Partly for reasons of politics, partly for reasons of gender prejudice, David has had to suppress her. In doing so, he has intensified the sense of martyrdom. With the removal of the perpetrator, the victim becomes the sole focus of attention.

All this is conjectural. We probably will never know whether David paid any serious attention to Fuseli's *Nightmare*. In a sense it doesn't matter. We can only guess in any case at the process whereby a picture comes into being. All attempts at a detailed account of the process are bound to be schematic and speculative. More important than trying to forge a link between the two is the recognition that Fuseli and David shared a common interest in the representation of the momentous in a stark and clear manner. In this sense a comparison between their works can be instructive even if no literal relationship can be established.

This point becomes more striking when we consider that there were artists throughout Europe at this time making images that shared these visual characteristics. In Rome the German painter Asmus Jacob Carstens was designing large mythological pieces that had a similar sense of monumental tragedy, most notably his *Night with her Children, Sleep and Death* (Fig. 15). Like David, he saw these paintings as answering the needs of his time, though the framework he used to sustain them was not revolutionary politics but Kantian philosophy.[12] In England William Blake was making abstruse but politically oriented monoprints of similar large-limbed doom-laden figures.[13] In Spain Goya included vivid images of darkness and fear in his social satires, notably those in his *Caprichos* (Fig. 16). This visual radicalism was not confined to painting and the graphic arts, either. It can be found in all aspects of visual culture at the time. Contemporaneously with David in France the architects Boullée and Ledoux were designing buildings that used unheard of simplifications, reducing houses to spheres, libraries to cylinders. All these designs – unbuilt and frequently unbuildable – were depicted in drawings that used darkness and starkness to emphasise their radical newness.[14]

The pictorial language that prevailed in the 1790s was a shared resource. It was used by different people in different ways. We need to be aware of it not so much to draw relationships between the works themselves, as to help us to understand the nature of the language being used by individual artists to say specific things in particular pictures, and to gain some indication of the level of engagement that these works have.

In the case of David's *Marat,* we need to consider how much the

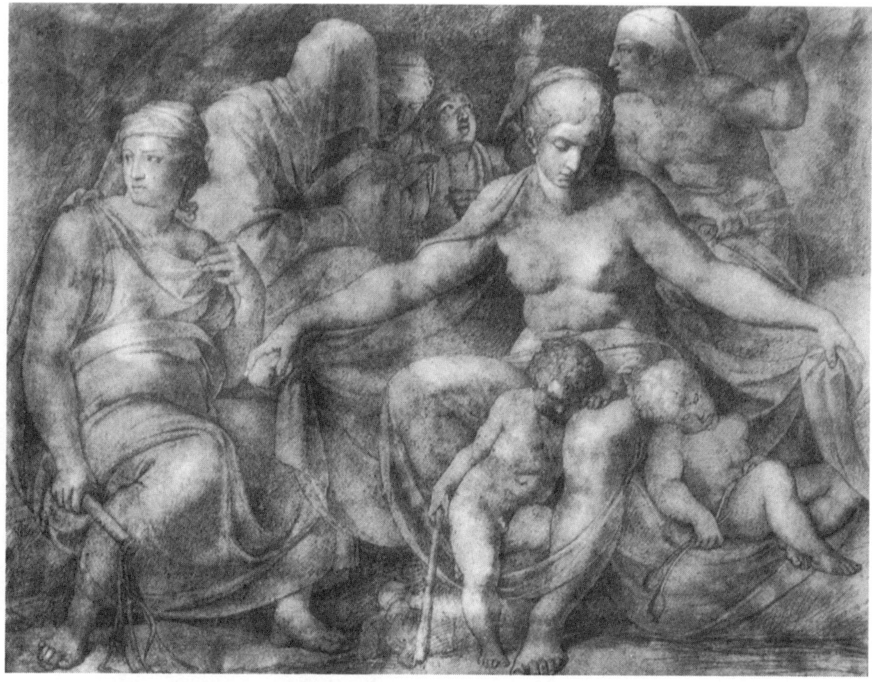

Figure 15. Asmus Jacob Carstens, *Night with her Children, Sleep and Death,* 1795, black and white chalk on tinted paper, 74.4 × 98.5 cm. Schloss-museum, Weimar. (Photo: Kunstsammlungen, Weimar.)

pictorial language of the time helped the artist to find the means of creating his stark, arresting image. Yet we should also remember that there is a specific context for it, as for all pictures, that precipitated its actual form. The extreme immediacy of the work comes from the need to put an urgent message across in the midst of a political event, the commemorative ceremony for a fallen hero. This was not a work designed for some timeless context, such as that which would have pertained in a church or an art gallery. It was not sup-porting a traditional faith, or an institution committed to the notion of the eternal value of great art. It did not have the luxury of being able to address an audience already predisposed toward meditation, whether of a religious or aesthetic nature. It was a political address for a particular occasion. It is this that gives the *Marat* its particular sense of urgency and makes it stand out now that it exists in the aes-thetic context of a gallery of fine art, the Musées royaux des Beaux-

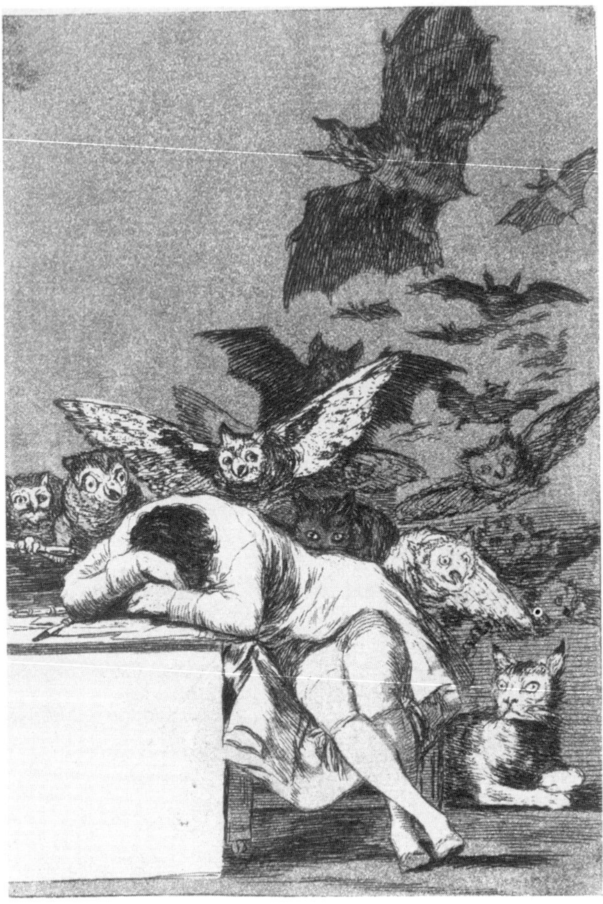

Figure 16. Francisco de Goya, *The Sleep of Reason produces Monsters,* from *Caprichos,* c. 1798, etching, 21.6 × 15.2 cm. British Museum, London. (Photo © British Museum, London.)

Arts in Brussels. Its effect would even be different, I think, if it were shown not in a royal institution but in a museum of the history of the Revolution, for there its polemical voice would have a context. Seen in the company of more refined and contemplative works it provides a shock, as though a door had been thrown open onto the street. This effect makes it all the more intriguing as an art object and perhaps helps to explain why it has continued to exert a fascination on those artists concerned with making radical statements, whether of a psychological or a political nature.

NOTES

1. Sir Joshua Reynolds, *Discourses on Art,* ed. Robert Wark (Pasadena, Calif.: Henry E. Huntingdon Library and Art Gallery, 1959), 60.

2. Jacques-Louis David, *The Death of Socrates (La mort de Socrate),* 1787, canvas, 1219.5 × 196.2 cm. The Metropolitan Museum of Art, New York. See Dorothy Johnson, *Jacques-Louis David. Art in Metamorphosis* (Princeton: Princeton University Press, 1993), 66–8.

3. Michelangelo, *Pietà,* 1498–9, marble, 174 × 195 cm. Basilica of St. Peter, Vatican City, Rome. See Anita Brookner, *Jacques-Louis David* (London: Chatto and Windus, 1980), 111.

4. Johnson, 23–9.

5. Heinrich Wölfflin, *Kunstgeschichtliche Grundbegriffe. Das Problem des Stilentwicklung in der neueren Kunst* (Munich: Bruckmann Verlag, 1915). The first English translation was Heinrich Wölfflin, *Principles of Art History. The Problem of the Development of Style in Later Art,* trans. M. D. Hottinger (London: Bell & Son, 1932).

6. Wölfflin, *Principles of Art History,* trans. Hottinger, 237.

7. Particularly in *Rococo, Classicism and Romanticism,* vol. 3 of *The Social History of Art* (London: Routledge, 1961), 137.

8. Kenneth Garlick and Angus Macintyre, ed., *The Diary of Joseph Farington,* vol. 5 (New Haven and London: Yale University Press, 1979), 1882.

9. Robert Rosenblum, 'Gavin Hamilton's *Brutus* and Its Aftermath', *Burlington Magazine,* 103 (January 1961): 8–16.

10. D. H. Weinglass, *Prints and Engraved Illustrations by and after Henry Fuseli* (London: Scolar Press, 1994), 55.

11. *Le Cauchemar de l'Aristocratie,* 1792, engraving by Benoît-Louis Provat after Jacques-Louis Copia; reprinted in Weinglass, no. 69D, 61. Weinglass comments, 'This composition appears to have been very popular: after engraving Copia's design, Provat then re-engraved it . . .'. David's picture, however, bears a closer formal resemblance to the second version of Fuseli's *Nightmare.* An engraving of this was made by T. Holloway and published on 1 June 1791. However, it is not clear that this engraving travelled to France, and there are no French caricatures based on it. See Weinglass, 60.

12. Albrecht-Friedrich Heine, *Asmus Jacob Carstens und die Entwicklung des Figurenbildes* (Strassburg: J. H. Ed. Heitz, 1928), 53–5.

13. David Bindman, *Blake as an Artist* (Oxford: Phaidon, 1977), 107–8.

14. Robert Rosenblum, *Transformations in Late Eighteenth Century Art* (Princeton: Princeton University Press, 1967), 123.

METHODS AND MATERIALS OF DAVID'S *MARAT*

The day after Marat's murder, Jacques-Louis David was called upon to paint the people's hero, and he immediately agreed. Like Madame Tussaud, he visited the body and the scene of the assassination. It was the hot month of July, and both artist and mask-taker would have had to work rapidly in the noting and taking of images. In the days immediately after the visit, David, who was also put in charge of the display of Marat's body and the grand ceremonies accompanying the funeral, would have been fully occupied, so that it is difficult to know exactly when he began the painting, but we do know that within three months it was ready to hang. How was this extraordinary image executed in so relatively short a time? One answer is that David's familiarity with very well established techniques and his intimate knowledge of each material and how they could be made to perform on the canvas enabled him to work with such speed and assurance.

For the first time the results of infrared reflectography reveal David's underdrawing on *Marat*.[1] These methods allow us considerable insight into how David set about the work. The present chapter combines such information from a scientific examination of this and other paintings by David with the documentary evidence of his pupils, colourmen, and other contemporaries writing on general painting practice, to discover what decisions were made as the painting progressed, why they were made, and with what result.

Few hints about the process of making this or any other painting came from David himself. He seems to have been deliberately evasive about his methods. Delacroix, thirty years after David's death, reports the latter's weariness when engaged in conversation about methods and materials: 'I knew all that before I knew anything at all', Delacroix quotes him as saying dismissively.[2] It seems, moreover, that Delacroix blamed David for encouraging an indifference toward painting technique amongst his followers and breaking the traditional links that painters had with their materials: '. . . bad results, neglect of preparations, canvases, brushes, execrable oils, carelessness on the part of the artist. David was responsible for this carelessness, because he affected to despise the material means'.[3] David's apparent dismissal of 'material means' has been a hindrance to the study of the methods and materials used in his paintings. There are few artists of such repute about whose techniques so little has been written.

It was less than just of Delacroix to chastise him for the lowering of standards of craftsmanship in painting, because David's attitude was not isolated. It certainly seems that by the 1790s, painters had a less intimate knowledge of their materials than their forebears. Several factors contributed to this situation. First, the increasing success of colourmen in the last part of the eighteenth century stemmed from painters' desire to be more than tradesmen. Painters throughout Europe had been attempting since the Renaissance to raise the status of painting from craft to liberal art, and that of the painter from craftsman to intellectual.

Second, the rise of painting academies in the seventeenth and eighteenth centuries with their emphasis on training in that most cerebral aspect of the artist's work, drawing, had also worked toward this goal. Undoubtedly David's championing of neoclassical line, with its attendant dismissal of rococo frivolity, played its part in the denial of material means. Delight in the sensuality of loose brushstrokes or liquid glazes could be equated with the more intuitive approach of mannerism,[4] which produced in turn an increasing reluctance to discuss the procedures of painting. Such an attitude contributed to a secrecy, and consequent ignorance of painting methods. Moreover, David's revulsion at the teaching of the Academy, which came to a head while he was working on *Marat,* reinforced his rejection of those methods that were taught. He condemned, for example, the artificiality of the poses students were given to draw: 'What time you will lose in forgetting those poses, those conventional movements, into which the professor's force the model's torso. . . .'[5]

Last, the industrial revolution made the distancing of the artist from the messy business of his craft seem all the more possible, with the mechanisation of looms, machine-ground colours, and so on. Alongside the proliferation of the middle men, colour merchants, at the end of the eighteenth century, these changes offered the artist the prospect of a divorce from the dirty, manual preparations that had been a necessary part of workshop life.

Nevertheless, whatever the promises that these economic and industrial developments brought, practical matters had to be considered within the artist's studio. If David chose to distance himself from talk of the physical aspects of painting in public, he still had to make technical decisions at every stage of the painting process for the *Marat*. Moreover, whatever David's affectations, there is no doubt that he was a superb craftsman, with a very exact sense of the characteristics and quality of his materials, as the beautiful condition of this painting still shows two hundred years later.

A painter always has to make a series of choices when realising his or her conception in the physical, two-dimensional form of a painting. Many of these choices would be determined by factors outside David's control. The dimensions of the painting, the type of support and priming used, the lighting and placing of the model, the method of applying the design, the palette, the brushwork — any of these matters might, at least partially, be decided by factors such as the proposed function and location of the painting, or the availability of materials or tools. Or the decisions may have been automatic ones, made unthinkingly from methods learned in his earliest training, before he 'knew anything at all'. It is one of the aims of this chapter to examine what or who determined the methods and materials used in *Marat,* as well as the reasons for their use and how successful they were in conveying the desired effect.

DAVID'S TRAINING

What did David's knowledge of Boucher's studio and his training under Vien teach him of the métier of painting? In the 1760s many of the raw materials were still being prepared within the painter's studio, rather than being purchased from a druggist or pigment seller. As a pupil of Vien's, David might have helped to prepare canvases and grind pigments, then set palettes and clean brushes: jobs that would have taught him a great deal about the qualities of the material.[6] (The way a pigment mixes with the medium, for example, its weight, the variations in its colour on different surfaces, its behaviour in mixtures with various colours, its opacity, its permanence, would prove invaluable, if habitual, knowledge thirty years later.)

After an initial period of working on these menial tasks, the emphasis of a young artist's training was on learning to draw. During all the time that David spent with Vien in Paris, attending the French Academy, and afterwards in Rome, daily practise in drawing was compulsory. A pupil learned to draw from his master's drawings, inanimate objects, classical statuary, and engravings. Only when competent, possibly several years later, was a pupil allowed to draw from life, and finally move on to painting. Vien prided himself on employing a live model, at least three times a week, which was unusual in the 1760s but was a practice that David continued consistently.[7]

PREPARATORY DRAWINGS

Returning to the painting of *Marat* in the summer of 1793, we can see what remains of the practices David had learned twenty-five years before. No firmly attributed preparatory sketches survive for the painting. If we consider the extreme speed with which he is known to have worked on some occasions, such as the sketch of Marie-Antoinette on the way to the guillotine (done on the same day that he first displayed the paintings of *Marat* and *Le Peletier* in the Louvre courtyard), it seems likely that he would have made sketches of the body and perhaps of the furniture of the room when he visited the scene of the murder; or that he made studies from memory of seeing Marat alive the day before the event.

Other than the pen-and-ink detailed study of Marat's head, the only drawing relating to the painting shows nothing of the furniture that is known to have been in Marat's room (Fig. 17).[8] It is undoubtedly the type of sketch that might have been made as a preliminary idea for the composition, but its very closeness to the form of the final painting militates against it being a first study.[9]

THE ARRANGEMENT OF THE MODEL AND PROPS

So what can David's first ideas for the composition of the *Marat* have been? The painting has been much admired for both its naturalism and the carefully orchestrated geometry of the forms. Perhaps David's last image of Marat alive, formed when he visited the man on the day before the fatal stabbing, was still strong in his mind. However, he ignored most of the furnishings and decoration in Marat's room, and instead selected and adapted a few props to suit his own purposes. Whether he contemplated other moments in the drama we do not know: he chose to portray neither the moment of assassination with Charlotte Corday, dagger in hand, nor the lesser drama a few moments later, when the servants rushed to his aid, disarmed his assassin, and helped raise the body from the bath, but instead, the dying hero, still in his bath, and viewed as if solitary. This choice of pose and the deliberate paucity of props may largely have been determined by having to produce a pendant to his earlier portrait of Le Peletier. A painting that depicts the display of Marat's body at his funeral in the Cordeliers church shows that he had been posed in more or less the same attitude as he appears in David's painting (Fig. 2). Since David was in charge of the funeral arrangements, this might be expected, but the fact that it was possible to display the body in this manner indicates that it was a relatively natural position for the fall of the head and arm of a dead man, given the right support. Both here and in the painting the position of the figure is not as 'dead' as that of Le Peletier: it is still seated upright, and though the forward arm hangs limply down, the face is not slumped but turned toward us, propped quite naturally by the headrest, with the torso adjusting only slightly to this turn of the head.

This picture of the funerary display also reminds us that David rejected the shoe-shaped bath in which Marat had been killed and chose instead a rectangular form more suited to the dignity, austerity, and aesthetics required for the subject. The minimum of props surround the figure in a deliberately barren setting: no classical furniture was manufactured for this painting.[10] The simplicity of the wooden case, also visible in the picture of the funeral, has been emphasised, and is the roughest of packing cases, made of flimsy, knotted wood, and knocked together with a few undisguised nails – a suitable table for *l'ami du peuple*. Great care was taken in the

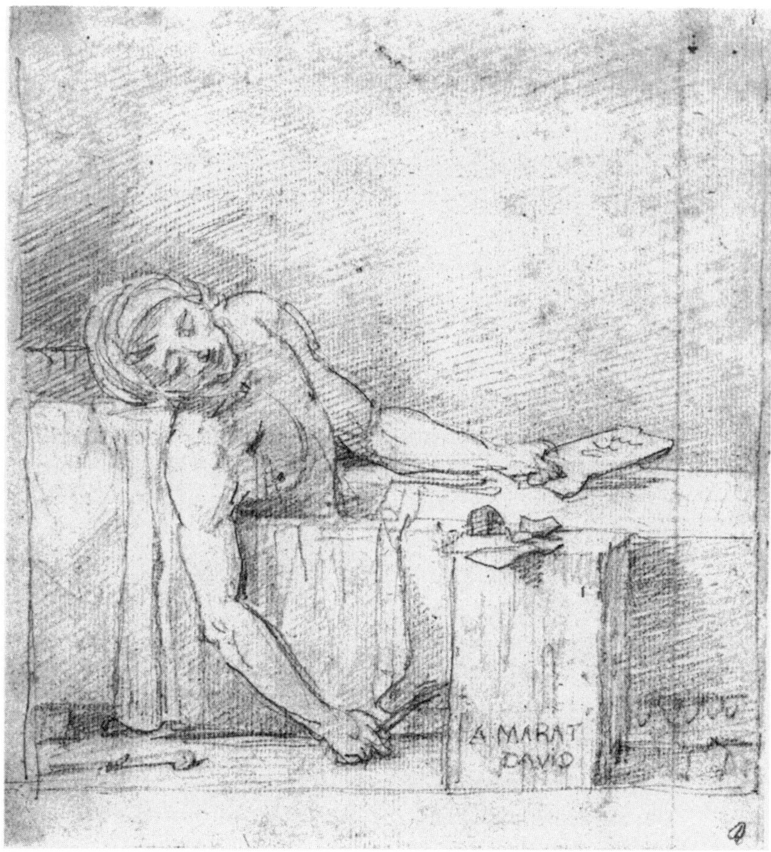

Figure 17. Jacques-Louis David (attrib.), *Marat stabbed in his Bath,* n.d., pencil, 16.2 × 14.9 cm. Private collection. (Photo: Courtauld Institute of Art.)

exact placing of the box within the composition. The underdrawn lines, seen by infrared, show two things to confirm this: first, the outlines of the box, which were ruled rather than drawn freehand (Fig. 18), have been moved and adjusted during the drawing. Black chalk lines just to the right of the present right edge of the box indicate either that the position of the box was changed, or that it may have been viewed slightly from the side in the first version, rather than face-on, and that this was the shaded side. What difference this change in position would have made to the confrontational quality of the image we can begin to judge if we look at the position in the drawn sketch, which also shows the shadowed right side of the box. This point raises again the question of authenticity of the sketch, since its possible concurrence with the underdrawing implies that it was executed before the final frontal position of the box had been determined.

Another pentiment discovered was the knot of wood in the upper right quarter of the box, which, when first drawn, was in the lower left quarter of the box. The latter may have been shifted in order to disassociate it from the inscription (it was placed above the first 'A' and 'M' of the first line), but its inclusion at all shows the precision with which the painting was being arranged so that every aspect was legible.

There has been some debate about David's procedure. Did he work from a combination of his conceptual sketch of the position of the body and a live model? It has been suggested that he might have used the wax effigy, made by Mme Tussaud and her uncle, on which to model his figure of Marat, based perhaps on the strong lighting and pallid hues of the figure in David's painting. However, a glance at one of David's studios shows the powerful effect of controlled light on the models set for his pupils (Fig. 19).[11] In another illustration of one of David's ateliers, a man can be seen adjusting the blinds on the highly placed windows, to restrict and focus the shaft of light (Fig. 20).[12]

In both paintings, the model is seen on a raised platform, and the intimate viewpoint of the *Marat* means that David must have set the 'bath' and model at eye level.[13] Many paintings executed by David were preceded by drawings of the composition as nude figures. The most surprising part of this procedure was the practice of drawing the nudes onto the canvas itself, before painting the clothing over the top. This approach is dramatically illustrated by the unfinished painting on canvas of *The Oath of the Tennis Court* (Fig. 13). Unlike *The Oath of the Tennis Court, Brutus,* and the *Horatii,* where compositional drawings, sketches, and squared-up studies exist to show the working out of various aspects and problems before David committed himself to paint, for the *Marat* there is only the highly finished pen-and-ink drawing of the dead man's head, and the black chalk sketch of the whole composition, already mentioned.[14] It might be supposed that the accelerated pace with which this painting had to be produced would cause David to bypass his normal careful preparations on paper. How-

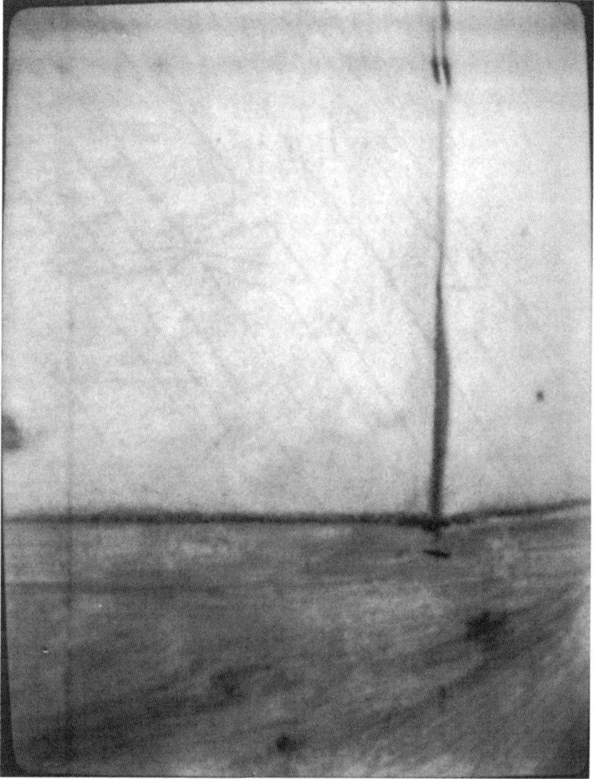

Figure 18. Detail of packing case in David, *Marat,* taken from infrared reflectography. (Photo: Freya Maes, Brussels.)

ever, this does not seem to be the case. The recent infrared examination of the painting revealed a definite grid of lines at 12.5 centimetre intervals. This find indicates that David used a squaring up process, which, of course, leads us to believe that there must have been a preliminary compositional drawing that was squared up for transfer. Such a process was a common technique of design transfer, and one that David had used quite often in previous paintings. This transfer is a point in the process of putting the painting together in which assistants could have been used, had David chosen to do so. A sketch executed by the master was covered in a grid of squares, and a similar grid of proportionately larger squares imposed (in charcoal or chalk) over the canvas. The sketch could

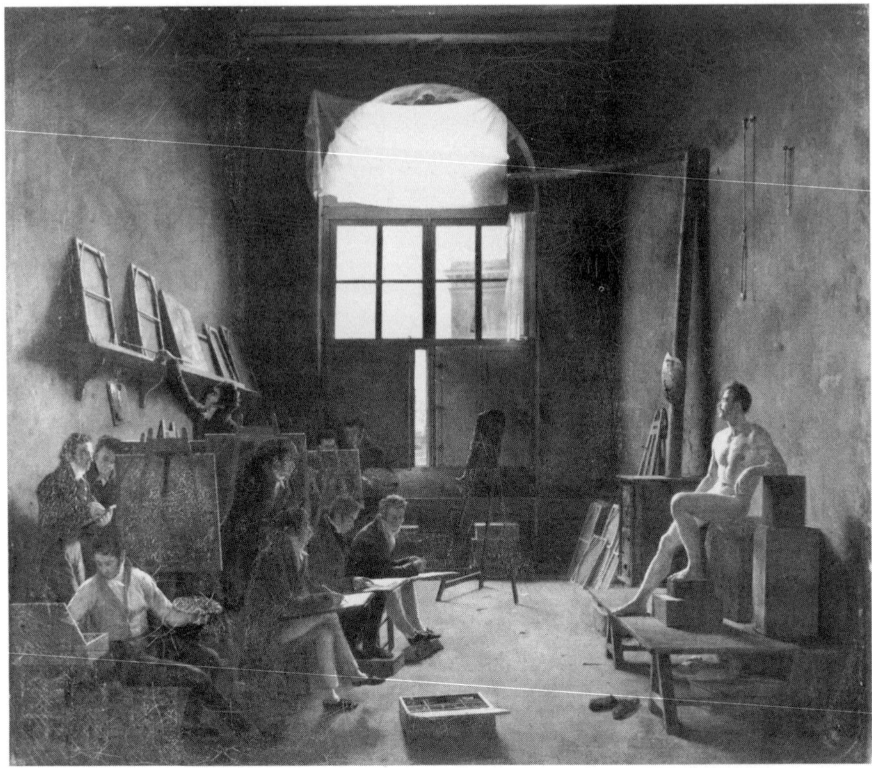

Figure 19. Léon Cochereau, *Inside David's Studio,* c. 1814, oil on canvas, 90 × 105 cm. Musée du Louvre, Paris. (Photo: Réunion des musées nationaux.)

then be copied, square by square, in its abstracted shapes, onto the canvas.[15] The painting of Le Peletier, had it not been destroyed, would very likely have shown similar grid lines. A squared-up copy of the drawing done by a pupil, Anatole Devosge, exists, perhaps imitating the lines that had been superimposed on the original, and at least showing the sort of system David would have used (Fig. 4). The finding of a grid under the *Marat,* however, does not imply that assistants did the drawing on the canvas: indeed, not only was this against the common practice for this type of major work, but, looking at the free style of the drawing discovered by means of infrared reflectography, we can surely refute such a proposal.

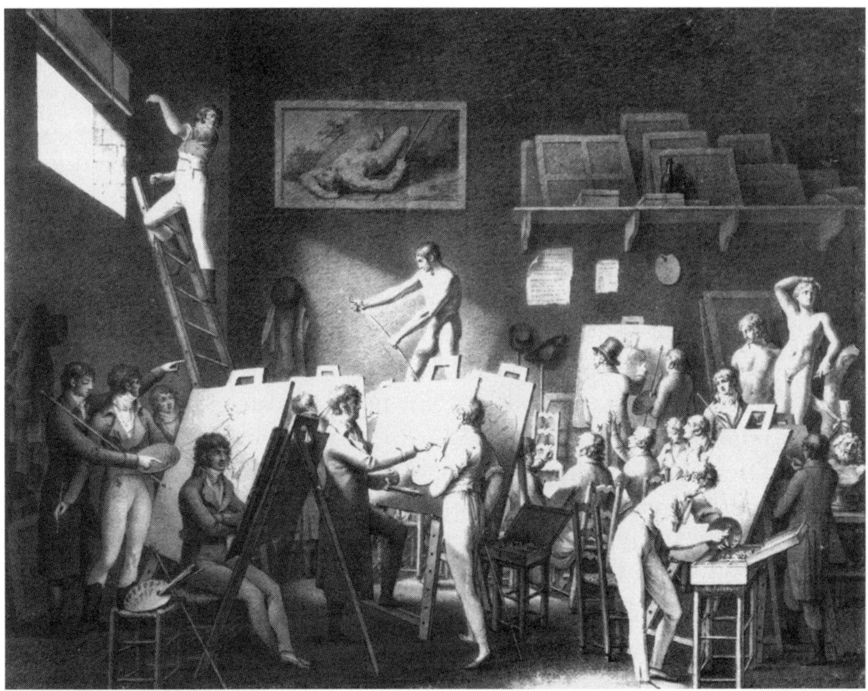

Figure 20. Jean-Henri Cless, *David's Studio,* c. 1804, pen and wash, 46.2 × 58.5 cm. Musée Carnavalet, Paris. (Photothèque des Musées de la Ville de Paris.)

THE CANVAS

Once an idea of the composition had been decided upon, the painter would have had the canvas prepared.[16] The canvas for *Marat* was relatively small, but both economy of time and the single figure subject probably suggested the size of the painting. The proportions may also reflect a genre that falls quite appropriately halfway between portrait and history painting.

Canvas was, of course, an obvious choice of support for the painting. There was no other support that would have served this important propagandistic purpose as well or better. Wooden panels had been used with increasing rarity during the eighteenth century for easel paintings. The coarse texture of the canvas surface compared to the smooth finish of wood was of less concern than portability to most artists at this time.[17]

It would be interesting to know how particular David was about the type of canvas he painted on for *Marat,* and who supplied it to him. Both the dimensions of the canvas and the type of weave affect the finished look of the surface paint, the consequent style and viewing distance, and the overall composition and form within the painting.

The type of material was either hemp or linen, both being popular with French artists in the latter part of the eighteenth century, with hemp being a little cheaper and more common at this time.[18] Hemp can be refined to give it a very similar appearance to linen, and there are records of David using hemp as a support. The state of war may have made certain materials such as fine linen and refined hemp inaccessible. What perhaps is most informative is that David seems to have used the lightest weight of canvas among his contemporaries, perhaps with an eye to its transportability. The canvas for *Marat* was a very regularly woven fabric, of medium to fine quality, which would give an even appearance on the surface – a particularly important consideration in some passages of *Marat,* for the various textures of cloth, flesh, and still life. A coarse canvas weave showing through the very thinly painted areas of some passages on the box, for example, would have interfered unacceptably with the representation of the wood grain.

The canvas was, in all probability, stretched on a square-ended frame, with corner supports, such as those shown propped up in David's studio (Figs. 19 and 20). In the late 1760s an important advance was made in the technology of stretchers. Keys, or wedges, were introduced to the corners of the stretcher joins, allowing canvases to be kept taut in different circumstances (such as low humidity or high temperatures), so they would not have to be removed from the stretcher restretched.[19] Mobility was increasingly a desirable characteristic of a painting, and although David's original stretcher may not have had wedges, when he later took the painting to Belgium, restretching it onto a strainer with wedges might have been one of the factors contributing to the painting's present good condition.

THE PREPARATION OF THE CANVAS

Once tacked onto the stretcher, the canvas would have been given a layer of hot glue, or size, both to protect the linen from the oil and to give it a taut, drumlike surface on which to apply the ground. Within the later part of the eighteenth century, there had been a significant change in the nature and colour of the ground layers on the canvas.

A great variety of colours had been used, until this time, for both single and double grounds within the seventeenth and early eighteenth centuries, but white had been used rarely. A common combination used in the later part of the eighteenth century consisted of a brown-red priming, rubbed with pumice stone to obtain an absolutely smooth surface, and then covered with a second priming of lead white mixed with small quantities of charcoal, black, and umber. It was this formula that both Boucher and Vien were using in the 1770s when David was first in contact with these painters. Several paintings attributed to Boucher, recently analysed, showed this structure of a thick red ground, followed by grey.[20] The purpose of the first layer of thick red earths had a largely practical function of filling in the weave of the canvas with cheap, bulky, and fast-drying material, and the second, upper layer was largely to modify the colour and set the tone for the painting. It is significant that David's canvases were markedly finer in weave than his predecessors', perhaps to eliminate the necessity for a double ground, and the colour of the upper ground was certainly changing in the 1770s and 1780s to white. Hubert Robert, Vigée le Brun, and David were all using at least an upper ground of white fairly early on by this time.[21] If a finer canvas was used, the bulky underlayer was not necessary, and it was a short step to the use of a single, white ground (put on in several layers), consisting usually of chalk and lead white.[22] One reason for this preference was that the white ground provided the best possible basis for a firm outline drawing. Another was its luminosity.

The painting of *Marat* was prepared with at least an upper white ground, which can be seen at the lower edge. Not only did David make his clear outline drawing on this ground, but he exploited its brightness in the final painting, making use of the ground in the way in which a watercolourist uses the white of the paper – that is, as a light in the final painting. The advantage the oil painter has over the watercolourist is that he can employ both the light of the ground – for the half-lights – and white paint for the highlights. Here David did exactly this. The light of the ground can be seen clearly in the half-lights of the flesh, through the rough brushwork of the *ébauche,* providing a warm and luminous underlayer. Why David employed this technique is a matter for conjecture. It was not a new method: he would have seen its effectiveness in the paintings of Rubens, for example, where a pale ground was employed to give an essential light to a painting destined for a dark location. David may have had the eventual location of this painting – the National Convention hall – in mind when choosing this technique. Another possibility is that the white ground showing through some of the scumbled brushwork may have brought the painter closer to emulating the effects achieved by the sculptor or wax-modeller.

THE UNDERDRAWING

The infrared reflectography examination of *Marat* resulted in some exciting finds.[23] The infrared is absorbed by the carbon black drawing lying under the paint and shows as clear black lines on the video screen. One of the discoveries made by this means was the precise location of the drawn grid under the paint. Hints of the grid can be seen on the surface; the spacing of the grid and the implications of its presence were discussed earlier.

An idea of the style and appearance of a missing compositional drawing might be gained from the most important revelation – the underdrawing. In many of David's unfinished paintings, the preliminary outline was made with paint, often using a red or yellow ochre or umber applied with a fine brush. It is fortunate that for the underdrawing of *Marat,* he used a black pigment, since it shows up beautifully in infrared, which presents the original outline on the canvas, hidden, as David intended, for two hundred years.

The underdrawing, used mostly to outline the main features, seems to have been done with a black chalk drawing tool.[24] The artist's lines, soft and broad, fine and feint, bold and intense, resemble closely his chalk drawings made on paper.[25] Many artists of the period used such a tool: it was a metal holder, with adjustable 'claws' at both ends, into which the lumps of natural black (or red, or white) could be placed, having been sharpened to a good point. Graphite, another drawing tool sometimes used by David, may have been more expensive, even though it was coming into much

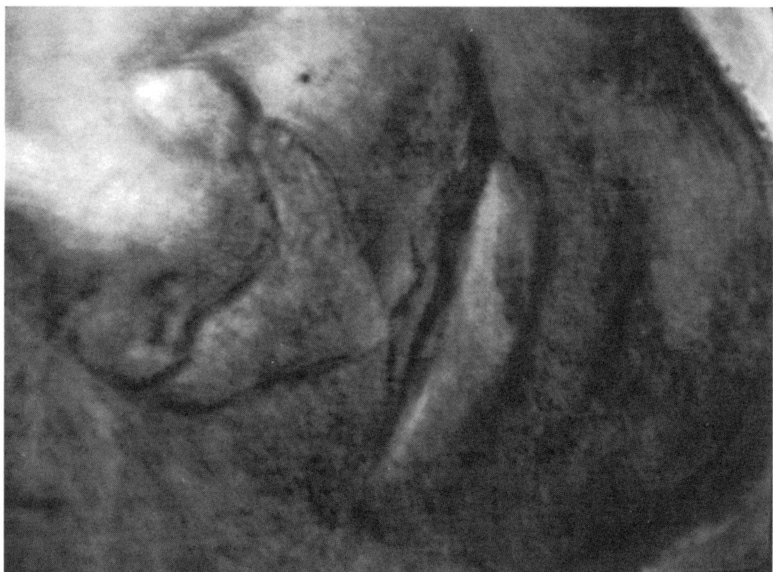

Figure 21. Detail of underdrawing of nose, lips, and shadows of nose in David, *Marat,* taken from infrared reflectography. (Photo: Freya Maes, Brussels.)

more common use in the 1790s, because the main European source for good graphite was Cumbria in England, and supplies at this point between the two countries might have been interrupted.[26]

The underdrawing is done with an assured hand, sketching in the lines of the body, but David made several alterations as he went along. On the face, the outlines of the lips, eyes, and nose show only minor adjustments, and the lips can be seen to have a more lifelike slump of a face on its side, rather than the even-lipped mouth that was created in paint, which gave Marat, finally, a gentle, almost smiling expression. Surprisingly, the outlines of the shadows of the face are delineated also, and hardly blocked in, but given merely a brief indication of shade with a few hasty strokes (Fig. 21). The importance of the dramatic, Carravagesque lighting in the final composition is obvious from the way the shadows are given such prominent treatment at the drawing stage. Despite the assurance of much of the drawing, the painter made many small adjustments to the lines at certain points, one of which is the elbow of the lower arm. He seems to have had difficulty in settling on its exact position.

One disappointment of the examination was that it did not reveal a full-length nude lying in the bath. From David's treatment of the figures in many paintings, most notably the unfinished *Oath of the Tennis Court,* it would not have been surprising to find that he had drawn in the whole of the naked torso. It is still not a certainty that he did not do such a drawing, since he sometimes drew with a fluid red earth paint,[27] or white chalk, neither of which would show in infrared light.

Other than the face, the outlines of the nude torso are lively, and not fixed. There are several significant alterations from the drawing in the painted version. Perhaps most interesting are the changes to the hands and the shift in the upper side of Marat's chest, upwards, by approximately two centimetres from the drawn line. The first position of the man's chest was originally slightly lower down in the body, with his left nipple clearly outlined (Fig. 22a). This means that even if he squared up from a sketch, David was still working out the exact placing of the drooping body. The muscle of the upper arm was bulging and more full of life in the first, drawn version. The arm nearest to us was slightly more in control of the pen, and the hand holding the letter seems to have been more open and less clenched in the initial drawing (Fig. 22b).

Some of these alterations are difficult to interpret, particularly in complicated areas such as the fingers of the hands. If we look at the hand holding the letter, the most obvious reading is that the first drawing showed all four fingers, with the position of the thumb slightly lower down. Moreover, at least two early versions define the edge of the letter held by the hand further to the left, the one furthest to the left bringing the paper right under the crook of the thumb and covering the first two fingers. So did the painter simply draw in all four fingers, never intending that they should show? This seems unlikely since the drawing of the whole hand, rather surprisingly, does not go under the letter, with the implication that the model held the letter while David drew him. One explanation of the change, from four fingers to three, is that the artist realised he needed the first finger to support the letter, at the point when he moved the paper to the right, and in a more upright position, in order to display all the writing: the right-hand edge of the letter was also expanded in paint to accommodate the lettering. Almost equally persuasive, however, is the argument that there was an ear-

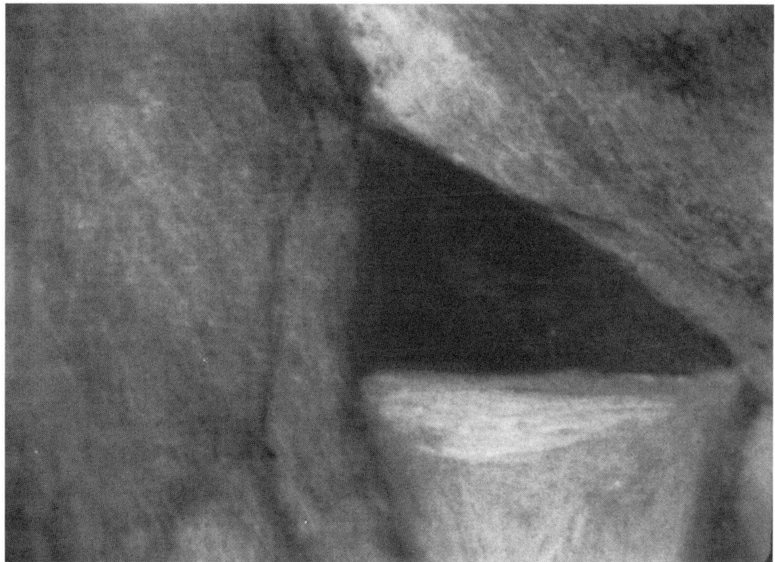

Figure 22a. Detail of Marat's left nipple in David, *Marat,* taken from infrared reflectography. (Photo: Freya Maes, Brussels.)

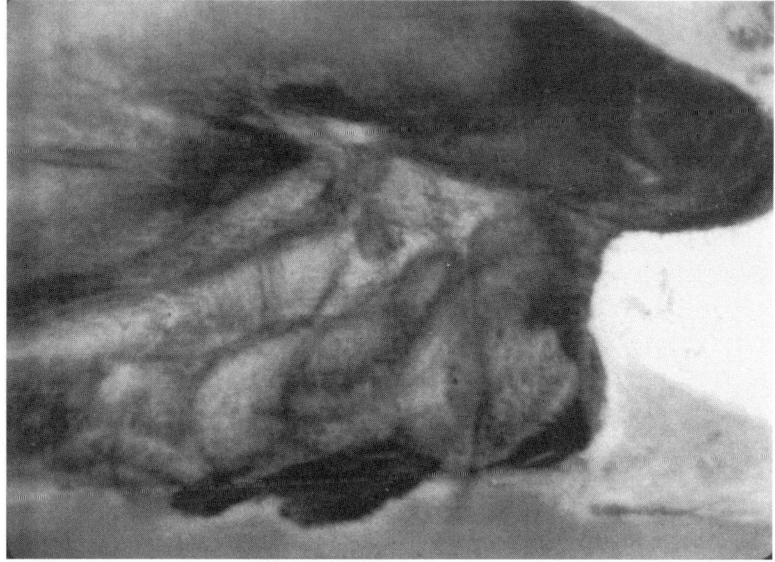

Figure 22b. Detail of the underdrawing of Marat's left hand in David, *Marat,* taken from infrared reflectography. (Photo: Freya Maes, Brussels.)

lier version, before the position of the letter was being worked out, where only the last two fingers of Marat's showed beneath the paper, and his hand was, in that earlier version, more open than it is at present.

It is obvious from both infrared reflectography and examination of the surface that the position and size of the letter was changed. Most significant is the expansion of the proper upper edge of the letter, and slightly at the lower left corner, to turn the whole piece of paper toward the viewer, in order to accommodate the inscription and increase its visibility.[28]

There are other revisions that require explanation. Why, for instance, did David change the position of the knot of wood, carefully drawn in the lower left of the box? As suggested earlier, it may have been moved so that it did not interfere with the lettering of the inscription and, once more, could give greater legibility at a distance. What is interesting is its presence at all at this point in composing the picture. It demonstrates that though David might have been working on the general position of the forms, he was also aware of the detail and the textural characteristics to follow in paint. It was to the white canvas, with its clear black outline, that David would have brought his broad brushes to paint the *ébauche*.

THE *EBAUCHE*

The *ébauche,* or pochade, was normally a coloured sketch made with broad brushes on the canvas. It had evolved from what a century before might have been referred to as 'dead-colouring', which was a first lay-in of the main lights and darks, with a limited palette of earth colours. The *ébauche* was painted with more diluent added to the oil medium than the upper layers of paint, making it faster drying and easier to apply. This rough underpainting was intended to be covered, modified by smooth overlayers, both opaque and glazed. The freshness and spontaneity of the *ébauche* might be lost in the final piece, and it is perhaps this quality that some painters were trying to capture at the end of the eighteenth century by using it as part of the finished painting.[29]

The *ébauche,* or coloured sketch, is visible in almost every feature of the *Marat.* In the background it has been left, exposed entirely. The brown paint was laid on with a dashing motion of slightly curved brushstrokes (*frotti*), which are scumbled lightly over the underlying white ground. This rapid manner of laying paint in on relatively unimportant areas was not new, as noted earlier, and David was not the only painter to be employing it in paintings in the late eighteenth century.[30] What made its use so startlingly successful here, in this hybrid of the portrait genre, was the contrast with the clean, polished highlights of the figure. Elsewhere, in the halftones of the flesh, David has barely covered the turbulent brushstrokes of the flesh, using both their warm colour and broken texture as a strong contrast to the smooth highlights of arms and shoulders.[31] One explanation for the use of the rough, *frottis* brushwork in the completed picture could be that he was anticipating the engraving of his work, and that, just like the intensely cross-hatched shadows of the pen-and-ink drawing, he was making signals to the printmaker about the depth of the shadows. It has been suggested that he was emulating the work of the much admired sculptors of antiquity, carving, in paint, smooth out of rough;[32] but it could equally be the result of a general interest in the encaustic methods of the ancients described by Pliny.[33] The palette used for the sketch normally consisted of a few earths – ochres, siennas, and umbers – together with black and white. Here, the underlying brushwork appears to be monochrome, done entirely in a brown colour, resembling umber.[34]

THE FINISHED PAINTING

Oil paint can be manipulated in various ways. No analysis of the medium has been carried out on *Marat,* but David is likely to have used either linseed or walnut oil. Walnut oil yellowed less with time but was slower to dry, and it was used most frequently in lighter paint. The faster drying linseed oil, diluted with turpentine, was undoubtedly the medium for the *ébauche,* but the good preservation of the lights in the painting may mean that he used walnut for the upper paint layers. The relatively slow drying time of either medium – though only a few days in summer – would give the painter time to manipulate the paint on the surface. Little pots with both oil and turpentine were kept alongside a painter (Fig. 20), allowing him to add some diluent to the pigments on his palette for thinner paint, or to add oil for a glaze, during the process of painting.

It is possible to build up a picture of David in his studio, standing at his easel, about to embark on the second and final stage of painting. His model was placed on the platform, in some kind of rectangular enclosure, draped to represent the bath, and with a second support to the left, cleverly disguised with a patched sheet, to support the drooping head. The plain wooden box was placed in front. Not all of the smaller items were necessary at this stage: it is plain from looking closely at the painting that the quill and inkpot, for instance, were painted on after the underlying paint was dry.[35] The whole of this scene was lit with a controlled shaft of light, from the windows to the upper left of the model.

Only one of David's brushes shows in the Luxembourg self-portrait of 1794, but he clutches a number of others in his right hand, along with a palette. He does not hold a mahlstick in this portrait, indicating that it represented him at the *ébauche* stage. It seems likely that he did use one for the final touches, looking at the equipment used by his pupils (Fig. 20). The Paris painter and colour merchant J. F. Watin described the largest of painters' brushes, which were made, 'either from the hairs of a boar on their own, or from the hairs of a boar mixed with those of a pig; they should be straight, rounded in shape, and their surface should look flat'.[36]

Despite the flat surface of the brush described here, it seems that Watin was talking not about the 'poche', but about the brushes for the final painting and the difficulty of getting good ones. The other brush listed as part of the artist's equipment was the 'pinceau,' made of badger hair and slotted into quill holders that ranged in size from the large quill of a swan to the tiny one of a skylark!

THE PALETTE

David's palette, represented in his self-portrait of 1794 as a slightly oval and relatively small surface, made of a light but strong wood, such as apple or pear,[37] probably represents the portrait painter's tool. Looking at depictions of his pupils at work, we see that a much wider range of pigments seems to have been set out for the more advanced stage of painting. The neoclassical severity of the subject of *Marat* may have suggested the use of a simple and restricted range of colours. Apelles, according to Pliny, was supposed to have used only four pigments – black, white, yellow, and red – and it would have been possible for David to have used a similarly austere range of colours here; for example, black and yellow to mix the green, and red and black for the brown.

Practical reasons persuaded many artists to employ a limited number of pigments, in addition to conforming to the classical ideal. Portrait painters, in particular, often had to be mobile, travelling to the sitter: for this purpose they had painting boxes in which to carry equipment. Raw pigments were mixed with the oil medium, either by artist or colourman, and carried around in small containers made from pigs' bladders. The oil paint inside could be squeezed out only by pricking the little leather bag with a tack. This left the painter with a series of sticky bags to pack away at the end of the painting session, and may have encouraged the painter to use the minimum necessary to record a likeness. David had long been important enough for most sitters to come to his atelier, and since *Marat* was painted in the comfort of his own studio at the Louvre, with numerous assistants to prepare and maintain his colours, the choice of pigments was not a problem. Examination of the painting under a microscope showed that he used a wider range than followers of Apelles.[38]

The flesh consists of large quantities of almost pure lead white, merely varied in thickness over the rough underpaint to achieve the different tones. The white of the drapery (also lead white) is cooler than the white of the flesh, largely by using the underlying colour of the *ébauche*. Two reds are used: scarlet vermilion, appropriately, for the bright spill of fresh blood; and a translucent crimson lake, probably cochineal or madder,[39] used for shadows on the blood, and sparingly on the lips of the dying Marat. For the wonderfully warm ochreous colour of the wooden box, David did not use a yellow at all, but dragged a light brown, probably raw umber, over the light of the underlying paint.

The most surprising colour of the painting is the green drape over the bath. David had rarely used green in any of his previous paintings, and certainly had not given it such prominence. The colour green had always presented some problems for painters, in that there were fewer green pigments than other hues, none entirely satisfactory. Green earth was too dull, malachite rare, verditer and verdigris were rather bluish greens and unstable. So greens had to be mixed, blue or black with yellow, and it was not always easy to find the right combination. In 1704, the invention of Prussian blue had given painters a wonderfully adaptable, slightly greenish blue to mix with yellow ochre, Naples yellow, or organic yellows, and these produced a wide range of natural greens. Analysis of other paintings by David shows that Prussian blue was indeed in use on his works,[40] and when examined closely, the mixture for the green cloth in *Marat* appeared to be Prussian blue and Naples yellow with some orpiment.[41]

The arsenic-based pigment orpiment has been found in many paintings of this period. Its poisonous nature would have been well known to David, but it was obviously worth taking the risk of using it, either to help dry the paint (as it was known to do), or because it was a brilliant yellow colour that could give the precise green that David wanted.[42] David has managed to achieve a solid, middle colour with his precise mixture of the two yellows and dark blue.[43] The opacity and solidity of this particular mix of green might have been used because it described the heavy nature of the drape better than blue, red, or black: it has a dull, even common property about it, appropriate to a man of meagre possessions. However, the fact that it is the complimentary colour to the red of the blood may have been the deciding factor: David could have been seeking the bold effect that would have resulted from the contrast between red and green, allowing the viewer to see, even at a distance, the small areas of red.

Of the methods and materials used in this painting, it is probably his brushwork, the extraordinarily smooth effect of some passages contrasting with the vigorous brushwork in others, that has drawn most comment. Over the *ébauche* David would have worked first on the flesh. Leaving the sketch to show in the midtones, he laid in the lights with a broad, heavily loaded 'brosse', and at the same time would have worked in the shadows in a cool grey tone. The highlights have been laid on similarly, with the broader brushes, using the final twist of the brush to end in a thick deposit of paint at the lightest point. For example, on Marat's forehead, the area catching the most light, there is a marked ridge of impasto. This highlighting not only worked because it was the lightest tone in the flesh, but it is also the highest impasto in the painting, so that although it is not as light as the whites of the drapery, the artist has literally made it stand out.

The cool greys of the shadows were applied with a much thinner, more fluid paint, and they allow the underlying sketch to show through. In much of the white drapery, the same techniques were employed, with the opaque white highlights being broadly brushed over the underpaint, and covering them completely, while the cool shadows were brushed on with much thinner paint. The green cloth on the bath provides a marked contrast to the lucid and lively passages of flesh and white drapes. It is a solid, middle green, brushed over to cover the underpaint almost completely. It provides a nice foil for the very different texture of the wooden box, which stands in front, and was achieved by dragging a thin, warm brown, using the sort of broad brushes ('poches') employed in the background.

The finer paint brushes, or 'pinceaux', would have been employed for the painting in of the eyes, nose, and mouth, the glazing of crimson over the lips, and the touches of blood. They would have been used to give crisp lines to the knife edge and the shaft of the quill pen and the writing on the letters.

David was not using new techniques in his brushwork. It is the way he combines them that is innovative. The daring stretch of background rough brushwork, left exposed; the juxtaposition of a highly finished passage to half showing *ébauche;* and the fine finish of the small features of pen, inkpot, and linen patch all contribute to the extraordinary impact of the final image. The present good condition of the painting is a tribute to David's thorough knowledge of his materials and excellence as a technician. David is known to have restored paintings himself, and as he was a severe critic of crude restoration methods being used on old master paintings by contemporaries, his concern for the permanence of his own paintings might be assumed.

Examining the means by which David put together the *Marat* has raised several questions. The rather voyeuristic means of infrared reflectography gives the sense of watching David at work drawing the model, altering the pose, making minute, but all-important adjustments to the fingers, arms, torso. Interpretation of the changes is not always straightforward. Was David searching for the right degree of naturalism – bulging muscles, fingers gripping, and the exact position of the body in relation to the viewer? Or were the problems to do with the precise moment between life and death?

Was the most important communication of the painting the legibility of both the image and the letters? Perhaps it was a combination of all of these thoughts that he was hoping to express.

Looking at the way in which the painter manipulated his materials has brought a fresh approach to the image. We can see that at each stage in the making of the painting David's choice of the means has affected the final product. From canvas and its preparation to the dual textures of rough and smooth in the brushwork; from the manipulations of model and lighting within the studio to the use of green and red colour contrasts; from the first working out of form to the final touches and adjustments – all these technical decisions have shown David's careful management of the spectator through the orchestration of his materials.

NOTES

1. For conducting the infrared reflectography and for making the photographs from the screen I am very grateful to Freya Maes, at the Musées royaux des Beaux-Arts, Brussels. I would also like to acknowledge the generous help from Frederick Laan, assistant to Mme de Wilde, at the Musées royaux des Beaux-Arts.

2. E. Delacroix, 15 September 1854: 'J'ai su tout cela quand je ne savais encore rien'. André Joubin, ed., *Journal de Eugène Delacroix* (Paris: Plon, 1932), 2: 265.

3. Delacroix, 11 January 1857: 'Mauvais produits, négligence dans les préparations, toiles, pinceaux, huiles détestables, peu de souci dans l'artiste'. Joubin, 3: 12.

4. Thomas Crow notes that in the early 1780s, critics like Carmontelle felt that 'the eye . . . must not be fooled by affected postures, silken textures, or sensually liquid play of the brush; these were the resources of mechanical artisans . . .', *Painters and Public Life in Eighteenth-Century Paris* (New Haven and London: Yale University Press, 1985), 221.

5. See J. L. Jules David, *Le peintre Louis David (1748–1825), souvenirs et documents inédits* (Paris: Victor Havard, 1880), 57, quoted in Crow, 230.

6. P.-A. Hennequin, c. 1780, a former pupil of David's, described setting palettes for his master in *Un Peintre sous la Révolution et l'Empire: Mémoires de Ph.-A. Hennequin écrits par lui-même;* réunies et mis en ordre par Jenny Hennequin (Paris: Calmann-Levy, 1933).

7. Anita Brookner, *Jacques-Louis David* (London: Chatto and Windus, 1980), for reference to Vien's *Mémoires*.

8. Antoine Schnapper, *Jacques-Louis David, 1748–1825,* Exhibition catalogue (Paris: Editions de la Réunion des musées nationaux, 1989), 287, no. 120.

9. However, infrared examination of the underdrawing has brought new evidence to bear on this attribution.

10. An antique candelabrum, discovered by Gavin Hamilton, was used in David's *Hector* in 1783, and other furniture was especially commissioned by David as props.

11. The light was effectively tunnelled in David's studios within the Louvre, which were 45 feet long and 30 feet wide, with windows only at one end.

12. Delécluze had described David's studios as being at the north side of the Louvre. Painters preferred northern light for its even and cool quality.

13. David was in charge of a large number of pupils at this time, and the model may have been one of these pupils whom he sometimes employed rather than paying a professional.

14. Doubts were raised about its attribution to David in Schnapper, 287.

15. Diderot and D'Alembert's *Encyclopédie, le Dessin* (1754–63) illustrates squaring up. The black chalk sketch has not been squared up.

16. David's large studio may have prepared its own canvases, although commercially prepared canvases were available. Lefranc had been trading in Paris since 1775, for example. See Anthea Callan, 'Artist's Materials and Techniques in 19th-Century France' (Ph.D. thesis, University of London, Courtauld Institute of Art, 1980).

17. David occasionally used a wood support: portraits of his brother-in-law and sister-in-law in 1795 were on panel, but they were executed in the country near St. Ouen, where canvas may have been scarce.

18. Katrina Vanderlip de Carbonnel, *A Study of French Canvases,* Journal of the American Institute for Conservation, vol. 20, 1981.

19. Anthea Callan pointed out the illustration of a keyed stretcher in the 1771 edition of Diderot's *Encyclopédie* that had not been in the 1765 edition.

20. C. Hassall and E. Sheldon, UCL Painting Analysis reports C263, 264, and 265, 1991, on Boucher's paintings *The Flower Gatherers, The Grape Gatherers,* and *Fishing* at Kenwood House.

21. As revealed by technical analysis of paintings by Vigée le Brun (UCL Painting Analysis) and David (UCLPA; Chicago; Ottawa; Malibu), as well as visual observations of Hubert Robert's paintings (D. Chesterman).

22. M. Leonard, Conservation Report on *The Farewell of Telemachus and Eucharis,* 1818, oil on canvas (J. Paul Getty Museum) claimed that painting had a commercial lead white ground, as did many of David's later works.

23. I am very grateful to Christina Masschelein-Curry for examining the painting with Freya Maes and me. Her collaborative notes and comments on the underdrawings have been extremely helpful.

24. In some places, slight traces of a smoother line, possibly made with a brush, could be seen.

25. See, for example, the drawings for the *Oath of the Tennis Court*, 1791–2 (Versailles).

26. The colourman Massoul mentions the shortage of good graphite in France. C. de Massoul, *A Treatise on the Art of Painting and the Composiiton of Colours, Containing Instructions for all the various Processes of Painting*, (London: 1797).

27. The painter Thomas Couture describes the 'sauce' of red earth, which was commonly used for drawing.

28. The lettering is still legible at approximately four metres distance (communication from C. Masschelein-Curry).

29. A self-portrait of Lemoyne, *L'Intérieure de l'attelier de femme peintre* (Metropolitan Museum of Art, New York), holding a set of large, coarse brushes, shows the artist about to paint the *ébauche* with brushes at least two centimetres wide, and with rather crude and blunt ends. The term 'pochade', of course, relates to the 'poche' or housepainter's brush, and these allowed the painter to block the image in, over a large surface, with rapidity.

30. *Portrait of Madame Trudaine de Montigny*, 1792, is an obvious example of this method. Other artists had been using a similar technique, such as Vigée le Brun in *Portrait de Hubert Robert*.

31. David would have seen similar contrasts of smooth and scumbled brushwork in the works of Rubens, both in Rome and in Paris.

32. Michael Peppiatt, *Imagination's Chamber: Artists and Their Studios* (London: Gordon Fraser, 1983), 27.

33. Comte de Caylus, a close friend of Vien, had interpreted Pliny's descriptions of encaustic methods. Vien also experimented with encaustic. See J. Mills and R. White, *National Gallery Technical Bulletin* 9 (1985): 60.

34. J. L. Jules David, 'David a passé sur sa toile un large frottis de bitume' ('David brushed a large amount of bituminous browns over the canvas'), *Notice sur le Marat de David* (Paris: 1867).

35. Again, this observation is important when considering the author of the drawing, which does not show the quill on the table.

36. '. . . ou du soie de sanglier seul, ou de soie de sanglier, mêlée a celle de porc; elles doivent etre droites, en forme ronde, et leur surface doit présenter une forme plate', J. F. Watin, *L'Art du Peintre, Doreur, Vernisseur*, 4th ed. (Paris: 1785), 10.

37. Ibid., 2nd ed., 8.

38. Examined at ×35 magnification. The painting could not be removed from the wall for this process. (Again, I am grateful to Frederick Laan for arranging this examination, and for Mme de Wilde's kind permission.)

39. Leonard, Conservation Report. Madder was identified on *The Farewell of Telemachus and Eucharis*.

40. Ibid. It was found, for example, to have been used for the blue of

Telemachus's robe, and on the *Portrait of Jacobus Blauw,* 1795 (National Gallery, London) and the *Portrait of Suzanne Le Peletier de Saint-Fargeau,* 1804 (UCLAPA).

41. Hennequin, 57.
42. Massoul, in his *Treatise,* advised: 'Yellow orpiment combined with Indigo makes a very good Green'. It could, however, turn black if mixed with ultramarine.
43. Leonard, Conservation Report. David appears to have been using a new green, chromium oxide, in *The Farewell of Telemachus and Eucharis,* painted in 1818 only four years after chromium oxide's invention.

THE CORDAY-MARAT AFFAIR

NO PLACE FOR A WOMAN

This chapter explores David's manipulation of Charlotte Corday's identity, from his decision to eliminate her actual presence from the painting to his means of characterising her, metonymically, within it. We are dealing with his blanking out of this woman as the perpetrator of the crime, resulting in her invisibility. In this respect David treated Corday differently from the way in which he had evoked Pâris, the assailant of Le Peletier, in his first martyr portrait. Pâris, also absent from the image, has his name on the sword/murder weapon (Fig. 4). Corday's name is not on the kitchen knife, but on a letter. This is not altogether surprising. The effect, nevertheless, is to identify Corday with a private dimension of writing, rather than with the public arena of heroic and political action. In eighteenth-century French art a letter most often signified the absent lover. It does not surprise us, therefore, that those unfamiliar with this historical incident should interpret this painting as a crime of passion by the absent woman whose name is revealed on a letter.

Pâris committed suicide the day after murdering Le Peletier; he obliterated himself. Before going to the guillotine on 17 July Corday, by contrast, spent four days in prison, during which time she wrote letters, stood trial, arranged for a portrait of herself to be painted, and worked at producing the notion of herself that she wished to hand down to posterity. It was for public consumption, and her place was for the history books of the future.

David makes her part of a private world and a name to note on a letter, but only in order for its owner to be erased from the people's memory by the more compelling script of MARAT and DAVID. In Corday's eyes she was the one and only agent of a sublime crime and a female agent at that. She alone was to be identified with this act. For David and the Jacobins she was part of a Girondin conspiracy, and her female and individual presence could be lost in sinister prerevolutionary and counterrevolutionary anonymity. In this David would have been supported by the Marquis de Sade. De Sade made a speech two weeks before the painting's completion, insisting that 'a dark veil should forever enshroud her memory; above all those who have dared to present her as an enchanting symbol of beauty should be stopped'.[1]

There was no question of David representing the attractive femininity of Corday that had been widely disseminated by the moderate press.[2] David did, however, have to deal urgently with Corday's own self-image. This was not an 'enchanting symbol of beauty' but something more powerful and enduring. Her request for a portrait to be painted of herself might be seen as vanity, as countering any process of defacing her appearance, but more than this, she wanted to be perceived as a force for justice, vengeance, and peace. She did not ask to be remembered for her act of so-called parricide, but for the act's consequences, that is, for the state of peace that would follow Marat's total disempowerment. I would argue that between July and October 1793 David inevitably had to reckon with Corday's construction of herself, and that her own writings played their part in the later stages of the painting's development.

For the most part, this chapter necessarily examines the painting's evocation of Corday in David's terms, that is, in linguistic terms, through the letters he represented in the painting.[3] My starting point, however, is a discomfort with the absence of any representation of Corday herself and the compulsion I experience as a woman, and as a directed spectator, to resurrect her into the missing narrative. Up to a point this compulsion overrides the recognition that this painting is an allegory, a symbol, an icon.

The exclusion of Corday from the pictorial space of David's painting has been related to men's exclusion of women from other forms of public life in October 1793, but we should be careful not to make this a simple equation. I prefer to see the construction of Corday in David's work in relation to the fears of both men and women, in the summer of '93, regarding, specifically, educated women who threatened to intervene in history and subvert the role of gender as a defining element of Jacobin ideology.

The work of writers of women's history frames my study of Corday's place in David's *Marat*. These authors have raised issues of women's exclusion from public spaces and activities in revolutionary France; they have listened to the female and male voices of protest against such exclusions; they have explored issues of women's moral agency and passivity, sexual subjectivity, and self-denial in relation to notions of Nature and 'natural' woman.[4]

PLACING CHARLOTTE CORDAY IN RELATION TO DAVID'S *MARAT*

When David was commissioned to produce a virtual pendant to *Le Peletier* it was already inevitable that his portrait of Marat would, like the earlier work, be a painting of a single figure, that it would not be a narrative of a contemporaneous event but an icon for public acclaim, which would exhort people to a state of virtue. It is not likely that David ever conceived of a representation of the assassination itself or the inclusion of Charlotte Corday in the act of stabbing Marat. Yet, ever since 1793, artists of varying political affiliations have attempted to construct a causal relationship between those items in David's painting that function as clues to the deliberately withheld narrative. These clues are the long-bladed kitchen knife on the floor, which Corday bought at a shop in the Palais Royal and which would have borne her fingerprints;[5] Marat's chest wound that she so effectively and so purposefully inflicted; the bloodstained bath water; and the letter in Marat's blood-drained hand.

That Marat is releasing his dying breath is not really in doubt. The blue thumb of the hand holding the letter and the limp body that leans out toward the spectator make his imminent death clear. That he is not yet quite dead is signified by the right hand still gripping the quill. This much of the narrative is visible. That he has been attacked by a woman of opposing political views is by no means self-evident. In mid-October 1793, however, the reference then was clearly to a recent event, which had already been much represented in prints and much discussed in texts during the preceding three months, and there would have been an expectation of the beholder to reconstitute, from the related fragments represented, the missing narrative that he or she knew only too well, to fill in the blanks, and to give the expected response.[6]

So powerful is the sense of absence of any feminine element from this painting that it is hard to imagine a place for Corday in relation to Marat. There is in fact no space to position her within the painting, certainly not behind the bath, as the scumbling technique negates this as room space. She has to be in the space of the spectator, outside the picture frame, having plunged the knife with her right hand, confronting the vulnerable figure of Marat as he lies back in the bath.

One of the most interesting efforts at visualising Corday's presence is the wood engraving by Léopold Flameng (Fig. 23). Published by Jules Janin in *Histoire de la Révolution française,* it was reproduced for *L'Illustration* in February 1865, and again in Louis Blanc's *Histoire de la Révolution française,* 1868–72. David's image has been reversed, extended horizontally to the left to include the sabot shape of the bath and create the light and space of a domestic interior. The most obvious inclusion is the fleeing figure of Corday, knife now in right hand, left hand fisted with determination, hair spiked and streaming behind her – a faceless, avenging fury. The artist has solved the problem of positioning Corday and keeping her beauty invisible by making her disappear offstage, but only by altering the story (Corday was not able to escape), by redefining the shape of David's composition (from vertical to horizontal), and by assuming that it would have been a natural movement to plunge the knife into the far side of Marat's chest (which I doubt).[7]

The print by J. L. Delignon, after a drawing by Du Vivier, and dating probably from the Directoire period to judge by Corday's costume, comes close to my own mental construction of what David might have done and of the pitfalls he would have had to avoid, had he ever considered a two-person composition (Fig. 24).[8] It positions Corday in the foreground close to the spectator's space. Like the Flameng, it too depends heavily on the David. Marat's head turns full toward the spectator and makes a similar appeal. The writing board is similarly placed across the bath, which is likewise not sabot-shaped, and in both images there are the white and

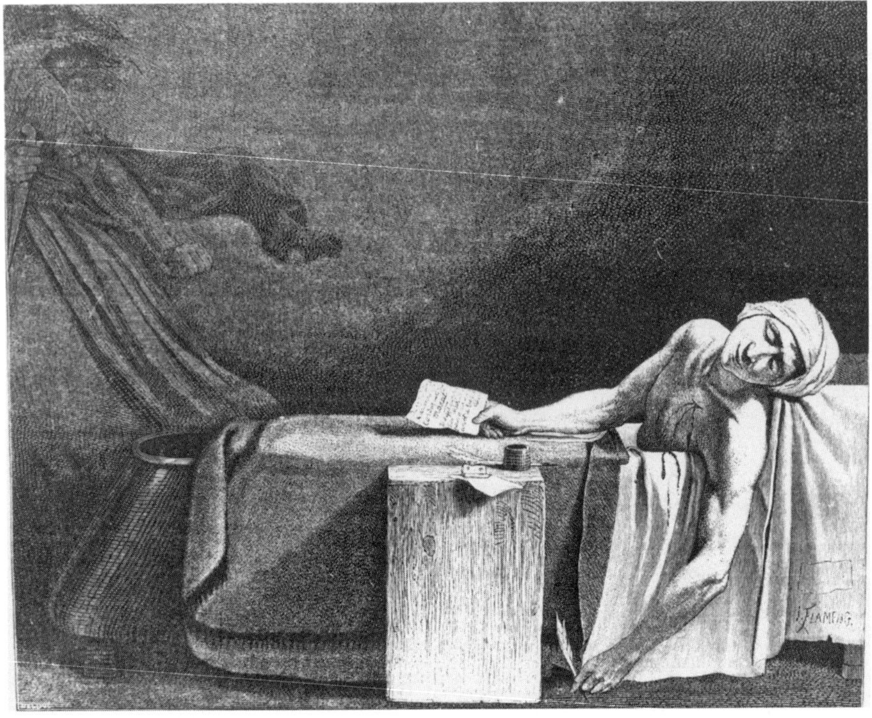

Figure 23. Flameng, *Death of Marat,* after the version of *Marat* in the collection of Le Prince Napoleon, reproduced in *L'Illustration* 25 February 1865, wood engraving, 18.5 × 15.5 cm. (Photo: T. Gretton.)

darker sheets and drapes over the bath. The letters are also prominently displayed in both. The whole surface has a balanced arrangement of verticals and horizontals in the window frame and divisions, the wall panelling, the squared-up floor area, and the side table that all echo the rectilinear emphasis of David's forms. In place, however, of David's upended box as writing table, we have the upright, dramatically silhouetted figure of Corday, her dress, hair, and profile shown *à l'antique,* and her eloquent gesture of accusation mimicking many such gestures in ancient history paintings. In the Du Vivier, Corday accuses Marat with an extraordinary extended arm, as her index finger all but touches the diseased body. But it is not at all clear whose side we should be on. This image produces precisely the kind of confusion between competing sites

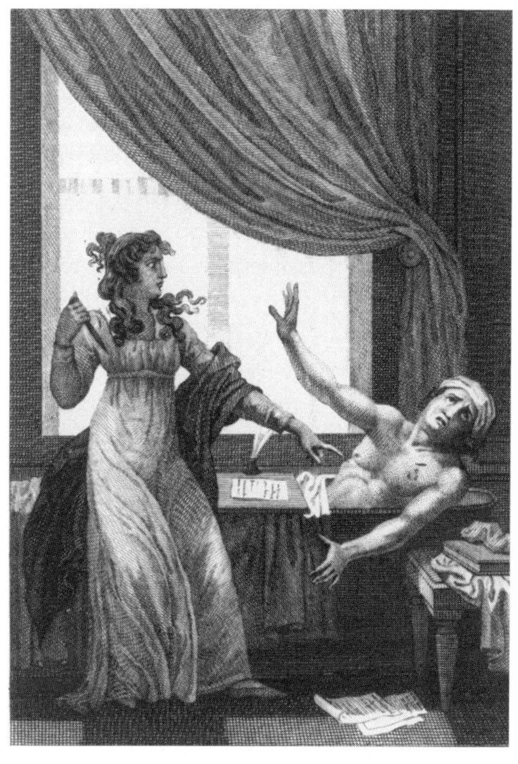

Figure 24. J. L. Delignon, after Du Vivier, *Marat frappé à mort (Marat struck dead),* late 1790s, engraving, 11.1 × 6.6 cm. British Museum, Chèvremont Marat Collection, London. (© British Museum.)

for virtue that David needed to avoid at all costs. His representation of Marat had to be unequivocally positive and virtuous and his evocation of Corday unequivocally negative and treacherous.

CREATING AN ANTIREPUBLICAN IDENTITY

What does the blanking out of Corday direct us to do? In part it directs us to reconstitute her, through the metonymic function of her letter, contrasted with Marat's letter in a system of polarities of vice/virtue, aristocrat/people, dissimulation/truth, female/male. Corday's actual letter, the second one she wrote to Marat, read: 'I wrote to you this morning, Marat, have you received my letter, can I hope for a moment's audience with you, if you have received it. I hope that you will not refuse me, seeing how important the matter is. It is enough that I should be quite wretched to have a right to your protection.'[9] David selected from this and adapted the wording to suit his purposes in fabricating Corday's identity.

First, there is allusion to the opposing politics of Corday and Marat and a construction of opposing moral characters: Marat is simply referred to as citizen, 'citoyen Marat' and as 'MARAT'; Corday, in her strong flowing script, as 'Marie anne Charlotte Corday', as she named herself at her trial. The absence of 'citoyenne' suggests the contrast between the male republican citizen and the female aristocrat. The date on her letter is written in the Gregorian calendar form, whereas the republican form, 'L'an II' (not yet in use in July '93), is identified at the base of the box with Marat and David. This has the effect of denying Corday's republicanism despite her statement that she had been a republican long before the Revolution. David reveals her use of 'votre (bienveillance)' at a time when the singular 'ta' would be the citizen's mode of address. By the end of October there were requests for *tutoiement* to be made official.[10] Corday's supposed literary pretensions and education are succinctly represented in David's selection of the phrase in her letter that used the subjunctive: 'il suffit que je sois/ bien Malheureuse . . .' ('it is enough that I should be/ quite wretched . . .'). Marat's direct and plain-speaking language, by contrast, is shown in his own letter, in a less assured script, to those who were to take money to a widow in need: 'vous (?) Donner(a?) (ez?) cet/ assignat à cette/ mère de 5 enfans/ et dont le mari est mort (parti?) pour la deffense de la patrie' ('you will give this *assignat* to this mother of 5 children and whose husband died defending his country') (Fig. 25). David changes the last word of Corday's actual letter from 'protection' to 'bienveillance' (again a more erudite word), thus removing any idea of Corday as feminine, as damsel in distress, and focussing instead on Marat's active benevolence. His thumb still holds on to this particular word and we now know from Libby Sheldon's research that this was a very careful and deliberate decision after earlier positionings of the thumb. Both characters are represented as writers. Marat worked for the Revolution as a journalist; writing was his trade; he used it overtly to expose and denounce traitors and the false values of the ancien régime. Corday's letter is to be read as duplicitous and treacherous; it is subtly worded to make Marat believe that she warranted his attention and benevolence.

The representation of Marat is all transparency (nakedness), gen-

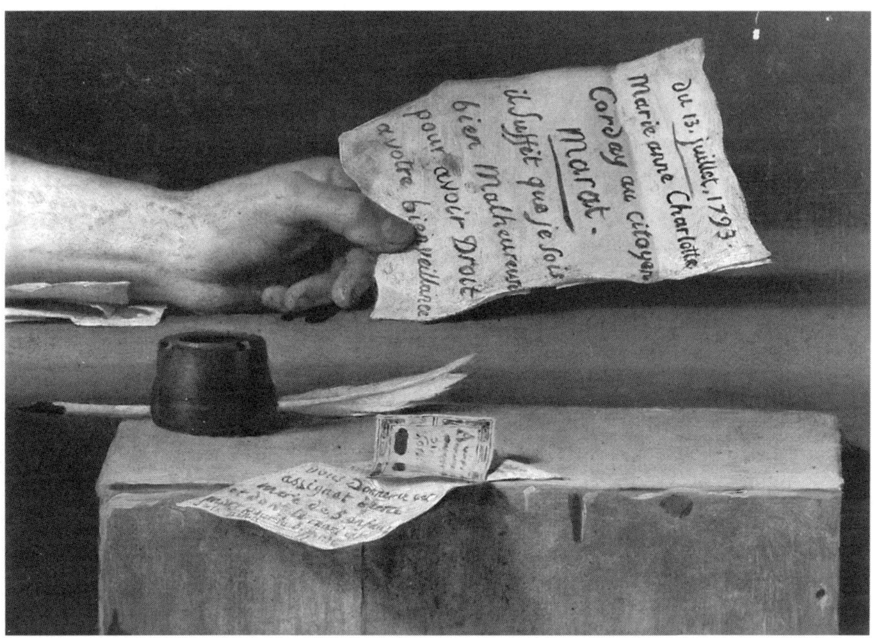

Figure 25. Jacques–Louis David, detail of *Marat,* 1793, Musées royaux des Beaux-Arts, Brussels. (Photo: © A.C.L. Musées royaux des Beaux-Arts de Belgique.)

erosity (his letter), self–denial (patched sheet), and hard work (two quills) on the people's behalf. That of Corday arouses the spectre of the hidden and manipulative power of the notorious *salonnières* and women of letters of the ancien régime, and it highlights the danger of linguistic perfidy, seemingly sincere language that in effect hid lies and conspiracies.[11] In these ways David constructed Corday's character and politics by invidious comparison with Marat's.

Second, there is a hostile construction of Corday's womanhood as opposed to that of the widow mentioned in Marat's letter. Corday, it was well known from the trial, was twenty–five but still unmarried and had spent her time reading and writing. The woman referred to in Marat's letter is a good republican who had reared several children and whose soldier husband had died fighting for his country. She is poor and needy; Corday only pretends to be 'malheureuse' and invokes Marat's help as a right. There was much rhetoric on the question of women's rights and woman's rightful role in society, and on the 'natural' order of society. Louis-Marie Prud'homme in his paper *Révolutions de Paris,* called on women citizens to

> be honest and diligent girls, tender and modest wives, wise mothers, and you will be good patriots. True patriotism consists of fulfilling one's duties and valuing only rights appropriate to each according to their sex and age, . . . always punish courageously . . . any crime which tends to disorganise society by changing sexes or indecently confusing them with anti-civic and perfidious intentions.[12]

Corday had also been condemned as a hybrid creature, acting against her sex, in de Sade's September *discours* – a creature 'of indeterminate sex, vomitted forth by the flames of hell to the despair of both sexes, belonging to neither completely'. She styled herself on great men from ancient history, not, as she should have done, on Cornelia, that paradigm of maternal duty. This was clearly transgressive of the expectations of her sex. When she was arrested in Marat's apartment she had her baptism certificate pinned to her *fichu* to assert her identity and 'to show what the most feeble hand is capable of when driven by total devotion'.[13] She also had the text of her speech, which she had intended to deliver as part of her original plan to assassinate Marat in public on the Champ de Mars or at the National Convention on 14 July. In this she compares herself to Alcides, a rather precious alternative name for Hercules, claiming similarity between his and her acts of destroying monsters.[14] Such comparison with the most masculine of men served to make her enemies' point, that such self-perception would only lead to behaviour that was monstrous and alien to the nature of republican woman/mother.

Prud'homme's and de Sade's speeches reveal anxieties about woman as disorder and as emasculator of men. It is arguable that fears of Corday as emasculator or castrator found expression in David's painting in the truncating of Marat's body in a bath of blood. Interestingly, Sheldon's researches have not revealed any underdrawing of a full-length male nude stretched out in the bath, indicating that David possibly never attempted a drawing of the lower body. If there is a case for reading castration here then there has been a reversal of the more usual psychic fiction of female castration, whereby women are transformed from human beings into wounded sacrificial creatures who were born to bleed. It is Marat who has been sacrificed here.

This horror of emasculation is also part of the broader fear of antirepublicanism, a fear of regression to a monarchical regime when the king was the only masculine figure surrounded by slavish, effeminised courtiers. In physically identifying with Corday, the spectator (perhaps especially the female spectator) shares Corday's transgressive nature in the sexual power conflict. Corday/spectator is fully clothed and empowered by the weapon; Marat lies beneath her, assumed to be fully naked (David has divested him of the dressing gown some say he was wearing), vulnerable, defenceless, a middle-aged man in distress. Perhaps to dispel such identification with Corday from the spectator's imaginings and any idea of disempowerment of Marat, David has given the exposed body parts, especially arms and shoulder, a masculine strength. Considering that Marat's body was profoundly and visibly diseased, it has not just been ennobled through denial of the evidence of skin blemishes; an exaggerated muscularity has also been invented for it, especially in the arm that still holds the quill, which suggests that the power of the pen is mightier than that of the knife, that this is not a weak man who could ever be overpowered by a mere woman. This man lives on and triumphs through the power of his writings, while the woman's courage and strength is nowhere visible.

COUNTERACTING CORDAY'S SELF-IMAGE

It is largely through Corday's letters to friends and family, through her responses at her trial, and through her intended public address to the French people that we gain an idea of her self-image. Fouquier-Tinville, presiding judge at Corday's trial, initially requested the immediate publication of her letters and speech, presumably in the hope that they would expose her as a Girondin conspirator. Although David claimed to be representing Marat as he had seen him the day before the assassination, it is my belief that Corday's writings were a determining factor in the development of the later stages of the painting.

Corday's letters examine her role in the revolutionary process and the view that she sees posterity adopting of her. For the immediate future she assesses the view of Marat's supporters: 'They are not exactly happy to have a mere woman of no importance to sacrifice to the ancestors of this great man'.[15] She dates the letter, significantly, 'the second day in preparation for peace', in the belief that her action will put an end to France's internal strife. This sentence is replete with irony. First, the phrase 'not exactly happy' was a gross understatement. Marat's supporters could not cope with Corday's insistence on taking sole responsibility for her action, and at her trial they repeatedly tried to force her to admit to being part of a conspiracy. The implication was that no woman could have had the courage to carry out an assassination unaided, and no woman would be capable of committing such an act out of political conviction. Second, Corday clearly did not see herself as 'a mere woman of no importance'. She was proud of her own ancestor, the playwright Pierre Corneille, and of her classical education, to which she made reference at her trial. She believed that a glorious place was carved out for her in the theatre of France's revolution, that she had been destined for great deeds and had now fulfilled her destiny.[16]

Third, her opinion of Marat was not that he was a great man, but rather a vile monster who had caused the bloodshed of hundreds of good French citizens and would continue to do so unless she stopped him. It was this image of a woman intervening in history, with justice on her side, bringing peace and salvation to France that she was at some pains to construct. She reinforced it through her comportment of stoic calm at her trial and her serenity before the guillotine. It had to be officially wiped out by David.

In the same letter to Barbaroux, Corday wrote of Marat's last words. The release of the final breath is a solemn moment, often accompanied in representations of dying ancient philosophers and heroes by last words of great significance. Charlotte Corday was well aware of this and goes to some lengths to put the record straight about the nature of Marat's dying words. She refuted the words that had been printed as his dying words: '. . . in any case these were his last words to me. After writing all your names . . . he said, to console me, that in a few days, he would have you all guillotined in Paris. These last words determined his fate . . .'.[17]

Evidently, what Marat would actually have been holding in his hand when the blow was struck was a list of names of men to be guillotined. This list had to be obliterated for fear of evoking the bloodthirsty devourer of men and of giving the slightest justification for Corday's act. Indeed, Marat is shown with his own blood spilling for the people.

Although David made his decision to paint Marat as he had seen him on 12 July writing for the 'salut public' and in 'honorable indigence', details of the wording of Marat's letter to a poor widow had not yet been finalised. Was it perhaps, in an effort to counter Corday's precise words in these published letters, which had also appeared in full beneath some of the pro-Corday prints, that David eventually represented Marat's dying words as those penned in the instructions to bring relief from suffering to a republican widow? Furthermore, in her letter to Barbaroux Corday relates that she has asked for any remaining money of hers to be given to the women and children of the brave men who had left Caen to rescue Paris. This act of generosity and support for women and children, wives of those fighting for their country, would appear to have been appropriated by David to characterise Marat.[18] Indeed, to reinforce the point, when presenting the painting to the National Convention, David called first on '. . . mothers, widows, orphans, oppressed soldiers to come and contemplate your friend . . .'.[19]

Finally, toward the end of her public address to the French people, Corday speaks of her death for killing Marat as intended to be useful to her fellow citizens. She sees it as her 'dernier soupir'. Did the phrase suggest the title for David's painting? She makes direct reference to the assassin of Le Peletier, distinguishing herself from Pâris, as if already seeing herself in relation to David's next painting: 'I shall not imitate Pâris by killing myself . . . I would like my dying breath to be useful to my fellow citizens, and for my head to be carried around Paris as a sign for rallying all the friends of the law!'[20] Again, any notion of Corday's devotion to fellow citizens with a 'dernier soupir' would have to be obliterated. What better way than by David appropriating such devotion for Marat's last breath and for the image of Marat to become a rallying point?

THE FUNCTION OF LETTER WRITING IN *MARAT*

Letter writing was an appropriate device for evoking Corday since many of the contemporary prints had represented her in her prison cell writing a letter to her father (Fig. 26). In these the image we often see is of an obedient daughter, normally submissive to her father's will. This is stressed in the first line of her letter, which is often left visible. It reads 'Pardonnés-moi, mon cher papa, d'avoir disposé de mon existence sans votre permission' ('Forgive me, my dear father, for having disposed of my existence without your permission'). This image of compliant woman, writing the sincere and affectionate letter to a beloved father, had to be countered in David's representation of her. Indeed, he was called upon to record 'une main parricide . . .'.

Arguably, what the letter does in *Marat* is to reduce Corday to a hand. The writing on the letter implies a hand behind it, unlike the latinized 'MARAT' and 'DAVID', and this in itself reminds us of prints of disembodied hands that were current in 1793 after the death of the king. She believed her hand to be 'driven by total devotion (to country)', but what was needed was erasure of filial and patriotic duty and promotion of Corday as 'une main perfide' and 'une main parricide'.

There are three linguistic messages in the painting: the first (Corday's letter) on the green cloth; the second (Marat's letter) reaching out to the spectator's hand across the edge of the upended box; and the third (David's lettering) inscribed on the lower area of the box but functioning also as the painting's title and signature by the artist's hand on the canvas surface. With these David is exploring three different temporalities. The tribute on the box has a universalising aspect, as if carved in stone. It immortalises Marat and sets David himself in humble position alongside him, reflected in Marat's 'gloire' for all time.[21] Second, the letter from Marat to the widowed mother reaches out to the spectator, urging us to take it, in much the same way as knife handles function in Chardin's still-life paintings.[22] It serves as intermediary between the painting and the spectator, between Marat and true republican citizens for the immediate future. The sense of immediacy is enhanced by a realisation that Marat's letter must protrude not just beyond the edge of the box but beyond the vertical surface of the canvas, since the bottom edge of the box is flush with the bottom edge of the canvas.

The third linguistic message is Corday's letter to Marat. It refers, however, to a past moment – the plotting of her forced encounter with Marat. It also invokes, more generally, the ancien régime and

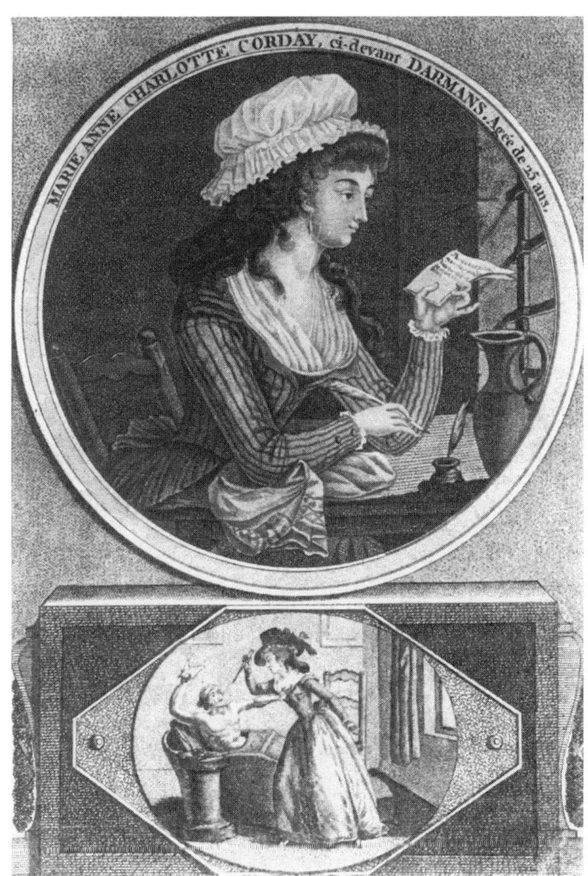

Figure 26. Quéverdo, *Marie Anne Charlotte Corday, ci-devant Darmans. Agée de 25 ans (Marie Anne Charlotte Corday, formerly Darmans, Aged 25)*, n.d., engraving, 14.5 × 9.8 cm. Private collection. (Photo: H. Weston.)

the falsehoods of a past era that Marat had exposed. Simply by virtue of being a letter written by a woman, it holds values considered feminine under a prerevolutionary regime, when women were perceived positively, as being the best — because the most sensitive and intuitive — letter writers.[23] Letters were also a site for intrigue, deception, and secrecy in an age of *honnêteté,* when social interaction depended upon masquerade and concealment. In the new republican era of transparency and direct speech, such notions of concealment and intimacy were held in contempt.

David manages a complete inversion of seventeenth-century Dutch and especially eighteenth-century French traditional representation of the letter theme, and in the process, he appropriates and transforms the act of letter writing to make it signify the republican, masculine virtue of magnanimity. It is these contrasts between regimes that David sets up with his painted letters, so that the whole painting functions as a rebuke to the sensibilities of the ancien régime.

In Louis-Léopold Boilly's *The Visit returned,* 1789, a man is represented in the private act of letter writing (Fig. 27). We presume it to be a *billet-doux* to the woman whose portrait hangs over the desk. We also presume this to be the same woman as the one on the left, accompanied by her maid, who has interrupted him. Not unusually the whole composition revolves around screens and concealment, secrecy, surprise, and speculation and all takes place in a well-furnished and generally comfortable apartment. David overturns these formulae in *Marat,* and by so doing he impugns the feminised society that produced and consumed an art of such privacy and sumptuosity.

SOLUTION IN EFFACEMENT

There is no evidence to suggest that at the time of making her decision to assassinate Marat in July 1793, any part of Corday's agenda might have included a 'feminist' issue of exclusion; exclusion, that is, from public spheres of activity that might threaten to take women away from home, husband, and the care of dependents. Nor was Marat's well-documented support for mothers and his concerns for women as objects of injustice a point at issue for Corday. Her reading of Rousseau had taught her to respect these attitudes. On this her views were not at odds with those of the Jacobin dictators. The fact that Marat incited women to denounce traitors – indeed, the powerful *Club des citoyennes républicaines révolutionnaires* had played an important part during May 1793 in stirring up anti-Girondin feeling – is more likely to have irked Corday and confirmed her in her resolve.[24]

From her reading of Plutarch, Corday had developed a special interest in the lives of great men of ancient Rome and Greece and had a deep admiration for Jean-Jacques Rousseau and Abbé Raynal.[25] She clearly also had a strong sense of what constituted virtue, justice, and right government. So, she might have been interested in the writings of another Girondin supporter, Olympe de

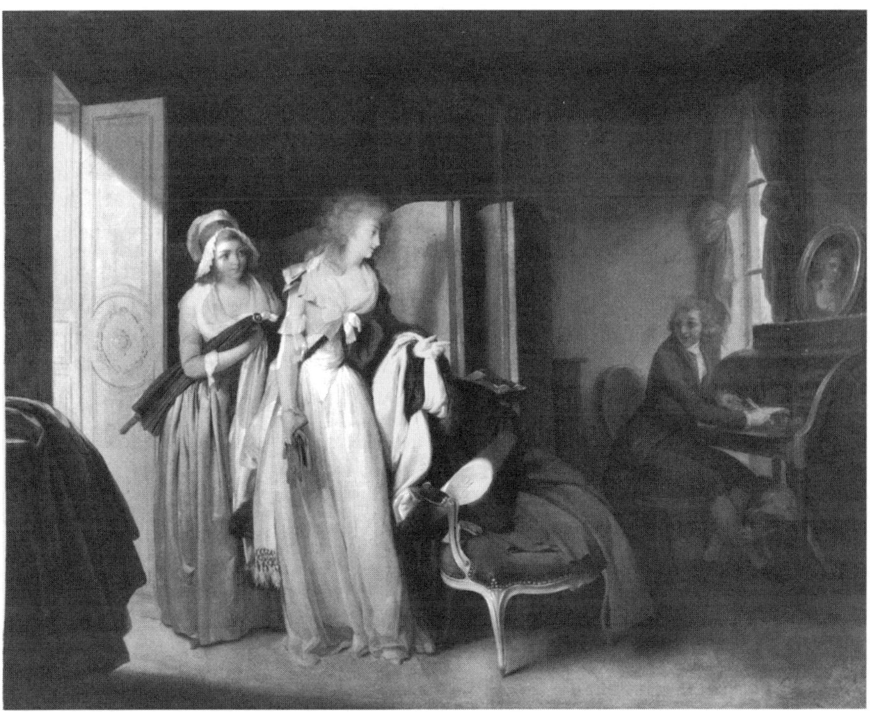

Figure 27. Louis-Léopold Boilly, *The Visit returned,* 1789, oil on canvas, 45 × 55 cm. The Wallace Collection, London. (Reproduced by permission of the Trustees of the Wallace Collection.)

Gouges, and her *Declaration of the Rights of Woman and Citizeness* (1791), or in the earlier essay by Condorcet, *On the Admission of Women to the Rights of the City* (1790). Both argued from a belief in natural rights that women were rational beings and were born equal with men, and that their exclusion from political rights was an 'act of tyranny' (Condorcet). Corday's concerns were not, however, for rights, whether natural, civil, or political, and her assassination of Marat, although recognised as an act of extraordinary courage, was nevertheless condemned by de Gouges as harmful to the women's cause, because it could only be perceived as a passionate and irrational act.[26] As far as women of the radical clubs, on the one hand, or women in the market stalls of Les Halles, on the other, were concerned, it was Corday's education, like that of Madame Roland and de Gouges, that counted against her. For the market women the women's cause was a matter of fixing maximum food prices – or not – and exposing hoarders and speculators. They idolised Marat because he was one of the few politicians who listened to them, took them seriously, and gave them a sense of purpose. The women of the *Club des citoyennes républicaines révolutionnaires* took care to distance themselves from Corday when a men's patriotic society tried, in September, to identify them with 'the Medicis, Elizabeth of England, an Antoinette, a Charlotte Corday', with any powerful women, in effect. Claire Lacombe, the society's leader, rejected such associations and accused the masculine sex of oppression of women, whereupon the Jacobin leaders mobilised the market women against the *Républicaines.* Their headquarters at Saint Eustache were promptly invaded by several thousand market women and events were so managed that women themselves were seen to be calling for the closure of women's clubs. At the end of October the Convention outlawed them all. Corday had nothing to do with these women's movements and issues, but for some, it was convenient to associate her with them after her death and thus justify the condemnation and exclusion of women from public political sites.

David had somehow to resurrect Corday as a threat, not simply to Marat, but by extension, to the welfare of French republican citizens. She was a threat because she had, in a particularly impressive way, defied the notion of exclusion and acted in a way perceived as being against her sex. Reports of her courage and beauty and serenity were compounded by myths that immediately grew around her. These focussed on the miraculous appearance of a blushing cheek, after her head had been cut off. The story goes that the executioner, Henri Samson, slapped the decapitated head on one cheek and the other cheek turned pink with shame or modesty, or as if she had 'turned the other cheek'. This account was published in the next issue of *Révolutions de Paris,* 13–19 July, and caused a sense of outrage against Samson, thereby arousing sympathy and awe for Corday.[27] Effacing her from David's image served both to conjure her up as hidden menace and simultaneously to leave the qualities of courage and beauty with Marat, together with the suggestion of a miraculous healing of his 'leprous' condition by effacing all traces of it.

The fear among Marat's Jacobin supporters of the potential of Corday's beauty to sway public opinion, contrasted as it was with the ugliness of Marat's 'leprous' condition, was well founded. It was sufficiently strong for the pro-Marat lobby to post up denunciations of her as hideous because of the hideous nature of her crime, while the *Gazette de France nationale* gave an official text 'correcting' all suggestions in the moderate press that 'crime and courage could march hand in hand': 'This woman, who is supposed to be really pretty, was not at all pretty; this was a virago, more fleshy than fresh, ungraceful, dirty, as are almost all female philosophers and intellectuals.'[28] David's way of contributing to the Jacobin construction of Corday as an unfeminine woman was to make her an articulate writer. By retaining the phrase with the subjunctive he underscored the notion of the bluestocking and thereby implied the dirty virago. Marat, meanwhile, is transformed into a beautiful noble creature.

How does David handle the question of Corday's virginity? It is slightly curious that he has included all her forenames on the letter. To her friends she was Marie. David might have used 'Charlotte' on its own, had he wished to diminish her in the way that Marie-Antoinette was diminished, for example, at her trial. Her name was cropped to 'Toinette' to disassociate her from names revered in a Christian context. It is worth remembering that the queen was on her way to the guillotine on 16 October, the same day that David's paintings of Marat and Le Peletier were put on display in the Cour du Louvre. She represented the cause for the state of corruption of France, Marat the emblem of its conversion to virtue. Thus, with the death of (Marie-Ann) Toinette came simultaneously the magical revivifying of 'Saint' Marat. Corday's names were used inconsistently during her trial and in official papers at the time, but she too was frequently referred to simply as Charlotte Corday, without the 'virginal' Marie.[29] Why would David allow the association with the Virgin Mary to stand in a painting where many saw Marat as a Jesus figure and the whole image as a sort of *pietà?*

As is well documented, Corday's body was taken after her death to the Hôpital de la Charité for examination by, among others, David. It was established unequivocally that she was still a virgin at the age of twenty-five, which made it difficult to charge her with sexual promiscuity! It did, however, enable her detractors to characterise her as unnatural for still being a virgin. The inclusion of 'Marie' and 'Anne' in the painting would have encouraged this interpretation.

Effacing Corday from the narrative allowed David to deny her subjectivity and responsibility for her action and thereby to demonstrate support for the conspiracy theory. As such she could be represented as part of an invisible, formless body, the threat of whose intervention is nevertheless palpable. Chantal Thomas compares the processes of exclusion and blame in David's painting with the Jacobin idea of a woman's place and quotes from the entry on Corday in the *Petit vocabulaire de la fémininité représentée*: '. . . in some ways and to a large extent the Jacobin conception of women functions like David's painting: excluded from public life, rendered invisible, they are at the same time made responsible for the evils that are stated there'.[30] Blanking Corday out did not remove her guilt. Women's responsibility for disorder was perceived to be in operation behind the scenes. For a woman to scheme in private and assert her presence and political views in public by taking the law into her own hands, as Corday had done, was to act against the natural order of society. Two weeks after the death of the queen, Deputy Jean-Baptiste Amar, member of the Committee of Public Safety, excluded women from all political societies. He asked:

> Is it possible for women to devote themselves to these useful and difficult tasks? No, because they would be obliged to sacrifice more important concerns to which nature summons them. Private tasks for which women are destined by nature itself are part of the general order of society; this order is the result of the differences existing between men and women . . .[31]

David contrasts Corday's threatening invisibility and unnatural public act with the visible body of Marat in its original, 'natural' state.

The will to efface Corday is carried through into public ceremonies honouring Marat. The women of the *Club des citoyennes républicaines révolutionnaires* were prominent at the inauguration of the wooden obelisk erected 'Aux mânes de Marat' on the Place de la Réunion on 18 August, 1793 (Fig. 28).[32] They had spent the previous month collecting money for this monument and had the honour of carrying the bath to be placed inside it. A bust of Marat was also installed, together with the chair, table, inkwell, quills, and papers. On the obelisk are the words 'une main perfide le ravit a l'amour du peuple' ('a perfidious hand snatched him from the love of the people'). The procession moved to the Cordeliers Club gar-

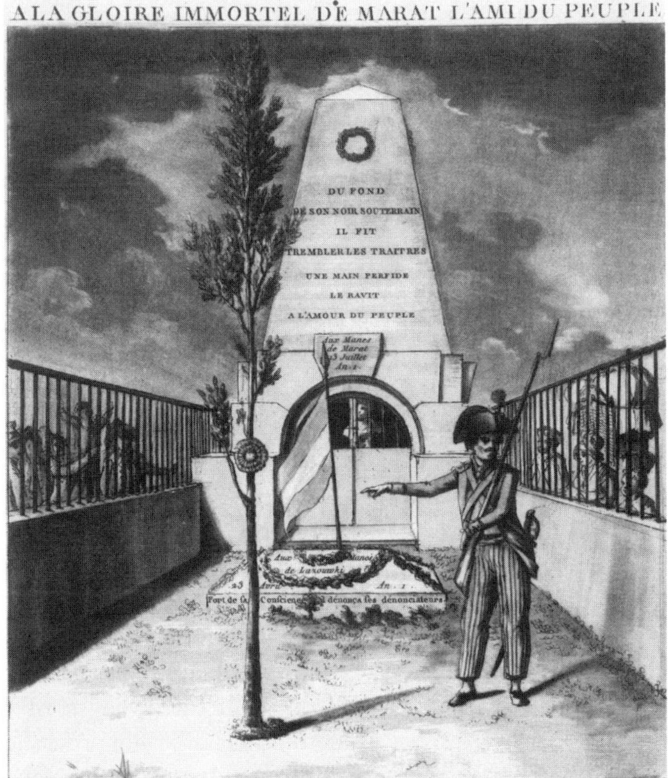

Ce petit Obélisque que le peuple dans sa reconnoissance a élevé aux manes du Vertueux MARAT, est situé sur la place de la Réunion, en face de la porte principale du Palais National; Ce palais occupé autrefois par le tyran: cette place ou c'est livré le 10 Aout 1792 ce combat à mort entre ses esclaves et les enfans de la liberté; Ce petit Edifice même qui renferme les cendres du patriote LAZOUWKI un des chefs des braves qui vinquirent en ce jour mémorable tout inspire aux vrais et bons Sans-Culottes des sensations douloureuse et satisfaisante invitant l'ame à se nourir de pensées sublime qui doivent tourner au profit de la liberté.
A Paris chez Villeneuve Graveur Rue Zacharie St Severin Maison du Passage N° 72.

Figure 28. Villeneuve, after Anon., *A la gloire immortel de Marat, l'Ami du Peuple (To the Glory of the Immortal Marat, Friend of the People)*, c. 1793, engraving, 22.5 × 17.1 cm. British Museum, Chèvremont Marat Collection, London. (© British Museum.)

den where there was a funerary oration, in which Corday was referred to as a fury whose hand had been directed by the perfidious men denounced by Marat. David, too, constructs Corday as a hand, the signatory of perfidious writing.

A feminist strategy for acknowledging Corday's moral agency and for counterblasting Jacobin effacement of her might be to consider her active participation in constructing that effacement. For there is a contradiction in her self-presentation. On the one hand she insists on her agency and responsibility for planning Marat's murder and for actually stabbing him to death. On the other hand she is so calm and detached, as if seeing the whole event from a distance, without her actual presence having had any importance. For her the act was preordained by her reading of Plutarch. There is nothing subjective in her action. It is as if the whole event happens in her absence. When pressed during her trial to admit that she must have practised the act of stabbing, she disclaimed all knowledge of how to do it: 'It just happened that I struck in that way. It was by chance . . .'.[33] She continued, 'I have never judged life except in terms of its usefulness'.[34] Now that her usefulness had been put to the ultimate test she no longer needed to assert her presence. Her total devotion to country had delivered France from a devouring monster. Her visibility was no longer of any consequence. David's portrait-as-absence might thus be seen as in keeping with her self-perception in the last days of her life.

It is in the details of the painting that we can see David's manipulation of Corday's self-image. She sees herself as equal to Hercules, that figure so closely bound up with the strength of the sans-culottes. David gives that strength to Marat's right arm. She sees her act as one of disempowering a beast, whose death can be celebrated. David shows Marat still alive, blood still dripping from the wound, lips still parted in utterance, forever not dead. Corday considers her act as devotion to her country, a useful act to be recognised at the moment of her *dernier soupir*. David takes this as title for his representation of Marat's last breath. She makes a final act of generosity by giving money to those fighting for their country. David makes this Marat's last act. She draws attention to Marat's bloodthirsty reputation by reiterating his last words to her of his intent to send Girondins to the guillotine. David disallows this and shows Marat's own blood as having been spilled for his country. So many of the artist's decisions contradict Corday's words that she emerges as a determining force by way of counterpoint in the later stages of the work's development. The power and identity she claims for herself find paradoxical expression in David's very attempts to eliminate her. In the final analysis the painting preserves Marat as forever not dead, but it also makes that death a foregone conclusion and allows the name of Marie Anne Charlotte Corday to be indelibly imprinted in the fabric of the paint as that of the woman who masterminded the crime.

NOTES

1. 'Il faut qu'un voile funèbre enveloppe à jamais sa mémoire; qu'on cesse surtout de nous présenter, comme on ose le faire, son effigie sous l'emblême enchanteur de la beauté'. De Sade, 'Discours aux mânes de Marat et le Pelletier', 29 September 1793. Quoted in G. Lely, *Vie du marquis de Sade, avec un examen de ses ouvrages* (Paris: Gallimard, 1952), 2:432–42.

2. See Jacques Guilhaumou, *La Mort de Marat* (Paris: Editions complexe, 1989), 21.

3. For the representation of Corday in nineteenth-century art see Michael Marrinan, 'Images and Ideas of Charlotte Corday: Texts and Contexts of an Assassination', *Arts Magazine* (April 1980): 158–75; Claudine Mitchell, 'Spectacular Fears and Popular Arts: A View from the Nineteenth Century', in *Reflections of Revolution. Images of Romanticism,* ed. Alison Yarrington and Kelvin Everest (London and New York: Routledge, 1993), 159–81; Marie-Claude Chaudonneret, 'Le mythe de la Révolution', in *Aux Armes et aux Arts!,* ed. Philippe Bordes and Régis Michel (Paris: Editions Adam Biro, 1988), 332–7.

4. I have drawn much from the work of Dominique Godineau, *Citoyennes tricoteuses* (Aix-en-Provence: Alinéa, 1988) and 'Minorités et exclus. Quels droits naturels pour les femmes d'un peuple libre?' in *Les Droits de l'Homme et la Conquête des Libertés. Des Lumières aux Révolutions de 1848,* Actes du colloque de Grenoble-Vizille 1986 (Grenoble: Presses univ. de Grenoble, 1988); Florence Gauthier, *Triomphe et mort du droit naturel en Révolution 1789–95–1802* (Paris: Presses univ. de France, 1992); Olwen Hufton, *Women and the Limits of Citizenship in the French Revolution* (Toronto, Buffalo, London: University of Toronto Press, 1992); Lynn Hunt, *The Family Romance of the French Revolution* (London: Routledge, 1992); and Chantal Thomas, 'Portraits de Charlotte Corday', in *La Mort de Marat,* ed. Jean-Claude Bonnet (Paris: Flammarion, 1986), 268–86, and 'Heroism in the Feminine: The Examples of Charlotte Corday and Madame Roland', in *Eighteenth Century: Theory and Interpretation* (Lubbock, Texas: Texas University Press, 1989), 67–82. For a study of the representation of women and women artists of this period, see Vivian Cameron, 'Woman as Image and as Image-Maker in Paris during the French Revolution' (Ph.D. thesis, Yale University, 1983).

5. David changed the colour of the knife handle from ebony black to white, to enable it to stand out against the dark floor.

6. On the concept of 'the blank' and its place in reception aesthetics, see Stefan Germer, 'In Search of a Beholder: On the Relation between Art, Audiences and Social Spheres in Post-Thermidor France', *The Art Bulletin* (March 1992): 19–36. See also Mattias Bleyl's conclusion in 'Marat: du portrait à la peinture d'histoire', in *David contre David: Actes du colloque,* ed. Régis Michel and Antoine Schnapper (Paris: La documentation française, Louvre, 1993), 2:381–99.

7. This print was probably done after the version of David's painting owned by Prince Napoleon and shown in 1863 at the Salon de la société nationale des Beaux-Arts, 26 bd. des Italiens (now at Versailles). I am grateful to Tom Gretton for drawing my attention to this print and, in general, for his constant willingness and enthusiasm in discussing this project.

8. According to François Chèvremont, *Index du bibliophile et de l'amateur de peinture, gravure etc.* (Paris: 1876), 417, this engraving was for an illustration to *Précis de l'Histoire des Français.* This print is part of a large collection of Marat/Corday imagery bequeathed to the British Library by Chèvremont, who devoted his whole scholarly life to Marat.

9. Je vous ai écrit ce matin Marat, avés vous reçu ma lettre, puis je espérer un moment d'audience, si vous l'avés reçue, j'espère que vous ne me refuserés pas, voyant combien la chose est intéressante, suffit que je sois bien malheureuse pour avoir droit à votre protection.

   B. M. Versailles, Ms Vatel F677/361/2, cited in Cat. Musée Lambinet, various authors, *Charlotte Corday. Une Normande dans la Révolution* (Versailles: 1989), 111–12.

10. See T. J. Clark, 'Painting in the Year Two', *Representations* 47 (Summer 1994): 42.

11. See Dorothy Johnson, *Jacques-Louis David. Art in Metamorphosis* (Princeton: Princeton University Press, 1993), 106–9.

12. Louis-Marie Prud'homme, *Révolutions de Paris, Feb. 1791,* quoted in Candice E. Proctor, *Women, Equality and the French Revolution* (New York: Greenwood Press, 1990), 56.

13. 'Je joins mon extrait de Baptême à cette Adresse pour montrer ce que peut la plus faible main par un entier dévouement', *Addresse aux Français, Amis de la Loi et de la Paix,* reproduced in Cat. Musée Lambinet, 210–11.

14. 'Si je suis coupable, Alcide l'était donc lorsqu'il détruisit les monstres; mais en recontra-t-il de si odieux?' ('If I am guilty, was not Alcides also when he destroyed monsters; but did he ever encounter such odious ones?') Ibid.

15. '[M]ais on n'est guère content de n'avoir qu'une femme sans conséquence pour offrir aux mânes de ce grand homme', Corday to Bar-

baroux, 16 July 1793. Text copied from facsimile and published by Vatel, *Procès criminel de Charlotte Corday* (Paris, Versailles, Caen), reproduced in Cat. Musée Lambinet, 212.

16. '. . . je prie ceux qui me regretteront de le considérer et ils se reouiront de me voir du repos dans les Champs Elysées, avec Brutus et quelques anciens . . .' ('I beg those who will miss me to consider this and they will rejoice to see me at rest in the Elysian Fields with Brutus and some other ancients . . .') Ibid., 213.

17. '[M]ais voilà les dernières (paroles) qu'il m'a dites. Après avoir écrit vos noms à tous, et ceux des administrateurs du Calvados qui sont à Evreux, il me dit pour me consoler, que dans peu de jours, il vous ferait tous guillotiner à Paris. Ces derniers mots décidèrent de son sort . . .' Ibid., 213.

18. For Corday's reputation for generosity and kindness, see Xavier Rousseau, *Les Cordays au Pays d'Argentan* (Argentan: 1938), chap. 18, 110–20.

19. 'Accourez tous! la mère, la veuve, l'orphelin, le soldat opprimé; . . . contemplez votre ami'. *Discours prononcé à la Convention Nationale par David, député de Paris, en lui offrant le tableau représentant Marat assassiné. Séance 24 brumaire, l'an II de la République française.* (D. and G. Wildenstein, *Documents complémentaires au catalogue de l'oeuvre de Louis David* (Paris: Fondation Wildenstein, 1973), no. 674.

20. 'Je n'imiterai point Pâris en me tuant . . . Je veux que mon dernier soupir soit utile à mes concitoyens, que ma tête, portée dans Paris, soit un signe de ralliement pour tous les amis des lois'. *Addresse aux Français,* 210.

21. For a penetrating study of David and the concept of 'gloire', see Valerie Mainz, 'History, History Painting and Concepts of *Gloire* in the Life and Work of Jacques-Louis David' (Ph.D. thesis, U.C.L., University of London, 1992). On notions of time in David's *Marat,* see Klaus Herding, 'La notion de temporalité à partir du "Marat" ' in Michel, 421–41.

22. For the significance of Chardin for David's painting, see Anita Brookner, *Jacques-Louis David* (London: Chatto and Windus, 1980), 114.

23. P. Pawlowitz, 'The Letter Theme: Fragonard and the Image of Woman', in *Eighteenth-Century Women and the Arts,* ed. F. Keener and S. Lorsch (New York, Westport, Conn., London: Greenwood Press, 1988), 189–200.

24. See Hufton, 33–6.

25. In Corday's letter to Barbaroux she refers to Rainal (sic) as 'mon oracle'.

26. O. de Gouges, letter addressed from her prison cell to the house of her friend, Cubières, 20 July 1793, quoted in Olivier Blanc, *Olympe de Gouges. Une Femme de Liberté* (Paris: Syros/Alternatives, 1989), 165–6, 219, n. 30. See also Thomas, 'Heroism in the Feminine', 72.

27. For discussion of the persistence of this myth, see D. Outram, *The Body and the French Revolution. Sex, Class and Political Culture* (New Haven and

London: Yale University Press, 1989), 118–21. Outram points to the similar chaste behaviour at the guillotine of Mme Elizabeth, Louis XVI's unmarried sister, also presumed to be a virgin.

28. 'Cette femme, qu'on dit fort jolie, n'était point jolie: c'est une virago, plus charnue que fraiche, sans grâce, malpropre, comme le sont presque tous les philosophes et beaux-esprits femelles'. *Gazette de France nationale,* quoted in Guilhaumou, 74.

29. On name cropping, see C. Thomas, *La Reine Scélérate. Marie-Antoinette dans les pamphlets* (Paris: Editions du Seuil, 1989), 152–3.

30. G. Lascault, *Figurées, défigurées. Petit vocabulaire de la fémininité représentée.* (Paris: 10/18, 1970, 1977), 33–6, quoted in French in Thomas, 'Portraits de Charlotte Corday', 276.

31.   Les femmes peuvent-elles se dévouer à ces utiles et pénibles fonctions? Non, parce-qu'elles seraient obligées d'y sacrifier des soins plus importantes auxquelles la nature les appelle. Les fonctions privées auxquelles sont destinées les femmes par la nature même tiennent à l'ordre de la société; cet ordre social résulte de la différence qu'il y a entre l'homme et la femme.

   Le Moniteur Universel, 31 October 1793 (10 brumaire an II), no. 40, reporting on the session of the National Convention of 9 brumaire (30 October 1793).

32. Now the Place du Caroussel, this had been the site of the guillotine between 21 August 1792 and 3 May 1793.

33. 'J'ai frappé comme cela s'est trouvé. C'est un hasard …'

34. 'Je n'estimais jamais la vie que par l'utilité dont elle devrait être.'

STAGING SACRIFICE
MUNCH, PICASSO, AND *MARAT*

Slumped in a bath that has become his tomb, Marat's last breath has just crossed his lips, yet that sharply cross-lit face transmits to us still 'une âme voltige'.[1] Between David's iconic masterwork and the awestruck viewer lies a veritable force field of emotions and imaginative transactions that this chapter seeks to explore. It does so at one remove by examining a sequence of images created by Munch and Picasso, each of whom returned more than once to the scene of Marat's murder. Their variants diverge in key respects from his, yet David's *Marat* stands as the source of an obsession whose nature and causes we shall try to uncover. At risk of preempting my conclusions, it will be proposed that David's sacralising image of the dying Marat invites a play of identifications in which is inaugurated a distinctly modern conception of the artist as a sacrificial figure. We shall venture to locate the origin of this persistent and durable modernist topos in the *Marat* itself.

The Freudian notion of phantasy supplies a theoretical model that is helpful in understanding what is at stake in an artist, Munch or Picasso, wanting to create a whole sequence of variant images on a single theme. 'Phantasies', write Jean Laplanche and J.-B. Pontalis, 'are still scripts *(scenarios)* of organised scenes which are capable of dramatisation – usually in a visual form'.[2] Narration, visualisation, and dramatisation are hence the defining properties of phantasies, whose function essentially is to provide a stage for the mise-en-scène of unconscious desire. It is also important for my purposes to note that phantasies are 'a *sequence* in which the subject has his own part to play and in which permutations of roles and attributions are possible'.[3] Typically, a phantasy is organised in such a way as to permit the subject more than one possible entry point into it; moreover, as the works to be discussed will demonstrate, it is possible, at one and the same time, to be both onlooker and participant in the phantasmatic scene.

An inherent theatricality meant that the actual event of Marat's death was amenable to phantasmatic elaboration in precisely the manner outlined. Marie-Hélène Huet argues persuasively that his assassination was constituted as theatre even before it had taken place.[4] An arch political demagogue who skilfully played to the instincts of the masses, Marat was constantly rehearsing the role of martyr. It is sufficient to recall an occasion in the Convention when he taunted his adversaries with a cry of 'Égorgez-moi!' No sooner had Corday obliged by carrying out this deed than a stream of theatrical productions began that has continued almost uninterrupted down to the present day. Any one of these could have acted as a spur for Munch or Picasso, who were both intimately involved with the theatre, and, as we shall see, their pictorial renditions of the event incorporate a number of overtly dramatic devices.[5] Indeed, the very factor of repetition involved in making a sequence of images could be construed as an attempt to emulate the temporality of a play with its usual division into separate acts or scenes. Repeated treatment of the same motif undoubtably also opens the way for an artist to indulge a variety of 'permutations of roles and attributions', as in phantasy.

As a sort of *locus classicus* before which anyone who aspires to represent the subject must first of all genuflect, we can ascribe to David's *Marat* the status of primal phantasy, or primal scene. Freud designated by these terms a restricted number of archetypal phantasies that seemed to crop up with great regularity in the course of psychoanalytic treatment, the prototype being the scene of parental coitus reconstructed from a dream reported by his patient the Wolf-Man. Laplanche and Pontalis state that primal phantasies are akin to myths inasfar as they all stage origins of one sort or another: in the case of the Wolf-Man they claim it is the subject's own origin that is represented to him.[6] As a consequence of the censorship whose function it is to prevent unacceptable ideas from entering consciousness, the primal scene was heavily disguised in the dream actually experienced by the Wolf-Man. The 'perfect stillness and immobility' that was such a conspicuous feature of the dream Freud explains as a reversal of the frenetic activity he presumes was observed by the infant.[7] Likewise, the 'strained attention' with which the wolves in the dream all look at the dreamer is, according to Freud, a turning about of the original situation in which he awoke suddenly, 'and saw in front of him a scene of violent movement at which he looked with strained attention'.[8] Marat's death is reworked and transformed by David in a quite similar fashion; an eerie stillness is present where moments before there had been unbridled violence. Following the analogy with the primal scene, an ambiguous blurring of positions between the spectator and the person being viewed – their propensity to exchange places – might also explain the uncanny intensity with which Marat, though dead, apparently beseeches the spectator.[9] Arrested in the split-second transition from a living, expressive face to the impassivity of a death mask, Marat looks at us with 'strained attention', the opacity of his gaze akin to that of a dreamer or somnambulist.

Of course, the death of Marat was no mere phantasy idly dreamt up by David. We do, however, need to bear in mind that the event itself was not directly witnessed by him, and thus it is not surprising to find that its representation is heavily conditioned by phantasy, since it had to be essentially imagined. Insinuating that Corday's assault on the naked and defenceless Marat is, at the level of the unconscious, no different to a scene of sexual intercourse is not as bizarre at it at first appears. Freud reminds us that the young child lacks either the requisite know-how or the experience to understand the sexual act and therefore interprets what it has by chance observed along the lines of its own sadistic phantasies. Apparently, even some of Marat's contemporaries were not oblivious to an erotic undertow in Marat's and Corday's lethal entanglement, though it is in the half dozen or more works by Munch on the theme that this symbolic equivalence is found spelt out unequivocally.

A 'DRAME INTERIEURE'

Death of Marat 1 of 1907 (Fig. 29) is the most elaborate work from a quite extensive body of images produced by Munch between 1906 and 1908 exploring permutations on the same basic theme of an alluring woman and her victim, who is invariably male.[10] Coinciding with a period of intense work for Max Reinhardt's theatre in Berlin, including the production of designs for Ibsen's *Hedda Gabler*, the setting for these cameos is a claustrophobic domestic interior covered with a sickly lime green wallpaper. Transferring Marat from his bath to a bed seems calculated to induce a disconcerting ambiguity in the mind of the spectator. Is this a murder as the plentiful blood and the body laid out like a corpse in a mortuary would indicate, or is it a scene of lovemaking as the nakedness of the two figures implies? Munch, as theatrical director, relishes our confusion on that score. However, he leaves us in no doubt as to the identity of the actors themselves: the character of Marat is played by the moustached artist and Corday resembles Tulla Larsen, his fiancée at the time of an incident in 1902 that lies at the origin of this sequence of works. In the course of a stormy argument, Munch fired a gunshot causing an injury to a finger on his left hand, which bled profusely and had to be operated upon. Munch grafts the death of Marat onto this autobiographic event before representing it in his painting, but the resultant transmutation from life into art distorts it to no lesser degree than the operations of the dreamwork previously described. Larsen, a bystander at an accidental injury that was in reality self-inflicted, is branded the perpetrator, or at least the root cause of his predicament. And, as a further consequence, the bowl of fruit she was offering him when the violence erupted becomes, like the letter in David's picture, a symbol of her treachery.

It helps to explain Munch's attraction to the Marat theme when one realises that it made possible the convergence of several thematic currents that had hitherto been kept separate in his work. Male submission to the superior power of woman had been something of a leitmotif to date. In this respect, the disposition of the two protagonists is significant, with the female occupying centre stage, having stolen the limelight that David trained on his hero, while the male is relegated to the shadowy wings. He lies supine and is to all intents and purposes emasculated, whereas the triumphant Corday is bolt upright, having become the phallus that he conspicuously lacks. On these grounds, the death of Marat can be assimilated with any number of staple themes in art and literature of the late nineteenth century involving the destruction of men by alluring women – Judith, Salomé, Delilah, and so forth – whose ubiquity has been seen as betraying anxieties about masculinity in an era that began to see traditional male privileges eroded.[11] Munch's own pride was reportedly wounded by rumours that he had sponged off Tulla Larsen, who was wealthier and from a more elevated social background than him. Personal experience might well have brought home to him the widespread perception of a patriarchal system in decline. The notion that masculine identity was threatened by a redefinition of gender relations could also have a bearing on the specific valence of blood in *The Death of Marat 1*. The blood-soaked sheets are placed immediately adjacent to the woman, whose hands we see are contaminated by blood and, as though Munch's abhorrence were uncontainable, the whole lower right-hand side of the canvas has been smeared a lurid crimson. Julia Kristeva writes that 'menstrual blood stands for the danger issuing from within . . . identity (social or sexual); it threatens the relationship between the sexes within a social aggregate and, through internalization, the identity of each sex in the face of sexual difference'.[12]

A second thematic strand pertinent to the death of Marat is the cycle of deathbed scenes from the 1890s based on Munch's recollections of the sickness and death of his sister. In *Death in the Sickroom* of 1893, our view of the dying person is obstructed, and the accent of the picture is upon the reactions of other family members present at 'the very moment of death'.[13] Every scenographic detail is subordinated to that end: the tilted plane of the floor and large expanses of space between and around the figures speak eloquently of their isolation and feelings of inner desolation in the company of death. David, fascinatingly, also chose to represent the subject of his painting in that emotionally charged instant, 'à son dernièr soupir' in his words, as Marat's limp hand loosens its grasp of the ink quill that had been his lifeblood, and he utilises the vacant section in the upper half of the image, like Munch, to register a poignant sense of absence and loss.[14] Munch retains this attitude toward the physical setting as the exteriorisation of an inner psychological state in his subsequent portrayal of the death of Marat. Arne Eggum draws attention to wavy white lines running across the upper part of the image that envelop the scene in a sort of atmospheric fog. Other details of the picture, most notably the ghostly Corday who stands before us sentrylike, are also inconsistent with a naturalistic reading of the scene and must be under-

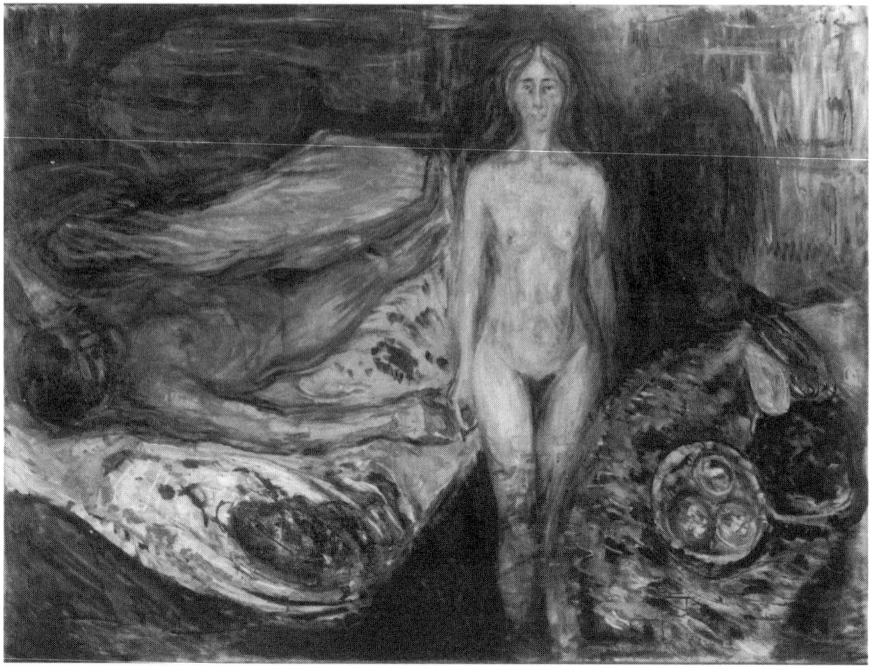

Figure 29. Edvard Munch, *Death of Marat I,* 1907, oil on canvas, 150 × 200 cm. Munch-museet, Oslo. (Photo: Munch-museet, Oslo/Svein Anderson and Sidsel de Jong.)

stood as figments of the artist's imagination in a drama played out on the stage of psychical reality.

With his arms flung out to either side, the male figure (Munch–Marat) takes up a crucifixion pose. Munch had previously depicted himself on a cross jeered at by an uncomprehending public in *Golgotha,* painted in 1900 while he was taking refuge in Kornhaug sanatorium. Such an affectation has obvious precedents in the fin de siècle visual culture: Gauguin took on board a Christ-like persona to publicise his plight as an outsider and scapegoat in such works as *Self-Portrait in Gethsemane* of 1889.[15] In the case of Marat, however, the Christ association might have been inspired directly by David, who sanctifies his hero by adapting the iconographic formula of a Deposition. A second version of the composition exhibited by Munch at the Salon des Indépendents in 1908 incorporates the drooping posture of the right arm from David, the aspect of his

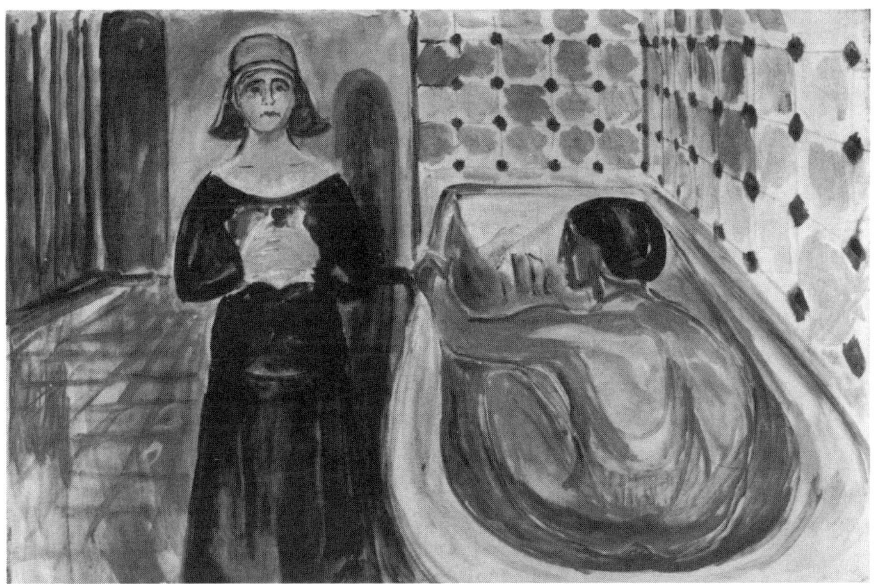

Figure 30. Edvard Munch, *Marat and Charlotte Corday,* 1932/35, oil on canvas, 80 × 120 cm. Munch-museet, Oslo. (Photo: Munch-museet/Svein Anderson and Sidsel de Jong.)

Marat that, along with the chest wound, most explicitly recalls a pietà. In his analysis of the Wolf-Man case, Freud describes how an identification with Christ enabled his patient to give vent to a masochistic wish that had also been expressed in the primal scene itself. Arguing that the Wolf-Man identified in phantasy with the passive, notionally feminine or masochistic, position in the originally witnessed scene of coitus, Freud writes that later on: 'His knowledge of the sacred story now gave him a chance of sublimating his predominant masochistic attitude towards his father. He became Christ – which was made especially easy for him on account of their having the same birthday.'[16] Plainly, Marat's death, like that of Christ with which it came to be compared, was ideally suited for the expression of such an attitude. It certainly seems to have been a key factor in its appeal to Munch, for it enabled him to represent the male artist, himself, as a sacrificial victim – at once hysterical, abased, masochistic.[17] Part of the interest of the Marat sequence for us resides in the fact that it exposes a causal link between the adoption of such a posture by fin de siècle artists and a problematic of the relationship between the sexes at this specific historical juncture.

Munch reiterates a number of the motifs discussed in connection with the death of Marat, particularly the sacrificial connotations, in an unpublished text of the same date that concerns a fictional – one might as well say, phantasised – visit to a slaughterhouse where the artist is witness to the butchering of an ox.[18] Before being led along a corridor to the room where it will be killed, the butcher embraces the beast with his arms around its neck and speaks to it like a duplicitous lover as 'Mon chéri'. The scene is evoked of a compliant and unsuspecting victim, Munch possibly, going innocently to the slaughter at the hands of a seductress. The story unfolds with a ritual solemnity: the ox is stunned and falls to the ground, then a knife is plunged deep into its heart and 'a sea of thick blood gushes out – the butcher places a glass beneath this red jet and fills it'.[19] As the narrative flows, so does the torrent of blood. One is reminded of the cult of Mithras in which devotees of the god would stand in a pit beneath the sacrificial bull so that its blood would spurt over them. Munch's account ends with the flayed carcass hung against a wall 'like the celebrated painting by Rembrandt' forming, one imagines, a sort of upside-down crucifix.

The Marat theme continued to exercise Munch's artistic imagination.[20] When the aged artist confronted his own mortality in an oil-painted version (Fig. 30) of 1932–5, he identified once again with the naked figure of Marat in a bath, which is now plainly also a tomb. To that fairly predictable association, he adds another, more surprising one: Munch encourages the viewer to read the rounded body of Marat with updrawn legs as a foetus bathed in amniotic fluid, his arm reached out like an umbilical cord toward the Woman who once more is split into a nurturing mother and an avenging destroyer concealing a dagger beneath her piously clasped hands.[21] The tomb–womb analogy conflates the end of life with its beginnings, death and the event of childbirth. If David's *Marat* can be said to licence the first of these associations through its deployment of a Christian iconography of the entombment, to what exent does it also permit the second? A serene expression replaces the ugly rictus of the dying man's face, and the skin blemishes that disfigured Marat in real life are nowhere visible. Bloodied drapes and instruments would not be out of place in a scene of childbirth, nor a baby in swaddling whose eyes are yet to awaken.[22] Marat may be dead, but it seems that David has not ruled out his future rebirth or resurrection.

CUT WITH A KITCHEN KNIFE

The first of Picasso's images to deal with the Marat theme is a small-scale painting of 25 December 1931 (Fig. 31), in which Marat squirms like an insect impaled on the end of a needle-thin stiletto. A copious stream of bright red blood issues from the wound to his chest. The attacker is a terrifying surreal monster whose powerful body arches over the diminutive Marat. Picasso had tried out this composition in an earlier drypoint etching of Orpheus, a conventional surrogate for the artist or poet, shown being torn apart by Maenads (Fig. 32). This visual link suggests that the victim in the later image might equally be a figure with whom the artist identifies. Another precursor work that reinforces this constellation of meanings is the celebrated *Crucifixion* of February 1930. Of roughly identical size to *Woman with a Stiletto,* it is executed in a comparable idiom consisting of crudely drawn outlines and searing expressionist colours, and it shares in the appetite for unremitting cruelty. The Magdalen who stands before Christ menacingly gnashing her teeth simply reappears as the devouring assassin in the later image. By the same token, one can readily imagine that the suffering Christ with the centurion's spear piercing his side has a filial connection with the dying Marat (in light of Freud's remark about birthdays, the precise dating of *Woman with a Stiletto* to 25 December is intriguing).

Ruth Kaufmann argued presciently in an article published in 1969, well before the current vogue in Anglo-American scholarship for the ethnographic surrealism of Georges Bataille, that Picasso's unorthodox treatment of the crucifixion as a primitive ritual accords with the intellectual agenda of Bataille's group.[23] She further established that a manuscript illustration from an article on the St. Sever Apocalypse that appeared in *Documents,* the journal edited by Bataille, served as a visual source for the crumpled bodies of the thieves in the foreground of the *Crucifixion.* For the Marat image it

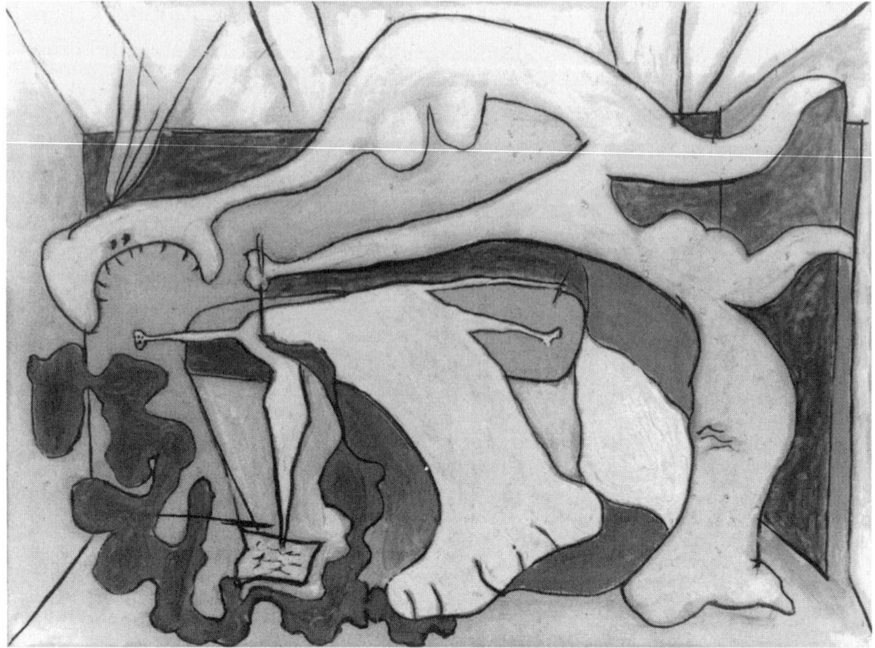

Figure 31. Pablo Picasso, *Woman with a Stiletto, Death of Marat*, 25 December 1931, oil on canvas, 46 × 61 cm. Musée Picasso, Paris. (Photo: Réunion des musées nationaux – Picasso.)

seems likely that a Hispanic manuscript illustration of an Aztec human sacrifice (Fig. 33), also reproduced in *Documents,* was employed by Picasso. The event it records is a gruesome one in which a sharpened stone was used to hack open the victim's chest and remove the heart still pulsating with blood. An accompanying article by Roger Hervé, an ethnologist, states that the Aztecs believed this bloodletting could nourish the gods in a sort of divine cannibalism. Picasso, preserving the maladroit style and even the colouring of the original, merely substitutes the high priest with Corday, who hovers above the victim, Marat, stretched across a bath-cum-sacrificial altar. While Picasso may not have been aware that Marat's heart was removed from his body after death and interred separately, in an attenuated echo of the primitive ritual, he quite probably was acquainted with a tradition that likened Marat, *l'ami du peuple,* to Jesus of the sacred heart.[24] In a scene of high melodrama from a play by Romain Rolland, for example, as news

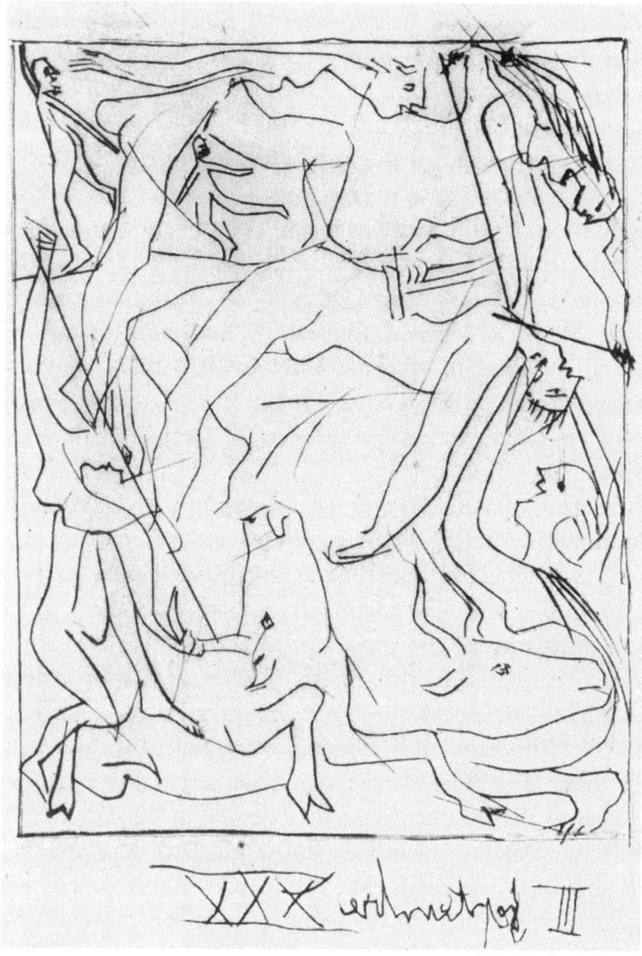

Figure 32. Pablo Picasso, *Death of Orpheus,* 3 September 1930, drypoint, 22.5 × 17.1 cm, unpublished figure for an edition of Ovid's *Metamorphoses.* Musée Picasso, Paris. (Photo: Réunion des musées nationaux – Picasso.)

of Marat's death reaches people in the street outside, a spontaneous chorus is heard: 'Ô coeur sanglant! Coeur sacré de Marat!'[25] Those hackneyed but nonetheless heartfelt words – bleeding heart, sacred heart – tap into a vein that draws together two remote cultures, exactly as Picasso does.

The unique flavour of *Documents* as a journal of the avant-garde owed much to the involvement on its editorial board and in the articles that appeared in its pages of professional ethnologists, as well as the more usual run of writers and artists.[26] One of the spin-offs of this rapprochement of ethnology and the avant-garde is seen in attempts by Bataille to reformulate contemporary artistic practice in terms of a notion of the sacred. Picasso was crucial to this project, and a special issue of *Documents* was devoted to his work in March 1930. At the heart of Bataille's conception of the sacred is the institution of sacrifice, his understanding of which derives in considerable measure from a study by the Durkheimian sociologists Marcel Mauss and Henri Hubert.[27] These authors claim that the essential meaning of sacrifice is revealed in those myths and religions where the god on whose behalf the sacrifice is performed, or one of his avatars, dies. The essence of sacrifice is therefore a *self-sacrifice*.[28]

The first of Bataille's numerous writings on sacrifice was concerned with Aztec human sacrifices, a form of theatre, Bataille insists, in which the audience avidly observes the macabre event and identifies with the victim. By means of a theatrical mimesis, whose similarity to the model of phantasy outlined earlier will be obvious, the sacrificial ritual enables us to see our own death represented to us. Bataille writes: 'It is a matter . . . of identifying with a character who dies, and believing ourselves to die whereas in fact we remain alive.' This theorising about sacrifice is extended to the situation of the modern artist in an essay on Van Gogh, whose self-mutilation Bataille regards as the equivalent of a sacrificial act.[29] The sovereign impulse that drove Van Gogh to cut off an ear Bataille sees reflected in his painting – in the motif of the radiant sun, for instance – which in much the same manner as the illustration of an Aztec sacrifice mediates for us the act that precedes it and, crucially for Bataille, is a guarantee of its total authenticity. One might suspect that a similar conviction and quest for authenticity lay behind Munch's repeated allusions to the self-inflicted injury to his hand.[30] Whether Munch consciously exploited the parallel with Van Gogh one can only guess, but it is significant that the incident is referred to at a time when he had begun using raw, impasto colour with renewed vehemence. This stylistic innovation, well exemplified in the *Death of Marat II,* is oftentimes attributed to the influence of Fauvist painting, but it might also have entailed Munch looking afresh at Van Gogh, who had certainly been a major source of inspiration in the past.

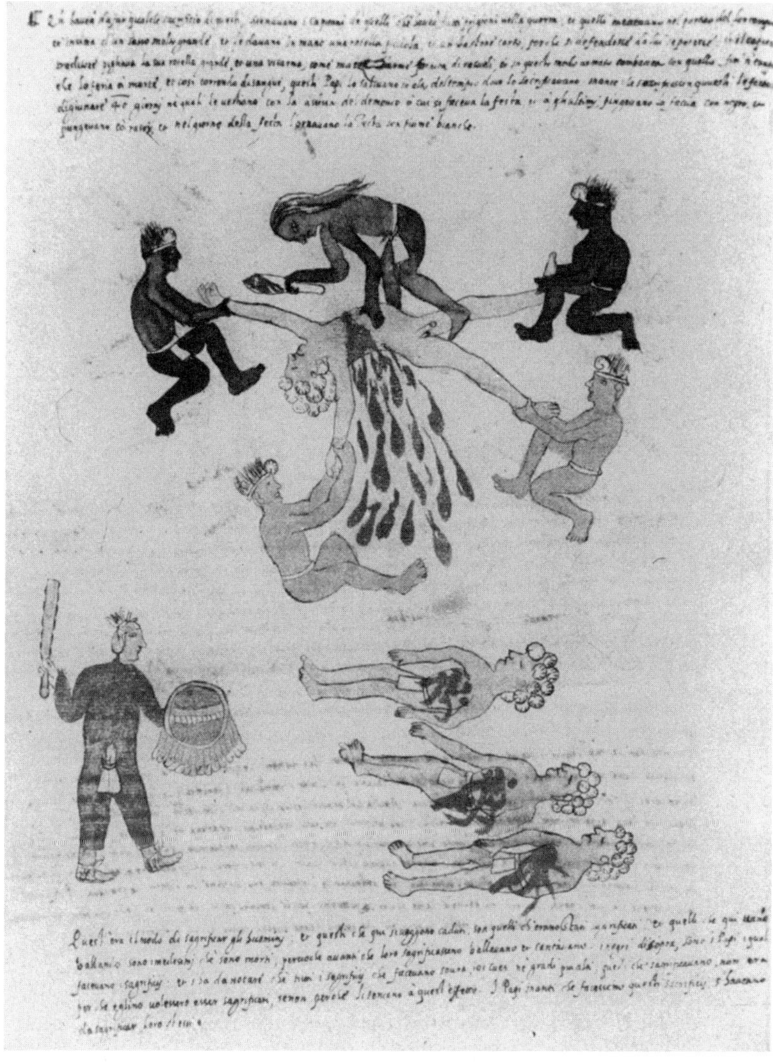

Figure 33. Aztec Human Sacrifice. Codex Vaticanus 3738. In *Documents,* no. 4 (1930): 207.

Bataille's essay might well have struck a chord with Picasso, who long before this had invoked the death of Van Gogh in order to portray the suicide of his friend, the poet Carlos Casagemas, as a martyrdom to art. When Picasso once again takes up the death of Marat theme in July and August of 1934, he stages it in a way that is

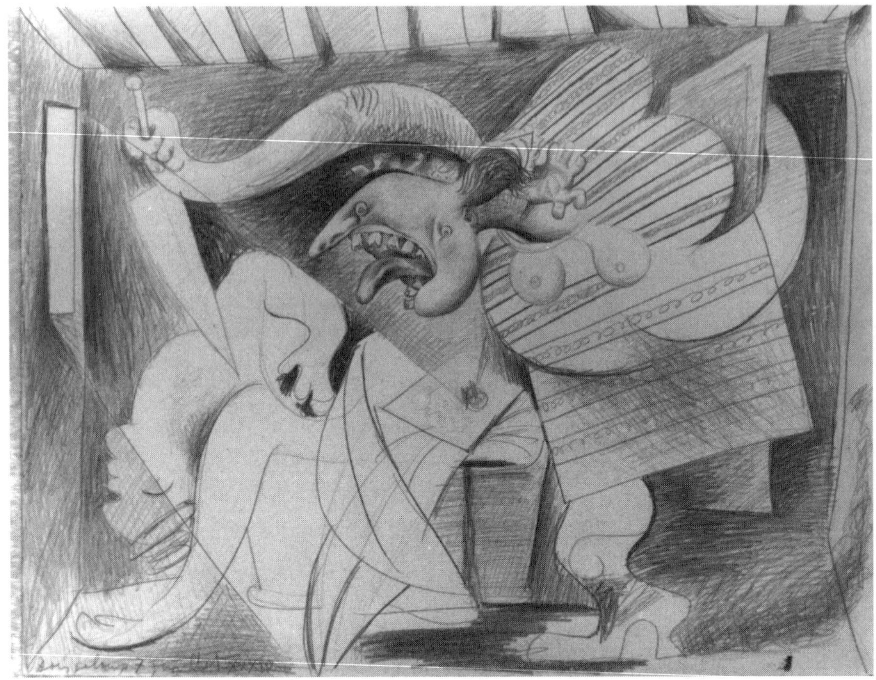

Figure 34. Pablo Picasso, *Composition (Death of Marat)*, 7 July 1934, pencil, 39.8 × 50.4 cm, Zervos VII, 216. (Photo: Réunion des musées nationaux – Picasso.)

consistent with Bataille's ideas about sacrifice. In a pencil drawing of 7 July 1934 (Fig. 34), he pointedly eschews the classical restraint and decorum of David. Corday, her mouth wide open to emit a shriek, bursts through an opened door and holds a generously large dagger at the throat of Marat, who lies recumbent in a bathtub with his head wrapped up in a turban.[31] Feverish pencil hatching adds to the feeling of intense agitation. As with Munch, the drama unfolds in a simple box-shaped room, lending an air of theatrical melodrama to the drawing. Lydia Gasman has observed that the figure of Corday poised on one foot strikes a ballet pose, which is perhaps also true of the graceful abandon of Marat himself, further enhancing the impression of a staged performance.[32] Comparison with Brassaï's photographs of the studio that Picasso occupied at Boisgeloup shows, moreover, that he has incorporated its distinctive wooden beams (the artist in the studio and associated activities of

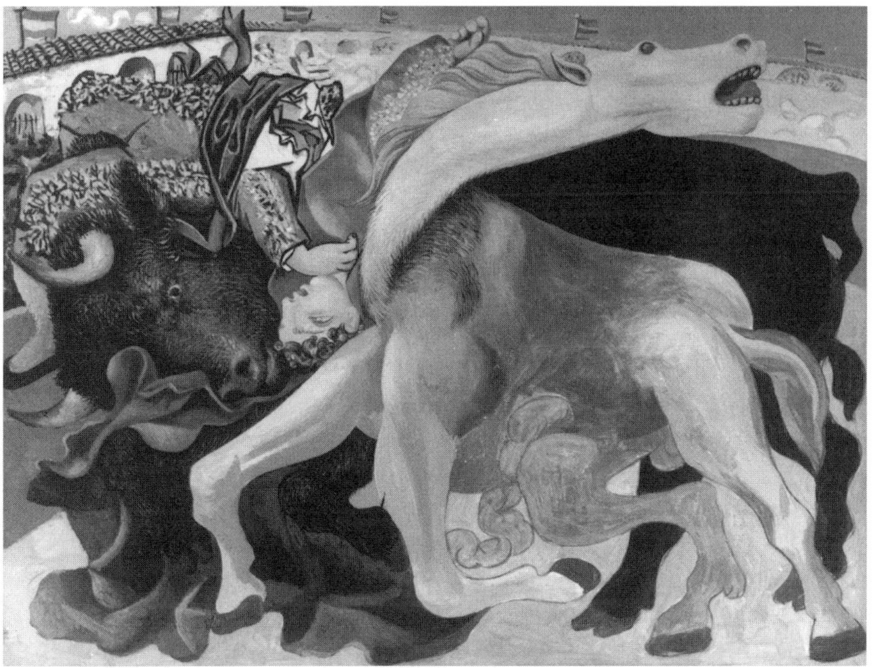

Figure 35. Pablo Picasso, *Bullfight: Death of the Torero,* 19 September 1933, oil on wood, 31 × 40 cm. Musée Picasso, Paris. (Photo: Réunion des musées nationaux − Picasso.)

art making comprise an important thematic grouping in the *Vollard Suite* of etchings, which overlap work on the death of Marat). It is germane to a reading in terms of artistic (self-)sacrifice that Picasso relocates Marat's death to a setting that, inasfar as it can be identified as the artist's studio, is marked out as the space par excellence of mimesis and representation.

That Picasso was fully cognisant of Bataille's views on sacrifice can be gauged from his parallel treatment of the bullfight. The gored matador in *Bullfight: Death of the Torero* of 1933 (Fig. 35) is arched across the horns of a bull that plays the role of altar, his flowing red cape a visual echo of gushing blood in the Aztec ritual (it is worthwhile recalling in this context that in 1932 Picasso was dubbed 'the toreador of painting' in an essay by his friend Gomez de la Serna). The supine pose of the matador is quite similar to that of Marat, who, in the later drawing, is trampled underfoot by a rampaging Corday whose bovine features – her whole misshapen head is like the jawbone of an ox – make her the natural counterpart of the bull. A more overtly sadistic eroticism surfaces in Picasso's bullfight imagery when the horse is shown being gored or disemboweled by a bull.[33] Once again this is analogous to the Marat drawing, since the extruded tongue of the assailant directed toward an area of shading on the body of her victim rather implies a reading of the scene as a sexual violation.

It emerges from Bataille's readings of specific artworks that sacrifice on the part of the artistic subject is generally conveyed by a thematics of castration.[34] In an extended analysis of *The Lugubrious Game,* Salvador Dalí's controversial reception piece among the Paris surrealists, Bataille discerned in the flagrant sexual imagery of the work 'the genesis of emasculation and the contradictory reactions it carries'.[35] Of Dalí, the male figure in the foreground whose shit-smeared pants disconcerted even his surrealist comrades, Bataille makes an observation that holds true for many a modern artist, asserting that 'a new and real virility is rediscovered by this person in ignominy and horror themselves'.[36] Munch, it was noted, depicts himself in *The Death of Marat I* as a sexless eunuch deprived of male genitalia. Picasso's earliest version of the subject alludes to castration by the fact that Marat's head is nearly encircled by Corday's mouth – she is about to decapitate him much as the female praying mantis does with her unlucky mate prior to copulating, a source of endless curiosity for the surrealists. And surely the same holds true for the dagger that hangs fatefully over the retracted, elongated neck of Marat in the July 1934 image, startlingly reminiscent of Alberto Giacometti's sculpture *Woman with Cut Throat* of 1932. Ensuing images of the minotaur amplify the castration theme and confer upon it a universal, tragic dimension. The Oedipal myth is explicitly invoked in a plate from Picasso's *Vollard Suite* (Fig. 36), in which the minotaur is depicted blinded and vulnerable, like Oedipus at Colonus. By accentuating its humanity, Picasso invites us to believe that the minotaur is a personification of himself, and he links it with the Marat theme by adding it to a plate that had upon it a drypoint etching of the *Death of Marat* (seen upside down at the left of the illustration).

The depiction of Corday as a castrating fury, while not without precedent in Picasso's work, may owe something to an article on

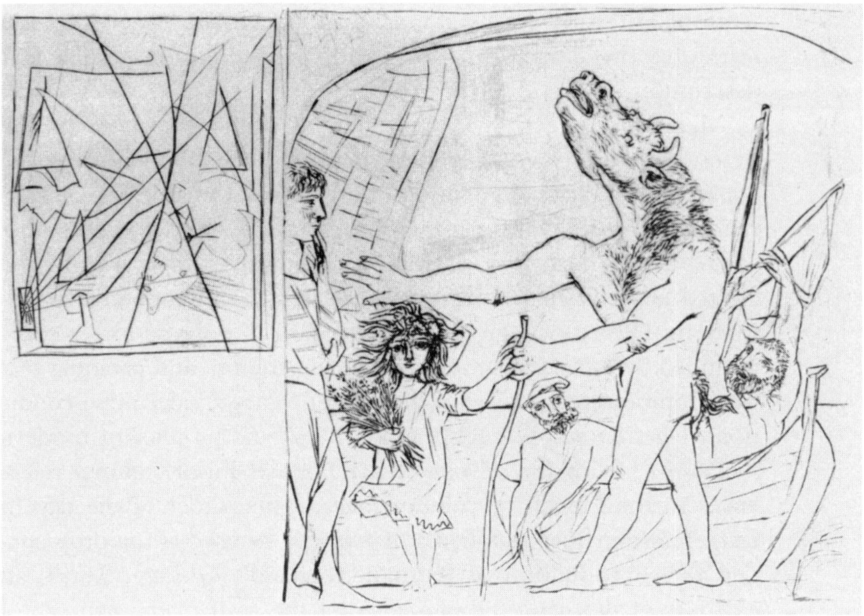

Figure 36. Pablo Picasso, *Vollard Suite (Blind Minotaur with Death of Marat),* 22 September 1934, etching with drypoint, 25.2 × 34.8 cm. Musée Picasso, Paris. (Photo: Réunion des musées nationaux – Picasso.)

the Papin sisters, Léa and Christine, which appeared some months earlier in the periodical *Minotaure.*[37] The author, Jacques Lacan, recounts in grisly detail how the sisters, whose recent trial for murder had held the French nation spellbound, erupted in a terrible orgy of violence one evening as the mother and daughter of a family in which they were employed as maidservants returned home. Without any warning or provocation, the normally meek, introverted sisters seized the two women, forming an 'atrocious quadrille', whereupon they savagely tore out their eyes like 'castrating Bacchantes', slit the victims' throats with a kitchen knife, and mutilated the bodies with bare hands. This frenzied outburst having run its course, they washed themselves and coolly returned to bed. Lacan, who had made a doctoral study of a similar case in which a young woman carried out a motiveless knife attack on an actress, diagnosed the pair as suffering from paranoïa. It may be that Picasso thought there were grounds for regarding Corday's crime as the work of a similarly deranged individual; at any rate, his composition reiterates the castration motif and other elements of Lacan's description.[38]

Marat's resurrection in the charged political climate of the 1930s, an event David may have foretold, is another factor to be considered in Picasso's adoption of the theme. On the sixth of February 1934, right-wing demonstrators had beseiged the Chamber of Deputies. The Left was fearful of a conspiracy to overthrow the elected government and reacted with strikes and counter-demonstrations. There was a growing polarisation of political forces compounded by a general atmosphere of uncertainty and paranoia that was propitious to a revival of the cult of Marat. Under these conditions, *l'ami du peuple* is reborn as a Messianic prophet of modern socialism.[39] With the advent of the Popular Front, cultural references to the French Revolution became the order of the day. In fact, Picasso in 1936 supplied a drawing to be used as the drop curtain for a production of Romain Rolland's *Quatorze Juillet,* an example of the genre he pioneered at the turn of the century of popular revolutionary drama in which Marat makes an entry in the climactic final moments.

A decision to represent the death of Marat at this time was, hence, inescapably a political one. In the early 1930s, Fernand Léger devised a theatrical scenario that he repeatedly tried to have staged during that decade. Called *La Mort de Marat, suivi de sa Pompe funèbre,* it was intended as an homage to Marat and in emulation of David, who had been responsible for choreographing Marat's funeral procession.[40] With fascism an ever-growing threat, artistic stances predicated on the unfettered pursuit of formal experiment within the laboratory space of the studio, as Picasso's had been, were now vehemently denounced. Everywhere, artists were being exhorted to abandon the ivory tower and rally to the socialist cause. In an address to the Institute for the Study of Fascism in Paris on 27 April 1934 the speaker, Walter Benjamin, reminds his audience that Plato had banished poets from his model state before insisting: 'The question of the poet's right to exist has not often, since then, been posed with the same emphasis; but today it poses itself.'[41] Far from being impervious to these reproaches, Picasso, because of his fame, was likely more vulnerable to them. The crisis of identity this provoked may have been a factor that caused him to cease painting during the following year, 1935, and the conflict between what he perceived as the formal imperatives of his art and the growing calls for an *art engagé* persists without resolution up until *Guernica*.[42] Though the whole series of works on the theme of the death of Marat are basically private, inasfar as they remained in the artist's personal collection, they can best be understood as part of an ongoing renegotiation of his relation to the realm of political action. By identifying himself with Marat in 1934, Picasso artfully stages his demise in the guise of an unassailable hero of the Left.

Just as Munch revisited Marat and Corday in old age, so too does Picasso as the coproducer of a short film titled *The Death of Charlotte Corday* in 1950.[43] Comprising a neatly symmetrical counterpart to his earlier treatment of the death of Marat, it also lays to rest a demon that had haunted him since the 1920s.

A MARAT, DAVID

A basic contention of this chapter is that Munch and Picasso elicit a phantasmatic structure that is latent within David's *Marat*. They read or interpret the picture for us, and stand in the same relation to it as Freud when he reconstructs post facto the phantasy that subtends the Wolf-Man's famous dream. Now, it might be objected that these artists simply exploit the death of Marat as a convenient vehicle for articulating neuroses that properly belong to a later era, and it is unfair, or worse anachronistic, to foist these onto David. Underlying the criticism is the belief that one can isolate in the *Marat* an uncorrupted, original meaning that is fully present in it. Psychoanalysis denies this very possibility. In fact, the concept of deferred action *(Nachträglichkeit)* first adumbrated by Freud in his account of the Wolf-Man's primal scene implies that signification is always assigned to an event retroactively through repetition or reworking. A further possible objection to our approach lies in the application of psychoanalysis to an artwork whose mode of address is so emphatically public: commissioned to hang in the Convention, it was meant to proclaim to all citizens of the Republic Marat's unselfish dedication to civic duty. But could we not regard it as a virtue of the psychoanalytic method as a tool for cultural analysis that it disregards any categorical separation between public and private realms? Cannot phantasies be operative on the level of collectively held attitudes, beliefs, and ideologies just as much as individual ones? And are not the displacements and disguises that an unconscious wish must undergo in order to be represented in a dream, or a work of art, justifiably compared by Freud to the censorship that political regimes impose on ideas they find unacceptable?

With that analogy in mind, it is reasonable to ask why David chose not to include Corday, unlike Munch and Picasso, when to have done so would obviously have been more fully informative with regard to the circumstances of his death. His motives were doubtless several, that is to say, overdetermined. First, David envisaged the picture as a pendant to his earlier portrait of Le Peletier, which presents its subject, an assassinated revolutionary like Marat, in dignified repose on his deathbed. Second, any excessive violence would have been incompatible with the stern, classical idiom clearly favoured by David. But one might suspect that her omission sprang from other sources as well. It has been seen that depicting Marat with Corday forces the viewer to confront a transgressive inversion of conventional masculine and feminine positions. All the horror provoked by the overturning of an order allegedly inscribed in nature is concentrated by the artists we have studied in the demoniacal figure of Corday.[44] It has plausibly been claimed that fears about the consequences of female empowerment after the Revolution played a part in the vilification of Corday during her trial and were a factor in the swift retribution meted out to her. Might it not also have dictated her exclusion from David's picture? Bearing in mind the range of associations of blood in Munch's image, however, one might speculate that a residual trace of these fears lies behind what one commentator refers to as 'le scandale du sang'[45] — the sea of blood glimpsed in the space between Marat's thorax and the edge of his writing board, also sullying the white sheet in front. Julia Kristeva, citing the work of anthropologist Mary Douglas, states that the system of taboos surrounding menstrual blood can be considered not only in terms of a loathing of impurity and defilement but also in terms of a positive 'power of pollution', and that such taboos may actually reflect displaced anxieties about women's power elsewhere in society: 'The power of pollution . . . thus transposes, on the symbolic level, the permanent conflict resulting from an unsettled separation between masculine and feminine power at the level of social institutions'.[46]

Women were firmly linked with blood in Marat's funeral procession: they paraded his bloodstained tunic like a relic of Christ's Passion, and 'in a symbolic gesture collected the blood which seemed to flow from it'.[47] If we allow for a symbolic connection with the feminine, then it is evident from the very abundance of blood in David's *Marat* that the spectre of the active, empowered woman and the fright she aroused could not be completely erased.

Without the physical presence of Corday one is free to imagine Marat as the agent of his own death, a reading that is fostered by the close proximity of the pen and dagger at the bottom of the picture. A *fait-divers,* the politically inspired murder that has become a virtual commonplace in our day, is thereby invested with the aura and tragic necessity of a sacrificial act. When the sacralisation of Marat actually begins is a matter of some dispute among scholars; nevertheless, the fully intentional association between the dead Marat and the Deposition of Christ inevitably reinforces the meaning of his death as sacrifice.[48] Amid the general suspicion of father figures after the toppling of the king, perhaps this portrayal was the only acceptable way heroic masculinity could be affirmed, in the form of the son's acquiescence in his own martyrdom.[49] In each of our case studies, self-sacrifice on the part of the artistic subject was consequent upon an identification with the dead Marat and the willed adoption of the pose of abased victim or martyr. Can we not also infer such an imaginary transaction in the careful juxtaposition of names — A MARAT, DAVID — inscribed on the wooden box at the foreground of David's picture? Fondness for the idealised subject of his painting shades imperceptibly into a desire to be like the dead man, to be one with him.[50] And, by extension, the metonymic chain linking the pen still grasped by Marat's hand to the nearby dagger, the instrument of his passion, also encompasses the brush held by the hand of the artist, David himself, but also more than a century later, Munch and Picasso.[51]

NOTES

1. Charles Baudelaire, *Curiosités esthétiques. L'Art romantique et autres oeuvres critiques,* ed. Henri Lemaire (Paris: Editions Garnier Frères, 1962), 89.
2. Jean Laplanche and J.-B. Pontalis, *The Language of Psychoanalysis* (London: Karmac and the Institute of Psychoanalysis, 1988), 318.
3. Ibid.
4. Marie-Hélène Huet, *Rehearsing the Revolution: The Staging of Marat's Death, 1793–1797,* trans. Robert Hurley (Berkeley: University of California Press, 1982).
5. A major cinematic *évènement* of the 1920s to mention in connection

with Picasso's attraction to the Marat theme is Abel Gance's epic film *Napoleon,* in which the surrealist Antonin Artaud plays a decidedly deranged-looking Marat.

6. Jean Laplanche and J.-B. Pontalis, 'Fantasy and the Origin of Sexuality', in *Formations of Fantasy,* ed. Victor Burgin, James Donald, and Cora Kaplan (London: Methuen, 1986), 5–34.

7. Sigmund Freud, 'From the History of an Infantile Neurosis' (1918), in vol. 9 of the *Pelican Freud Library* (London: Penguin, 1979), 263.

8. Ibid.

9. My point here is succinctly made in an etching by the contemporary artist Ian Hamilton Finlay, who simply reverses the inscription on the picture to read À DAVID, MARAT'.

10. The bulk of these images are reproduced in *Munch et la France* (Paris: Musée d'Orsay, 1991–2), illus. 181–3 and plates 45, 46; and in *Edvard Munch. The Frieze of Life* (London: The National Gallery Exhibition Catalogue, 1992–3), plates 77–83 and accompanying figures.

11. For a compendious survey of this topic, see Bram Dijkstra, *Idols of Perversity: Fantasies of Feminine Evil in Fin-de-Siècle Culture* (Oxford: Oxford University Press, 1986).

12. Julia Kristeva, *Powers of Horror. An Essay on Abjection,* trans. Leon S. Roudiez (New York: Columbia University Press, 1982), 71.

13. This was Munch's alternative title when the picture was first exhibited. The picture has been compared to a play by Maeterlinck, *The Intruder,* where the death actually takes place in a room next door. See Geneviève Aitken, 'Munch et la scène française', in *Munch et la France,* 226–30.

14. On the *Marat* as, essentially, a deathbed picture, see Robert Rosenblum, *Transformations in Late Eighteenth Century Art* (Princeton: Princeton University Press, 1978), 27.

15. So too does James Ensor, another artist whose work Munch regarded highly. Naturally, we must avoid assuming any conventional religious faith on the part of the artists concerned in identifying themselves with Christ.

16. Freud, 300.

17. I use the term hysterical rather than histrionic deliberately here to suggest that Munch adopted this condition – strongly associated with femininity – as a posture, much as Jan Goldstein has described for a number of nineteenth-century male writers. In Munch's account of the circumstances in which he came to injure his hand, he refers to his body in the grip of overpowering emotions, strongly reminiscent of the hysterical convulsions made famous by Charcot's patients at the Hôpital Salpêtrière during the period when Munch stayed in Paris. He writes: 'His entire body is shaking in a violent convulsion, he stares wildly at her, bends down, stretches out his arms . . .'. It is also relevant to note that a crucifix

pose was one of the typical so-called *attitudes passionelles* recorded in photographs of female hysterics. See Jan Goldstein, 'The Uses of Male Hysteria: Medical and Literary Discourse in Nineteenth-Century France', *Representations* 34 (Spring 1991): 134–65.

18. In French translation in *Munch et la France,* 364.

19. A woman holding a bowl filled with blood stands in the foreground of *The Operation,* of 1902 (Munch Museet, Oslo). A strongly ritualistic and sacrificial air prevails in this autobiographical work which, as Arne Eggum points out, provided a blueprint for the entire Marat sequence. See *Munch, The Frieze of Life,* 132.

20. A photograph in the collection of the Munch Museet in Oslo taken in 1908–9 while Munch was at Dr. Jacobsen's Clinic being treated for alcoholism shows him posed 'à la Marat', apparently naked in a bath with drapes and so forth. My thanks to Jeremy Stubbs for bringing this to my attention.

21. The picture is one of several variants in the Munch Museum, all featuring the same woman in contemporary dress. See Arne Eggum, *Edvard Munch og hans modeller 1912–1943* (Oslo: Munch Museet, 1988).

22. Such a conflation is common in early modern representations of the Nativity where the Christ child, newborn in the crib, seems to prefigure the Entombment. On this question, see Barbara Lane, *The Altar and the Altarpiece, Sacramental Themes in Early Netherlandish Painting* (New York: Harper & Row, 1984). My thanks to Christa Grössinger for pointing out this association and the reference.

23. Ruth Kaufmann, 'Picasso's Crucifixion of 1930', *Burlington Magazine* III (1969): 553–61. Like Francis Bacon in his *Figures at the Base of a Crucifixion,* Picasso avoids any hint of transcendence. His realm is one that Bataille would define as 'sacred horror'. Not surprisingly, both artists were obsessed by Grünewald's Isenheim altarpiece, which they preferred to southern European idealising representations of the crucifixion.

24. See F.-P. Bowman, 'Le "Sacré-Coeur" de Marat (1793)', in *Les Fêtes de la Révolution,* ed. Jean Ehrard and Paul Viallaneix (Paris: 1977). I am grateful to Tony Halliday for this reference.

25. Romain Rolland, *Le triomphe de la raison,* act 1, scene 3. Excerpted in J.-Cl. Bonnet ed., *La Mort de Marat* (Paris: Flammarion, 1986), 462.

26. See James Clifford, 'On Ethnographic Surrealism', *Comparative Studies in Society and History* 23 (1981): 539–64.

27. Henri Hubert and Marcel Mauss, 'Essai sur la nature et la fonction du sacrifice', *L'Année sociologique* (Paris: Félix Alcan, 1898), 462, 29–138.

28. For this reason, concludes Bataille, 'Human sacrifice is loftier than any other – not in the sense that it is crueler than any other, but because it is close to the only sacrifice without trickery, which can only be the ecstatic loss of oneself'. Georges Bataille, 'The Sacred', *Cahiers d'art* (1939), in

Visions of Excess. Selected Writings, 1927–1939, ed. Allan Stoekl (Minneapolis: University of Minnesota Press, 1985), 244.

29. Georges Bataille, 'La Mutilation sacrificielle et l'oreille coupée de Van Gogh', *Documents,* no. 8 (1930): 10–20. In *Visions of Excess,* 61–72.

30. Bataille cites in connection with Van Gogh's automutilation a variety of ritualised social practises, including the ablation of a finger in early human societies, of which visual records survive in the form of outlines on cave walls. At the Munch Museet in Oslo today an X ray of the artist's injured hand is displayed in a glass cabinet ostensibly as documentary evidence, but one wonders if this relic does not also answer to a more archaic desire.

31. This 'ange de l'assassinat' is, to my mind, uncannily like political caricatures of Margaret Thatcher, suggesting there may be a repertoire of negative visual tropes for representing the powerful woman that traverse the boundaries of high art and popular consciousness.

32. Lydia Gasman, *Mystery, Magic and Love in Picasso, 1925–1938: Picasso and the Surrealist Poets* (Ann Arbor, Mich.: Garland Publications, 1981), 418f.

33. See, for comparison, a picture of very similar date to the Marat drawing, the *Bull disembowelling a Horse,* of 24 July 1934 (Zervos, VIII, 215).

34. See Carolyn Dean, 'Law and Sacrifice: Bataille, Lacan, and the Critique of the Subject', *Representations* 13 (Winter 1986): 42–62.

35. Bataille, 'Le "Jeu lugubre"', *Documents,* no. 7 (December 1929). In *Visions of Excess,* 29 (Minneapolis: University of Minnesota Press).

36. Ibid.

37. Jacques Lacan, 'Motifs du crime: le crime des soeurs Papin', *Minotaure,* no. 3–4 (December 1933): 25–8. The connection is also noted in Neil Cox, 'Marat, Sade, Picasso', *Art History* 17, no. 3 (September 1994): 383–417.

38. The two sisters were sentenced to be guillotined, as was Corday, a fate that the wedge-shaped window at the side of the room may allude to.

39. Typical of this reappraisal was the eulogy delivered by Paul Vaillant-Couturier to an audience of Parti Communiste faithful in 1936. See Vaillant-Couturier, 'Marat, l'ami du peuple', *Cahiers du bolchévisme* (25 July 1936), in *Vers des lendemains qui chantent* (Paris: Editions Sociales, 1962), 219–22. A spate of monographs on Marat in the period testifies to the level of interest in him.

40. In a sketchy outline of what he envisaged, dated 1931, Léger describes his conception of the scenario as 'classique, d'esprit davidien'. A more elaborate set of notes and drawings for costumes datable to 1934 is reproduced in *Fernand Léger et le spectacle* (Musée national Fernand Léger, Biot, 1995). My gratitude to Sophie Bowness for sharing her expertise on these matters.

41. Walter Benjamin, 'The Author as Producer', an address at the Institute for

the Study of Fascism in Paris on 27 April 1934, in *Reflections* (New York: Schocken Books, 1978), 220.

42. On this question, see Sidra Stich, 'Picasso's Art and Politics in 1936', *Arts Magazine* 58 (October 1983): 113–18.

43. Details of this venture can be found in Marie-Laure Bernadac and Gisèle Breteau-Skira, eds., *Picasso à l'écran* (Paris: Musée national de l'art moderne, Centre Georges Pompidou, 1992).

44. The challenge for Paul Baudry wishing to glorify Charlotte Corday in his portrait of her for the Salon of 1862 (Musée des beaux-Arts, Nantes) was to neutralise awareness of this transgression. This he does by portraying her as a chaste heroine and emphasising her virtuous dedication to a selfless ideal. See Jean-Claude Chimot, 'Le Marat de David et la Charlotte Corday de Baudry', Société de l'histoire de l'art français, *Archives de l'art français,* nouvelle période, t. XXV (1978), 377–9.

45. J. L. Jules David, *Le peintre Louis David (1748–1825)* (Paris: Victor Havard, 1882), 285. Others have seen this blood as evoking the 'bloodbath' of the Terror, in which Marat was deeply implicated. Of course, it is scarcely imaginable that David would deliberately have done so; we would have to treat this as an instance of failed repression. Taking cognisance of the historical context of the Terror convinces me that the notion of a traumatic primal scene has manifold implications for our reading of the *Marat.*

46. Kristeva, 78.

47. Jacques Guilhaumou, 'La Mort de Marat à Paris', in Bonnet, ed., *La Mort de Marat,* 71. See also Lynn Hunt, *The Family Romance of the French Revolution* (London: Routledge, 1992), 76.

48. Apart from the Christ association, perhaps David meant to allude to the suicide of Seneca, the Roman Stoic philosopher who died from exsanguination by having his veins cut while in a bath. The invocation of sacrifice in the aftermath of Marat's death is examined by Philippe Roger in 'L'Homme de sang: l'invention sémiotique de Marat', in Bonnet, ed., *La Mort de Marat,* 141–66.

49. What I am implying here is that a historical parallel can be drawn between the postrevolutionary period and the situation in the late nineteenth century outlined earlier in connection with Munch. The compromised status of patriarchal structures of authority in the aftermath of the French Revolution is dealt with by Lynn Hunt, *Family Romance of the French Revolution.* Concerning prerevolutionary France, see Carol Duncan, 'Fallen Fathers: Images of Authority in Pre-Revolutionary Art', *Art History* 4 (1981): 186–202.

50. According to Freud, in mourning the individual identifies at the level of his ego with the lost or abandoned object, and thus 'the shadow of the

object falls upon the ego'. Sigmund Freud, 'Mourning and Melancholia', in vol. 11 of the *Pelican Freud Library,* 258.

51. In fact, as we have seen, this chain of associations is strongly implied by Picasso in the first of his versions of the death of Marat (Fig. 31), where, in spite of the exaggerated foreshortening, the stiletto plainly echoes the writing instrument that Marat holds and is moreover similar in shape to the sort of fine paintbrush that would have been required to inscribe the narrow contours of the image.

GLOSSARY

L'Ami du Peuple. One of the titles of Marat's newspaper.

l'ami du peuple. Title assumed by and given to Marat himself.

ancien régime. Name given to the French monarchical régime before 1789.

l'an II. Year II of the new republican calendar, which started in September 1792 when the Republic was established. Years started on 21 September, contained months (renamed) of thirty days and weeks or *decadis* of ten days. Year II began on 21 September 1793.

assignats. Loan certificates issued by the government of 1789, indicating that some of the nationalised property of church and crown was assigned to the certificate-holder. In 1790 the *assignat* became a sort of paper money with a fixed (but not guaranteed) value against gold. In the summer of 1793 it was still worth about half its face value.

le bien-aimé. 'The well-loved', nickname adopted by Louis XV and retained by Louis XVI, who wished to be perceived as the restorer of liberty.

Brissotins. Followers of J. P. Brissot, deputy and leader of the Girondins in the National Assembly. Brissotins fell from power in June 1793; their leaders were imprisoned and executed in October.

Committee of Public Safety. Began as a link between the Convention and Ministers early in 1793 but evolved into a dominant group of twelve men with full executive power and responsibility for instituting the Terror.

Commune de Paris. After the storming of the Tuileries Palace on 10 August 1792 the old Municipal Assembly of Paris, which was split between moderates and radicals, was replaced by this revolutionary Commune.

Convention. Replaced the National Assembly in September 1792 with the fall of the monarchy.

Directoire/Directory. System set up to govern France from 26 October 1795 (4 brumaire, an IV).

enragé. Name given to an extremely outspoken group of journalists and politicians who articulated a violent egalitarianism during the most radical phase of the Revolution.

Girondins. Deputies, many of whom came from the Gironde, who dominated the Assembly and later the Convention until June 1793. More moderate than their radical enemies, the Montagnards, they were arrested and eventually guillotined on 31 October 1793.

Jacobin(s) Club. A revolutionary club that met in the old Jacobin convent in Paris and forged links with similar clubs all over France. Its membership reflected the growing popular intervention in political life in the years 1789–94. It ended under the control of Robespierre and his supporters in July 1794.

Montagne/Montagnards. (Mountain, men of the Mountain). Radical members of the Constituent Assembly and Legislative Assembly that followed it, so-called because they sat on the high benches of the auditorium. They came to power after 10 August 1792 and the collapse of the monarchy, and they overpowered the Girondins in June 1793.

National Assembly. Proclaimed on 17 June 1789 by the Third Estate in defiance of the king, followed by the oath sworn in the Tennis Court at Versailles three days later and recorded by David.

Panthéon. Former church of Sainte-Geneviève, converted into a place for honouring heroes of the Revolution.

parricide. Act of murder of one's father and, by extension, revolutionary leaders.

Père Duchesne. Foul-mouthed fantasy folk hero and narrative voice in a number of down-market daily and weekly opinion sheets published after 1789. Hébert's was the most important.

Plaine. The moderate politicians who supported the government and sat on the lower benches at the front of the auditorium.

sans-culottes. Literally 'without knee-breeches' or the tight trousers worn by aristocrats, churchmen, and bourgeoisie. Artisans, shopkeepers, and others wore full-length trousers. The title was adopted by this latter group and those who spoke for them from 1792 to 1794.

Sections. Administrative divisions of Paris that replaced the parishes of the ancien régime. Revolutionary reforms created first twenty-four, then forty-eight sections.

Terror. Set of exceptional measures to force French men and women to obey the revolutionary government from late summer 1793 to July 1794.

Thermidor government. Government that came to power on the fall of Robespierre (9 thermidor, an II – 27 July 1794). It was replaced by the Directory on 26 October 1795 (4 brumaire an IV).

APPENDIX
CHRONOLOGY OF DAVID'S *MARAT*

1793

12 July   David visits Marat as a deputy of the Convention to obtain news of his health. He sees Marat at work in his bath. This sight was to be important for the formation of the subsequent commemorative picture.

13 July   Marat is murdered in his bath by Charlotte Corday. The news is announced to the Jacobins during a meeting that is being chaired by David.

14 July   David is called upon by Guirault, a member of the Convention, to organise the funeral arrangements and to commemorate Marat in a painting. The artist agreed: 'oui, je le ferai.'

David's overall activities were as follows:

1. Mortuary preparations and display of the body.
2. Funeral rites and burial.
3. Painting of Marat in his bath.
4. Exhibition of the painting, along with the one of Le Peletier, for purposes of public veneration.

15 July   David addresses the Convention describing his visit to Marat:

> . . . I found him in a pose that struck me. Near him he had a block of wood on which ink and paper were placed and with his hand emerging from the bathtub, he was writing his final thoughts for the good of the people . . .

Marat's body goes on public display.

16 July	David describes changes in the arrangements for the public display of Marat's body in the Church of the Cordeliers to the Convention.
19 July	Date on Quéverdo's engraving of Marat from death.
October	David declares to the Convention that the painting showed 'Marat à son dernier soupir'.
16 October	David shows the picture at the Louvre to his fellow artists.
14 November	David offers the finished picture to the Convention and requests that Marat be given the "honours of the Pantheon".

1794

10 May	The Convention orders the copying of both *Marat* and *Le Peletier* under David's direction for tapestries to be made of them at the Gobelin factory.

LATER HISTORY

1795

10 February	*Marat* and *Le Peletier* are taken down and returned to David as a result of changes in the Republic's views on public participation in the democratic process. Marat remains hidden in David's studio for the rest of the artist's life.

1826

14 April	*Marat* is shown at the sale of David's work following his death. It is seen by Stendhal.
23 April	Delécluze, David's former pupil and future biographer, sees and sketches the work, fearing that it may soon be destroyed. *Le Peletier* had been bought by members of the subject's family before the sale took place and was destroyed. *Marat* is not sold and remains with the family.

1835

10 March	*Marat* is bought at a second sale by Baron Meunier (the artist's son-in-law) and Eugène David (the artist's son) for 4,500 f.
May	*Marat* is shown in London in an exhibition of David's work in Leicester Fields that causes violent antipathy from Constable. 'David seems to have formed his mind from three sources, the scaffold, the hospital, and a brothel . . .'*

*C. R. Leslie, *Memoirs of the Life of John Constable* (London: Phaidon, 1951), 242.

1846   *Marat* is exhibited at the Bazar Bonne-Nouvelle as part of a small exhibition of the works of David and Ingres. Baudelaire's review of the show includes his famous description of the picture.

1860   Jules David, the artist's grandson, buys out Mme Meunier to become sole owner of the *Marat*. He makes a gift of one of the versions of the work in his possession to Prince Napoleon, who places it in his gallery at the Palais-Royale.

1867   In a publication Jules David states that the *Marat* in his possession is the original and the one in the Palais-Royale a copy.

1885   The dealer Durand-Ruel sells the Palais-Royale version (which he has acquired) as an original David to Terme.

1886   Death of Jules David.

1889   The continuing dispute about the versions of *Marat* causes Jules David's widow to instigate a trial, in which the status of her version is upheld. Durand-Ruel buys back the Palais-Royale version from Terme.

1893   *Marat* is bequeathed by Mme David to the Musées royaux des Beaux-Arts de Belgique, Brussels, in recognition of Brussels' reception of David when he was in exile. It is placed permanently on view.

1903   The Durand-Ruel/Palais-Royale version is acquired by the Musée de Versailles.

BIBLIOGRAPHY

1846. Baudelaire, Charles. 'Le Musée classique du Bazar Bonne-Nouvelle', *Le Corsaire-Satan,* 21 January. Reprinted in *Oeuvres complètes.* Vol. 2. Paris: Gallimard, Pléiade edition, 1976, 410.

1855. Delécluze, E. J. *Louis David, son école et son temps.* Paris. Reprint edited by Jean Pierre Mouilleseaux. Paris: Editions Macula, 1983.

1867. David, Jules. *Notice sur le Marat de Louis David Suivie de la Liste de ses Tableaux dressée par lui-même.* Paris.

1875. Chévremont, F. *Marat. Index du bibliophile et de l'amateur de peintres, gravures, etc.* Paris.

1882. Jules David, J. L. *Le peintre Louis David (1748–1825), souvenirs et documents inédits* Vol. 2. Paris: Victor Havard, 140–7, 331–4

1913. Saunier, C. 'Le Marat expirant de David et ses copies', *Gazette des Beaux-Arts,* 24–31.

1948. Dowd, D. L. *Pageant Master of the Republic: Jacques-Louis David.* Lincoln: University of Nebraska.

1949. Polak, B. H. 'De Invloed van Einige Monumenten der Ondheid op Het Classicisme van David, Ingres en Delacroix'. *Nederlandsch Kunsthistorisch Jaarboek,* 287–315.

1954. Hautecoeur, Louis. *Louis David.* Paris: Table Ronde.

1962. Lankheit, Klaus. *Der Tod Marats.* Stuttgart: Reclam.

1967. Rosenblum, Robert. *Transformations in Late Eighteenth Century Art.* Princeton: Princeton University Press.

1973. Verbraeken, René. *Jacques-Louis David jugé par ses contemporains et par la postérité.* Paris: Léonce Laget.

1973. Wildenstein, Daniel, and Guy Wildenstein. *Documents complémentaires au Catalogue de l'oeuvre de Louis David.* Paris: Fondation Wildenstein.

1980. Brookner, Anita. *Jacques-Louis David*. London: Chatto and Windus.

1980. Schnapper, Antoine. *David, témoin de son temps*. Fribourg: Office du livre.

1981. *David e Roma*. Exhibition catalogue. Rome: De Luca, 158–9.

1983. Herding, Klaus. 'David's "Marat" als *dernier appel à l'unité révolutionaire'*. *Idea, Jahrbuch der Hamburger Kunsthalle* 2 (1983): 89–112.

1986. Bonnet, Jean-Claude, ed., *La mort de Marat*. Paris: Flammarion.

1986. Traeger, Jorg. *Der Tod des Marat: Revolution des Menschenbildes*. Munich: Bestel.

1988. Bordes, Philippe. *David*. Paris: Fernand Hazan.

1988. Michel, Régis. *David: L'art et le politique*. Paris: Gallimard.

1989. Roberts, Warren. *Jacques-Louis David, Revolutionary Artist*. Chapel Hill and London: University of North Carolina Press.

1989. Schnapper, Antoine. *Jacques-Louis David, 1748–1825*. Exhibition Catalogue. Paris: Éditions de la Réunion des musées nationaux.

1992. Germani, Ian. *Jean-Paul Marat: Hero and Anti-Hero of the French Revolution*. Lewiston, N.Y. and Lampeter: Edwin Mellen Press.

1993. Michel, Régis (ed.). *David contre David*. Paris: La Documentation française, 2 vols.

1993. *The Death of Marat*. Exhibition Catalogue. London: UCL.

1993. Johnson, Dorothy. *Jacques-Louis David. Art in Metamorphosis*. Princeton: Princeton University Press.

1994. Clark, T. J. 'Painting in the Year Two'. *Representations* 47 (Summer): 13–63.

1996. Crow, Thomas. *Emulation. Making Artists for Revolutionary France*. New Haven and London: Yale University Press.

1998. Lee, Simon. *David*. London: Phaidon.